Further Praise for *People-Focused Knowle*

"Drucker may point the way of a knowledge economy, knowledge worker, but Karl Wiig instructs us precisely how to take advantage of a dynamic knowledge strategy. In **People-Focused Knowledge Management**, he simplifies the complex, makes the concepts relevant and actionable and leaves the (inevitable) results to us. Finally, we have a resource for creating a compelling knowledge value proposition linking economics, behavior and technology. For decades, his remarkable graphics and penetrating analysis has been a cornerstone for managerial excellence in all corners of the globe and all sectors of the economy. Few can match his roots and vision in this field; and no one will be disappointed with this newest triumph."
— **Debra Amidon**, Founder and CEO, Entovation International,
Ltd., and Author of *The Innovation Superhighway*

"Melding theory with application, Wiig has created an invaluable ready reference for everyone who works in the knowledge management arena. He is uniquely qualified to provide such a thorough and thought-provoking analysis of the role of knowledge and knowledge management in meeting the business challenges that we all face."
— **Alex Bennet**; Mountain Quest Institute; Co-Author of *Organizational Survival in the New World: The Intelligent Complex Adaptive System*; former Chief Knowledge Officer of the U.S. Department of the Navy

"This book distills the practical and theoretical wisdom of one of the true pioneers in the field of Knowledge Management. The constant interplay of case analysis and fundamental propositions signals the coming of age of the discipline. It takes seasoned practitioners and students alike to the strategic and systematic perspective of management that is required to release the power of knowledge in action."
— **Francisco J. Carrillo**, Professor of Knowledge Management, Center for Knowledge Systems, ITESM

"In **People-Focused Knowledge Management**, Karl Wiig goes beyond the boundaries of traditional knowledge management and integrates this with recent cognitive research on such diverse subjects as mental models, narrative, conceptual blending, decision theory, and sense making, in a very comprehensive treatment."
— **Steve Denning**, Author of *The Springboard*

"Karl Wiig's understanding of the human and organization dynamics of KM is unsurpassed. His decades of experience and insight are captured in this seminal work."
— **Carla O'Dell**, Ph.D., President, APQC

"When it comes to weaving together theory and practice, Karl Wiig is a master! **People-Focused Knowledge Management** illustrates this beautifully. In it he integrates management philosophy with company specific illustrations, cutting edge epistemological theory with specific knowledge management strategies, and current psychological research with operational details. The depth of Wiig's analysis is unusual, and the fact that he carries the analysis all the way to concrete actions makes this book an especially valuable addition to the growing literature on knowledge management. A feast for the mind as well as the enterprise!"
— **Sue Stafford**, Professor and Chair, Department of Philosophy, Simmons College

PEOPLE-FOCUSED
KNOWLEDGE MANAGEMENT

PEOPLE-FOCUSED KNOWLEDGE MANAGEMENT

How Effective Decision Making Leads to Corporate Success

KARL M. WIIG
KNOWLEDGE
RESEARCH INSTITUTE, INC.

ELSEVIER
BUTTERWORTH
HEINEMANN

AMSTERDAM • BOSTON • HEIDELBERG • LONDON
NEW YORK • OXFORD • PARIS • SAN DIEGO
SAN FRANCISCO • SINGAPORE • SYDNEY • TOKYO
An imprint of Elsevier

Elsevier Butterworth–Heinemann
200 Wheeler Road, Burlington, MA 01803, USA
Linacre House, Jordan Hill, Oxford OX2 8DP, UK

Library of Congress Cataloging-in-Publication Data
Wiig, Karl M.
    People-focused knowledge management : how effective decision making
leads to corporate success / Karl M. Wiig.
        p.   cm.
    Includes bibliographical references and index.
    ISBN-13: 978-0-7506-7777-6   ISBN-10: 0-7506-7777-5 (pbk.: alk.paper)
    1. Knowledge management — Social aspects.   2. Organizational
effectiveness.   3. Organizational learning.   4. Decision making.
5. Corporate culture.   6. Organizational behavior.   I. Title.
    HD30.2.W52 2004
    658.4′038–dc22

                                                      2004005921

British Library Cataloguing-in-Publication Data
A catalogue record for this book is available from the British Library.

ISBN-13: 978-0-7506-7777-6
ISBN-10: 0-7506-7777-5

For information on all Butterworth–Heinemann publications
visit our Web site at www.bh.com

05 06 07 08 09 10   10 9 8 7 6 5 4 3 2

Printed in the United States of America

CONTENTS

Chapter 1

COMPETING IN THE GLOBAL ECONOMY REQUIRES EFFECTIVE ENTERPRISES   1

Chapter 2

THE EFFECTIVE ENTERPRISE 26

Chapter 3

ACTIONS ARE INITIATED BY KNOWLEDGEABLE
PEOPLE: PEOPLE MAKE DECISIONS AND ACT
USING DIFFERENT KINDS OF MENTAL
FUNCTIONS   63

Chapter 4
MENTAL AND STRUCTURAL REFERENCE MODELS 100

Chapter 5
A KNOWLEDGE MODEL FOR PERSONAL
SITUATION-HANDLING 117

Chapter 6

Chapter 7

PEOPLE-FOCUSED KNOWLEDGE MANAGEMENT IN DAILY OPERATIONS 213

Chapter 8

PEOPLE-FOCUSED KNOWLEDGE MANAGEMENT EXPECTATIONS 248

Appendix A
EXAMPLES OF KNOWLEDGE MANAGEMENT ANALYSIS APPROACHES   281

Appendix B
EXAMPLES OF KNOWLEDGE MANAGEMENT PRACTICES AND INITIATIVES   298

Appendix C
Memory and Knowledge Categorizations   312

ACKNOWLEDGMENTS

This book could only be possible by the continued support by Elisabeth, my wife of many decades, who with her own research, deep insights, and collaboration has encouraged my investigations and allowed me to channel my efforts into this venture.

I am also grateful for the support of Serina Lai and her associates at Angel Net Universal Company, Ltd.

For the insights and contents of this book, I thank my many clients and professional collaborators over the past 40 years. They have continually pointed me in directions — and shown me solutions — that for the most part would have eluded me. I am particularly indebted to those organizations, some with which I have not worked, that by their examples demonstrate the enduring power of leadership that combines people-friendliness with business savvy, requirements for perfection, and intolerance for foul play.

Several of my teachers of the past changed and broadened my perspectives, providing lasting influences, even though some encounters were brief. I particularly wish to recognize Russel Ackoff, the late Donald Ekman, Edward Lawler, and Irving Lefkowitz.

I am also beholden to the researchers and thinkers in many fields whose works have influenced and strengthened my convictions. They made it possible to "stand on their shoulders," and many of their contributions are referenced in this book.

The book includes examples and case histories without attributions. Most are modified to fit the topics they illustrate, and some might be recognized by their originators. I am thankful for their contributions.

PREFACE

This book is based on some fundamental beliefs about what makes a great enterprise:

- Organizational performance is primarily a result of effective actions by knowledgeable people (Pfeffer 1995), and therefore good knowledge management is crucially important.
- People act effectively when they understand situations and the contexts within which they operate, are motivated, and have appropriate resources.
- When people are treated "right," productivity advantages may exceed 25 percent (Lawler 2003).
- Employees imitate as role models their leaders whose behavior reflects their basic philosophies.
- All employees must be held accountable for their actions, and everyone must be part of the enterprise's governance.

PEOPLE ACQUIRE, POSSESS, AND USE KNOWLEDGE IN REMARKABLE WAYS!

This book builds its case on our present understanding of how people work with their minds, the role of knowledge in conducting work, and how that translates into effective actions for the enterprise, the people themselves, and other stakeholders. It also builds on understanding recent cognitive science and management theories, resulting in new insights that have replaced conventional thinking and in premises such as the following:

- Conceptual integration (blending) of prior knowledge into new mental models that are applicable to new situations represents a unique human aptitude — not a preprogrammed function that operationalizes prior knowledge as has mistakenly been suggested by "Mind-as-Container" or "Mind-as-Machine" and similar metaphors (Bereiter 2002; Fauconnier & Turner 2002).

- Expertise is a tacit and abstract personal capability used to innovate, learn, act, and blend mental models and judge situations from theoretical and practical perspectives. It is not a result of an extensive "content of a mental filing cabinet" (Bereiter 2002).

- Innovation is a tacit mental function that involves conceptual integration or blending (Fauconnier & Turner 2002).

- To a much greater extent than was realized earlier, decisions are made by tacit activation of mental models that reflect experiences of similar situations when those situations are understood by the decision maker (Bechara *et al.* 1997).

- In the workplace, as in life, education in the knowledge era must provide deep understanding. Teaching cannot continue to provide just facts and shallow understanding sufficient "to tell what was told" (Bereiter 2002).

- Mental models range in abstraction from concrete routines, operational models, scripts, schemata, and general principles to highly abstract metaknowledge.

- Mental models are basically converted stories in the form of encoded descriptions of static scenes, dynamic episodes, procedures for work, complex situations, and so on.

- Stories provide integrated models for creating a cohesive understanding of complex domains.

- Stories are crucial for sharing understanding, acquiring and institutionalizing structural intellectual capital, providing effective education, and conducting knowledge diagnostics.

- People learn and remember stories and concepts better than facts.

FOREWORD

At the beginning of the twenty-first century, there is increasing evidence that the world sees the human mind as the new frontier. Mind-altering medications such as Prozak are commonplace. In two consecutive issues recently, *Time* magazine provided multipage articles supported by colorful pictures based on functional magnetic resonance imaging (fMRI) to illustrate mental functions that may be improved or changed to our benefit (Stein 2003; Gorman 2003). These and many other events indicate that we are clearly expected to better manage aspects of how we use or influence our minds to function, giving better performance and better quality of life.

Ever so slowly, we see that the general interest in the new frontier is penetrating the corporate world, although thinkers like Peter Drucker, Charles Handy, and Arie de Geus have told us so for many years. We are beginning to understand how we can provide stewardship and facilitation to make people work more intelligently and more effectively by building and making available knowledge and conducive work environments, cultures, and resources. However, most managers still consider technology and other physical resources to be critical success factors instead of focusing on the human mind. As long as they do not know how to "manage knowledge," they will find it simpler to focus on aspects that can be seen and counted.

In today's world each business and enterprise is constantly required to change; to be reinvented in order to provide new capabilities and perspectives; to be able to cope with new challenges; and to renew itself to adopt new approaches, keeping those that work well and discarding those that are outdated. All these changes are required, but at the same time we are reminded that we need to provide stable work conditions and set our strategies to support innovation in both traditional business areas and new "destructive" business areas in the interest of providing competitive advantages in tomorrow's world. These are considerable challenges that private companies, nongovernmental organizations, and nation states face — even individuals who seek to work in challenging positions. Those who step up to the challenges will likely survive, whereas those who shy away from them are likely to fail. To thrive and prosper will require considerable management skills and involvement of new professional skills such as *knowledge management (KM)*. It will also require the adoption of management philosophies and practices that emphasize the facilitation of effective work environments and performance-beneficial cultures.

No one suggests that management is simple or easy. Even under the best of circumstances — when nothing much changes and business goes well — managers must coordinate complex intertwined social, business, human, and mechanical processes. But such ideal conditions rarely exist. The real world — particularly today — involves constant changes on nearly every front. Customers, suppliers, competitors, products, services, employees, technologies, regulatory environments — the economic playing field itself — all tend to change. Changes include improvements and opportunities as well as external and internal challenges and problems. In this turmoil, managers at every level do their best not only to "keep the ship afloat" but also to improve performance to remain viable and successful. Under these circumstances, management is indeed difficult and complex. The old adage of "keep it simple stupid" (KISS) does not seem to work. Worse, KISS may often do harm by inappropriately narrowing the focus and ignoring significant implications. Many try to circumvent challenges and requirements by manipulation and the creation of false impressions. Those who insist on following such paths frequently find themselves in serious trouble, as is evidenced by many recent examples.

Old mainline approaches to business management and operations have less validity. Vibrant and novel management approaches and operational practices need to be pursued. Many of these have been practiced in outstanding organizations for centuries, although new perspectives and scientific findings provide additional foundations and conceptual supports.

The business environment itself is changing. Globalization and increased competition are emerging with new driving forces resulting from more sophisticated consumer populations. The new world is upon us, as numerous companies and public institutions realize. It has significantly changed the attitude of stakeholders of all kinds, of employees, of customers, of suppliers, of whole regions and countries where the economy and quality of life are supported by industries and institutions. Investors and sponsors of public institutions are changing their understanding of what constitutes appropriate operation. In many instances, it is realized that the complete approach to conducting business must be changed when the goal is survival and success. Business must be reinvented to build new value-creating paradigms, processes, products, and services. This is particularly important in the developed countries in Europe, North America, Australia, and parts of East Asia to support their quality of life.

In this environment, Knowledge Management provides a particular opportunity to help people work more effectively and intelligently in support of the enterprises in which they invest their own and their families' future and on which they depend for their livelihood. Sharper competition between companies, between countries, and between continents result in requirements for greater effectiveness of operations and service to customers and for creation of new products and services. There is increased understanding and agreement that the major driving force in this new environment is knowledge — that is, both personal and structural knowledge and other forms of intellectual capital assets. However, the situation is more complex than just building and applying knowledge. Competitiveness in the new world is directly dependent not only on the value and sophistication of the knowledge assets but also on how well they are renewed and utilized to conduct competent work. Consequently, it is necessary to deal directly with how people and organizations create and utilize the knowledge and understanding — know-how and thinking strategies — in their daily work lives. We need to learn and apply how these intellectual capital assets are engaged to analyze situations, make decisions, and execute actions to the enterprise's and individual's best advantages.

Neither these issues nor the approaches to deal with them are simple or straightforward, and our insights are limited. Hence, many of the perspectives expressed in this book will be subject to debate and change as we learn more. Models and philosophies for what makes enterprises successful vary widely. No two enterprises are the same or have identical requirements. To allow for such disparities, we examine basic knowledge-related premises for what makes the enterprise effective and viable. We will explore what it means to "act effectively." We will study factors and conditions that promote and maintain effective-acting behaviors and prevent dysfunctional ones. We will examine what it means for an enterprise to achieve "durable viability." We will focus on many aspects of how situations can be handled effectively. We will discuss how Knowledge Management can assist in achieving enterprise objectives. And we will explore some of the implications that may be expected from better people-centered Knowledge Management. In the appendices, we introduce models for implementing KM in proactive organizations and for showing what is required of KM professionals in terms of services provided and expertise needed.

Views vary on the economic and social roles of the enterprise, as well as on the relative importance of the roles and behaviors of key individuals and business leaders. Nevertheless, an emerging school of thought bases success and viability on business ethics and properly prepared and motivated individual contributors. That view is pursued here. It is our belief that motivated, contributing, and accountable knowledge workers are the linchpins that secure and sustain the successful operation of the enterprise machinery. However, they must be supported by well-designed organizational structures and infrastructures. They must also be provided with leadership and role models to help guide their behaviors.

Managing knowledge and managing in general are intricate endeavors that require the manipulation of human, social, and economic systems that are only partially understood. From systems-theoretic perspectives,[1] organizations are complex *open systems*[2] that cannot be fully *observed* and therefore cannot be *identified*. As a result, these endeavors cannot be *controlled* in any strict sense or even to our specifications.[3] Yet, we need to manage them — influence them — in order to shape their behavior and performance, bringing them closer to the desired objectives and expectations.

Unfortunately, some managers try to run their organizations with strict rules in the belief that a highly ordered operation will become "Newtonian" and that it can be controlled with practical means. National leaders have also pursued such philosophies and continue to do so. To some extent, legal systems and laws are designed to channel behavior to be predictable and not just appropriate.

Organizations vary greatly, and since they cannot be fully observed it is difficult, if not impossible, to perform rigorous investigations of processes such as the use of knowledge and how people think to determine what works, what does not work, and what may be improved to work better. However, in order to achieve effective performance, we still need to determine good approaches — particularly knowledge-related methods — as best we can.

As a result, in this book we present suggestions for what can be done and what may be expected from different actions under various circumstances and how such actions depend on personal and enterprise knowledge and other intellectual capital assets. It therefore should be clear that our suggestions are assertions and hypotheses based on the author's experience and interpretation of the experiences of others.

Whereas this book largely pursues systematic and analytical methods, we also recognize that synthesis and holistic perspectives are required to build the broad and overall understanding and vision required to create workable approaches that will provide the effectiveness needed to compete and survive.

An integrative systems view lies behind the perspectives provided in this book. This view recognizes the interrelations between the enterprise and its surroundings and markets. It recognizes that we need to consider mutual relations between areas within the enterprise such as its departments, its procedures and practices, its culture, its assets, and its people and their motivation, expertise, skills, and attitudes. It also recognizes the dynamic and often nonpermanent nature of entities, relationships, and behaviors.

Whenever possible, I have attempted to build on scientific findings and on established, commonly accepted, or seemingly logical premises. In many instances, scientifically obtained findings are stretched and extrapolated in "good engineering fashion" to synthesize frameworks, approaches, and actions. These constructs are often illustrations, examples, and models and are expected to generate beneficial target system behaviors.

The underlying premise of this book is based on the belief that the central actors in organizations and society are humans — not computers. Similarly, the major enablers of performance are knowledge and other intellectual capital assets — not information. People, and the effectiveness of their actions, determine success or failure. Hence, our emphasis is on people and their behaviors and roles in enterprise operations. This emphasis is further strengthened when we consider that our ability to act effectively is determined predominantly by our mental capabilities, especially by our personal knowledge, understanding, beliefs, and other mental constructs available to us at the point and time of action.

NOTES

1. This and many other terms and concepts are outlined in the Glossary. For more on systems perspectives, see Ackoff and Emery (1972), von Bertalanffy (1969), and Checkland (1999).

2. Organizations are *complex* open systems, in contrast to mechanical systems which are *complicated* closed systems; see Glossary.
3. In 1960, Rudolph Kalman presented the Kalman filter theory with observability and controllability as fundamental criteria for dynamic systems identification and operation (Kalman 1960a and 1960b). Feldbaum also used the concepts as part of his dual control theory (Feldbaum 1960).

1

COMPETING IN THE GLOBAL ECONOMY REQUIRES EFFECTIVE ENTERPRISES

PREMISE 1-1: THE GLOBAL ECONOMY DEMANDS EXCELLENCE

The global economy reaches everywhere. Enterprises throughout the world provide cost-and-feature competitive products and services wherever they find customers. They also seek partners and suppliers wherever they can obtain the most advantageous cost-and-quality combinations. Everyone has access to the same markets and the same suppliers. Under these conditions, any organization that provides deliverables in the competitive global market can only succeed through excellence — by being best among competitors — by delivering products, services, or combinations of these that are of the greatest value to its customers.

In addition to *being* excellent, advanced enterprises strive to remain leaders by *innovating faster than their competitors* since only learning faster than their competitors often means adopting what others — their competitors — already practice.

THE COMPETITIVE ENTERPRISE EXAMPLE

For 25 years Jones Development & Engineering, Inc. has provided advanced technology services to industrial customers in many industries. Jones assists customers in creating prototypes of complex high-performance products that utilize advanced technologies and materials. Jones's staff collaborates with customers to conceptualize, design, and engineer products that must perform well in very demanding applications. They also work with customers' customers to understand their problems so that they can properly address the issues they have. Most often, Jones starts work with customers in the initial conceptual stages of new product development followed by pilot production and product introduction. Later, Jones's staff assists by handing over production to customers' operations, often working for months in customer facilities to achieve full technology and expertise transfer.

Jones has grown steadily to become the international leader in its niche and works hard to maintain its leadership position. The company is very profitable with a large and faithful customer base. In many ways, Jones operates like many of its competitors, yet pursues practices that are proactive and deliberate and therefore quite effective, which sets them apart. Some examples of these practices are as follows.

- *Provide superior customer value* — Jones's management emphasizes the need to provide the best matches to the individual customer's needs and requirements, thereby providing the highest possible value to customers.
- *Understand customers* — Jones's employees recognize that it is absolutely necessary to understand their customers' business purpose, direction, objectives, and their marketplace and that Jones's products and services contribute to the customers' value creation and how to help customers succeed.
- *Understand technology opportunities* — Jones's employees work to understand how and why customers, and the customers' customers, benefit and are affected by different technology solutions.
- *Collaborate with customers to maximize value of assistance* — Jones's teams collaborate with customers to conceptualize and engineer new products. The teams consist of a mix of researchers, design engineers, and crafts people to allow immediate incorporation of insights into advanced solutions and practical assessments of how solutions can be built in the factory.
- *Develop relationships* — Jones's management emphasizes the need for employees to network and develop good relationships with customers, suppliers, and coworkers. They rely on these relationships to understand what is needed and what they can provide. Internal relationships are crucial for frictionless and effective operations and for support of workforce morale.
- *Understand the universe of product opportunities* — Jones's management and employees — professionals and crafts people

— are continually provided with opportunities such as participating in professional meetings to understand the importance of utilizing and benefiting from advanced technologies and materials.

■ *Ascertain that the company has command of state-of-the-art technology* — Jones invests in advanced technology expertise early — through benchmarking or acquisition of licenses and equipment — and experiments with promising technology in the factory for trials and familiarization before they are needed for customer work.

■ *Prepare employees to implement corporate strategy* — Through companywide information, education, discussion, and feedback programs, Jones's employees build understanding of corporate thrusts, direction, and strategy and of how they as individuals can assist in implementing the company's goals. Employees also understand how their future depends on their own performance and the company's long-term and durable success.

■ *Innovate faster than competitors* — Jones's management believes that to keep their leadership position they need to learn quickly and innovate faster than their competitors — in technology, in management and operational practices, and in strategy.

■ *Support personal learning* — By understanding why it is to their personal benefit, Jones's employees take it upon themselves to learn about advances in every field they think will be important for their work. They are recognized and rewarded as a group for practical curiosity, innovations, and their ability to collaborate and share insights. Jones's culture fosters agility, versatility, and flexibility in a noncompetitive, safe environment.

■ *Foster knowledge-focused mentality and culture* — Jones's senior management believes that each employee must understand, as second nature, how better knowledge is built and leveraged — through personal and company investments, through collaboration, and through deeply entrenched and practiced tradeoffs between short-term facilitation and long-term strength.

As a result of pursuing such practices, Jones Development & Engineering, Inc. has been able to maintain its global leadership position. In addition, it has become a role model for other proactive organizations that also work to become leaders in their market niches.

THE GLOBAL ECONOMY CHALLENGE

Many factors drive the global economy and make the world a challenging business environment with complex implications for most courses of actions. That makes it difficult for some enterprises to provide products and services with sufficient margins to stay in business. For others, it makes a much larger marketplace with near endless opportunities. Positive aspects of globalization provide new opportunities for enterprises and individuals throughout the world, including developing nation states. For the first time, many people are able to contribute and improve their quality of life regardless of their geographical location. Such changes are particularly noticeable for people who deliver knowledge-intensive products and services to customers in other parts of the world. Numerous examples can be cited where new international industries have emerged in geographical areas that earlier were quite isolated. Services ranging from software development to call centers are provided from locations that previously were isolated in Asia, Latin America, and Africa. In addition, sophisticated design and manufacturing that traditionally were performed only in industrialized nations have migrated into countries that earlier did not have the capabilities to deliver such products.

Globalization causes work itself to become more complex. Work must satisfy requirements for improved effectiveness and provide deliverables with new features and increased capabilities that provide the needed competitive value in the global marketplace. In response, competitive enterprises prepare their workforces better, automate or outsource many routine functions, and organize work in ways that produce new deliverables. In many situations, work becomes more sophisticated and expands to take advantage of new capabilities brought about by the increased availability of personal and structural knowledge. Efficiency is improved by automation systems that perform routine tasks, thus freeing people to apply greater expertise to more demanding and value-creating work. Application of advanced technology and development by sophisticated organizations continue the refinement of work in general.

Figure 1-1 presents an example of the globalization complexity. Nine independent factors indicate the diversity of influences that

Figure 1-1

Many knowledge-related, people-focused factors influence globalization opportunities and challenges — and the enterprise ability to succeed and individual people's ability to thrive. Copyright © 2001 Knowledge Research Institute, Inc. Reproduced with permission.

affect global economy opportunities and pressures. In the context of this book, it is important to understand that every one of these factors is influenced by the effective actions of people at every organizational level — by their competence, their expertise, and their knowledge. To a lesser, but very important, extent, technology, especially information technology (IT), also influences how these factors will change performance in the global economy.

Globalization causes work to change and become more complex, satisfying requirements for improved effectiveness and providing deliverables with new features and increased capabilities. To compete, enterprises strive to increase performance productivity on both micro and nano levels. They prepare their workforces better, automate many routine functions, and organize work in ways that create better deliverables. Automation systems perform routine tasks, thus freeing people to perform more demanding work, which inevitably enables them to add more features and options and to further complicate work. Work expands to exploit new knowledge capabilities.

THE WORLD REQUIRES US TO CHANGE

The world has changed in its features and its relationships and, perhaps more importantly, in the speed by which new changes and requirements are introduced. In the new millennium we have been awakened to different driving forces in local and international economies. Earlier, enterprises could exist comfortably within narrow geographical and market boundaries. Now most, even small enterprises,[1] are forced onto the globalized competitive playing field and are subjected to rules that often are quite different. Customers everywhere are more sophisticated and demand individualized products and services to a degree not thought possible a few years ago. Suppliers have access to well-trained and efficient workers in most parts of the world — some at very low costs — making it attractive to seek new alliances. New competitive products, technologies, and service capabilities are introduced into the market overnight. New business practices such as business-to-business (B2B), including supplier bidding systems, are emerging everywhere and are utilizing new vehicles like the World Wide Web. *Crafts people, professionals, managers, and whole organizations must act differently to maintain their accustomed lifestyles by delivering work that requires greater personal knowledge. Employee and customer loyalties are changing and are often reduced sharply.*

To survive and prosper, most enterprises find that they need to tailor their activities to unique situations. They need to act effectively and "intelligently" in order to provide customized goods and services and otherwise adapt to new contexts. Viability, success, and progress no longer depend extensively on exploitation of depletable resources. Instead, innovation and pursuit of knowledge-based practices and opportunities are new drivers, not only for new-type businesses, but also for traditional industries. In particular, enterprises realize that they must continually build and apply high-quality and competitive knowledge. They must make available and leverage competitive personal and structural — tacit and explicit — intellectual capital (IC) to facilitate the intelligent-acting individual and group behaviors needed to survive. As the economist Paul Romer states: "Knowledge-based innovation can provide almost unlimited potentials for success and economic growth" (Kelly 1996; Romer 1993).

Knowledge-Intensive Work

The Misunderstanding of Knowledge-Intensive Work

The degree of knowledge intensity of work may often be quite misunderstood. Many distinguish between manual work (which they indicate is *not* knowledge-intensive) and knowledge-intensive work as if work that results in manipulation of physical objects does not require intensive application of high levels of expertise. To provide a different view, consider the machining center operator who is preparing the final metal cuts on a high-technology part in which hundreds of thousands of dollars of work have already been invested. One error by the operator may destroy that piece. Or consider the European aircraft company that started a new carbon fiber composites plant and planned to train new workers by only transferring engineers (the "knowledge workers") from the old plant. In this case, it took six months and the transfer of expert manual laborers before the new plant could produce a single part that passed inspections. And consider that the roustabouts on North Sea oil platforms spend more than 60 percent of their time on paper and computer work.

We find high degrees of knowledge intensity in work performed by effective and high-performing people everywhere. Often, these people are not consciously aware that they apply deep knowledge since it is tacit and highly automatized and has been acquired through implicit learning over long periods. A clear example is the master blacksmith who has learned his craft over a decade or more.

Researchers who analyze how intellectual work is performed are appalled by the general lack of understanding of how people use their minds to work. "*How people work is one of the best kept secrets in America*" is a statement that expresses this sentiment (Suchman 1995). Only in the last few years have we started to understand and focus on the intellectual functions performed by knowledge workers when they perform knowledge-intensive work. As a result, in many instances we are now just starting to understand the complexity, power, and business value of how proficient knowledge workers apply the knowledge they possess to analyze and interpret challenges and deliver high-quality work products. We are also learning more about how we can support knowledge workers to be more versatile by providing them with additional knowledge when needed and how we can reduce the need to educate or train them to become proficient in many rarely encountered or lower-level tasks that can be automated to assist them or be executed autonomously. These are the knowledge-related functions that we often complement with knowledge-based system (KBS) applications.

Knowledge Intensity

Knowledge intensity of work is a function of several factors. Increased knowledge intensity is a function of how much knowledge and understanding a person must possess and apply when required to perform competent work and to be prepared to deal with uncertainties and surprises. It consists of at least four factors:

- *Level and complexity of knowledge and understanding required to perform regular work.* The amount of knowledge needed to deliver competent work under normal conditions is part of determining the degree of knowledge intensity. Requirements for greater knowledge result in higher knowledge intensity, as we should expect.
- *Level of expertise required for competent handling of work-related variabilities.* The degree of knowledge intensity is influenced by the variety of challenges that a person must be prepared to handle competently. Consider the spectrum of alternative scenarios the private pilot faces when there are uncertain weather conditions and congested airways at her destination.
- *Severity of consequences of potential work errors.* Knowledge intensity increases in high-value situations where the consequences of errors are large. Airline pilots and surgeons, for example, must be prepared to deal competently with wide ranges of issues and problems to avoid serious errors. In addition to executing their normal tasks, they must continuously, and often tacitly, watch out for indications of potential problems or anomalies and know how to handle them to avert disasters. Competent managers — even ditch diggers — face similar challenges.
- *Swiftness of action.* Work that requires quick actions (e.g., fighter pilots engaged in combat) requires that all required knowledge and understanding must be present in the person's mind. Work that is slower (e.g., insurance underwriting) is less knowledge intensive and can rely on external knowledge from coworkers, computer-based work aids, etc.

At this time, we do not attempt to provide measures of knowledge intensity of work, although that could be of value to set priorities for where and how to invest in knowledge building and management.

Work Is Becoming Increasingly Complex and Valuable

Work is changing, and so is the workplace. Apart from increased work complexity, the workplace itself is equipped with sophisticated work-aids that often take considerable understanding to handle and exploit. Work-aids include IT-based infrastructure capabilities and task-specific aids such as mathematical analysis models, knowledge bases (KBs), and work guides for complicated work processes. There are increases in communications support for e-mail and groupware capabilities. With some communications capabilities, many people find that their normal work is frequently interrupted and that such disruptions make it difficult to perform their work as intended. Given these and other changes, effective work requires that people must have greater proficiency to deliver the quality expected. Workers need to possess — or have access to — knowledge in different ways, such as through collaboration, expert networks, or communities of practice (CoPs).

Some knowledge may be routine, tacit, and automatized; other knowledge may be tacit at higher abstraction levels; yet other knowledge may be accessed via computers or consultation with colleagues. People must deliver proficient work in spite of interruptions, they must be able to take advantage of complicated work-aids, and they must be capable of innovating and improvising when customized demands require it. More importantly, they must integrate their work with adjacent functions and departments, include interdisciplinary perspectives and expertise where required, and understand how they, as individuals, teams, or departments assist in implementing enterprise goals, objectives, and strategy. Workers at all levels, to the extent that they affect outcomes, must also understand customer requirements regarding quality, service supports, and many contractual aspects such as delivery or inventory conditions. In the Tayloristic[2] era, these considerations were not important but have become increasingly significant.

Workers on the assembly line — be it in an aircraft factory, food plant, or computer company — are constantly making small tradeoff decisions that affect quality, rework and costs, or speed of delivery. Within a work day, each individual will face many different tradeoff challenges of varying degrees that cannot be foreseen and therefore cannot be planned for in advance. From managerial perspectives, assembly work may look routine, but it actually contains complexities that must be resolved competently to implement the desired enterprise direction.

Continued progress and improvements have led to a continued increase in supplier capability and efficiency. This trend is energized by customer demands for better and less expensive goods and services and stronger competitors. As indicated in Figure 1-2, these changes result in more complex work. Complexity results from the need to deliver ever higher quality and better customized products and services — to customers and, increasingly, colleagues and downstream business processes within the enterprise itself. Competent delivery of complex work products requires additional knowledge — greater abstract understanding and, in many cases, totally new knowledge. Whereas better knowledge is important, it cannot by itself deliver the desired performance. Information technology and structural intellectual capital (IC) such as systems and procedures, business models, management and operational practices, and organization of work, all contribute to effective delivery of complex work, as does worker motivation.

In Figure 1-2 the changes in work complexity are indicated as a frequency diagram where work is divided into six categories, from simple to complex. A fair amount of traditional work ("past work") tends to have relatively low complexity levels. For this reason it is possible to replace some people-work with intelligent automation that gradually takes over routine work such as payroll, inventory control, and commodity purchasing, thus leaving workers free to deal with more demanding challenges.

For organizations to just "stay in the game" in competitive and productive terms, it is essential that activities in categories 1, 2, and 3 be automated as far as possible. They should at least be embodied in the structural IC of the organization. This is the focus of many KM-IT activities today. However, as should by now be obvious, KM-IT systems are merely quicker ways to address yesterday's business challenges since KM-IT, for the most part, only automates what has been well known from past experiences. In general, it is not possible to automate new challenging work about which we still are learning and do not fully know how to handle. On the other hand, today's routine work is often work that was complex yesterday. Such change requires human intelligence and mental capabilities such as conceptual blending, as we will discuss in Chapter 5.

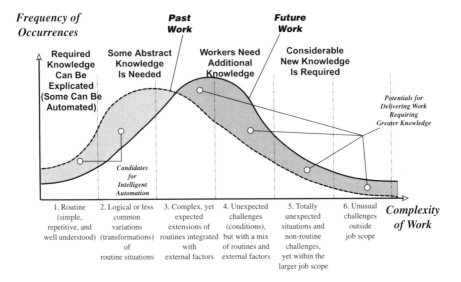

Figure 1-2

Future work is becoming increasingly complex as routine and almost-routine work is automated. Copyright © 1999 Knowledge Research Institute, Inc. Reproduced with permission.

Enterprises ask employees to undertake increasingly complex work by changing job descriptions and service paradigms (see Chapter 7). To deliver competent work, employees at all levels not only need to have task knowledge, but also need to understand their new responsibilities in the broader organizational context. Placing improved operational knowledge at the point-of-action leads to reduced costs and an effort to deliver routine work — work is executed quicker with fewer problems. To obtain the desired effectiveness in more complex situations, a person's job-related understanding must be increased by building additional concepts and mental models in the forms of scripts and schemata to metaknowledge.[3]

An example of work displacement and resulting nano-productivity gain is found among oil refinery operators.[4] Advanced computer control has automated most normal and many abnormal operations, leaving operators with new responsibilities. Operators are asked to seek out better operating conditions, anticipate and understand upstream changes and disturbances, diagnose emerging problems, decide how to handle them, carry out compensating actions, and monitor the effectiveness of their interventions with an eye on how to continue operating the process in the best way. The operators have been provided with new conceptual and methodological knowledge, much in the form of mental models. They have assumed selected tasks from process engineers and maintenance professionals who now can pursue complex work that previously was not well covered. As a result, refined products are now closer to specifications, production rates are higher, energy consumption per barrel of product is lower, and maintenance problems are reduced. Performance productivity is improved on the individual, department, and organizational levels.

Complex Work Creates Greater Value

The complex work required to create and produce sophisticated goods and services with better quality and increased customization has greater value than less complex work required to provide simpler deliverables. Within the enterprise itself, non-routine and novel challenges also have greater value than routine tasks in that, by their very nature, they address more important opportunities or challenges than do routine matters. The more costly, difficult, and risky work will not be undertaken unless it also has the potential for creating greater value.

The Six Major Challenges

The evidence is clear that to survive and succeed, enterprises must change their approaches to conduct successful business in the globalized economy. Whereas gradual change has always been required to adapt to new conditions, the pace is now accelerating and incremental change is no longer sufficient. There are many reasons behind the needs to change (see Figure 1-1). Additional challenges and greater detail are indicated in Figure 1-3, which illustrates the six major challenges: (1) work is becoming more complex; (2) competition is more demanding; (3) new management approaches are introduced; (4) changes occur quicker and quicker; (5) workers demand greater involvement; and (6) education and training follow new directions.

1. **Work is becoming more complex resulting from**
   — Continued efforts and advances to streamline business and automate routine tasks.
   — Increased demands to create and deliver better and more competitive products and services.

Figure 1-3

*Enterprise performance is a function of many factors. Copyright © 1999
Knowledge Research Institute, Inc. Reproduced with permission.*

— Greater sophistication of management and operating practices that require new approaches.

Increased work complexity necessitates that people must be better prepared and support systems that must be better suited to handle new tasks with proper competence. In particular:

— People need to possess — or have access to — work-domain knowledge and metaknowledge with higher competitive quality, thereby allowing them to deliver complex work with the necessary degree of proficiency.

— Support systems must be better integrated with business (and other systems) and must be smarter by increased application of artificial intelligence (AI) and other advanced methods. These changes will improve the quality of current information services. More importantly, they will lead to increased offloading of intellectual work for people by automating simple reasoning tasks.

It is realized that most work is increasingly knowledge intensive — requiring expertise to deliver competitive products and services. These changes make traditional work management and organization less effective in the new environment.

2. **The nature of business has changed, and the competitive environment is more demanding as a result of changes caused by:**
   — Increased dependence on intellectual capital (IC) assets — that is, assets of personal competitive knowledge, expertise, understanding, and assets of structural intellectual capital — to create and deliver competitive customized products and services. This contrasts with earlier business models that were focused on financial and physical capital.
   — Pressures from globalization. Quality and highly competent suppliers from across the world are able to transcend geographical boundaries to compete nearly everywhere.
   — Competitive differentiations based on product uniqueness, which are increasingly being based on product capabilities supported by related service arrangements that often are highly targeted and customized.
   — Better informed customers who have an improved understanding of their needs and therefore impose greater requirements on suppliers. Today, customers also have a greater choice of suppliers than previously.
   — Competitors who are increasingly becoming more sophisticated and smarter.

3. **New and more complex management, operational, and technical approaches and practices are introduced to deal with the new challenges.** Many practices are based on practical experiences with what works and what doesn't. Others are based on new theoretical insights from fields ranging from information and management sciences to cognitive and social sciences. Together, they give enterprises greater competitive capabilities and an improved ability to perform and succeed. The new tools constitute a challenge by themselves since they require new understanding, initiatives, and efforts. The tools include:
   — New generation knowledge management (NGKM)[5] practices that cover modern management theories and practices, human capital management (HCM), intellectual capital management (ICM), and the dynamic facilitation, manipulation, and control to create, organize, deploy, and apply knowledge to meet enterprise objectives. Emerging KM practices are based partly on recent cognitive science understandings of human capabilities, such as conceptual

blending and concepts for learning, conceptual skills transfers, decision making, problem solving, and personal motivations. The new practices are significantly based on successful experiences when applying KM in advanced enterprises.

— People-focused knowledge management that becomes more explicit based on a better understanding of the nature of intellectual, knowledge-intensive work, how situation-handling and effective actions rely on knowledge such as mental reference models, and people's actions and behaviors in general. It also becomes more explicit by the realization that enterprises do not behave and respond as machines — they are social systems.

— In the proactive enterprises, intellectual asset management mentality[6] that is becoming a cultural cornerstone caused by the widespread concern for how better knowledge is built and leveraged — through personal and company investments, collaboration, and deeply entrenched and practiced tradeoffs between short-term facilitation and long-term strength.

— Integrative management that involves proactive perspectives and integration of strategic, tactical, and operational views and activities between business units, departments, and individuals. Integrative management relies on extensive and effective communication, the introduction of incentives, and cultural changes to motivate required behaviors. It also introduces asset-based management mentality, principles, and measurement systems applied to intangible assets to maximize their value over time.

— Advanced information management and technology (IM&IT), which focuses on intangible as well as tangible asset-based management principles for information and includes a wide range of technologies such as:
  — Artificial intelligence (AI) for automatic reasoning
  — Collaborative and groupware environments
  — Content management
  — Corporate history repositories and other approaches
  — Customer relations management (CRM)
  — Data mining
  — E-learning
  — Electronic performance support systems (EPSSs)
  — Enterprise resource management (ERM)

— Enterprise value creation (EVC)
— Extensive automation of routine business functions
— Interactive computer-based training (ICBT)
— Internet and intranet portals
— Knowledge management support systems (KMSSs), including knowledge capture systems and knowledge deployment systems
— Supply chain management (SCM)

The introduction of new management approaches and capabilities facilitates efficient and effective work; that is, execution of individual and group activities. Some approaches also provide direct support — even offloading — of mental tasks such as summarizing and organizing information and, to some extent, reasoning.

The new management approaches are not automatically easy to adopt. For many managers, professionals, and crafts people, pursuing and implementing the new directions and practices present problems. The approaches require depths of expertise and involvement in professional disciplines that often go beyond current business practices. The ability to handle the new approaches requires learning and development of new perspectives by managers and staff — efforts that may exceed the energy and availability of the people involved. Hence, only highly motivated and proactive parties appear to adopt the new approaches.

4. **The rate of change is higher than at any time before.** New technologies, new business conditions, new regulatory and legal requirements, new practices, and new demands are being introduced more quickly than ever before. These changes require proactive stances to detect future needs and very different approaches to plan, create, and implement solutions.

5. **Workers demand greater involvement and are less satisfied with traditional employment situations.** Only a small fraction of enterprises treat their employees "right" (Lawler 2003). Typical business–employee relationships are impersonal and provide little understanding of, involvement in, and sense of contribution to the enterprise's strategy and direction. As stated by Dawn Lepore: "Employees will work for money but will give a piece of their lives for meaning!" (Anonymous 2001a)

6. **Needs for conventional training and education often exceed allocated time.** The knowledge economy requires frequent

updating of both personal and structural knowledge to adapt to new demands and conditions. However, many — perhaps most — organizations expect their employees to maintain and renew their personal knowledge on their own time (Shellenbarger 2001). This often creates moral and family problems, and can decrease the motivation and effectiveness of the workforce. Computer-based training material — e-learning — is frequently provided but appears to be less effective than is often perceived, and many companies report bad experiences, with low knowledge retention and other problems ranging from cheating to negative attitudes (Anonymous 2001b).

Instead of wide separation of work from education and training, many organizations now pursue "just-in-time training" as part of regular work using sophisticated computer-based knowledge support systems, shadowing, "buddy coaching," and tailored e-learning accessible to managers, professionals, and crafts people. However, these approaches require new practices, application of new technologies, and revision of work in general. They often provide better knowledge transfer as we now start to understand it from new cognitive psychology findings (see Chapters 3, 4, and 5).

Four Management Initiatives

Tackling the six challenges requires drastic changes — at times with a need to reinvent the business — rethinking and redesigning operational and management practices, incentives, controls, and culture, and above all learning how to obtain, retain, and serve customers to their best advantage. For many enterprises, the challenges have been met by pursuing four management initiatives:

1. Provide systematic and comprehensive knowledge management distributed widely throughout the enterprise and guided (*not controlled*) from central management. KM is backed up by monitoring, incentives, and detailed understanding of knowledge mechanisms to ascertain appropriate actions everywhere.
2. Pursue integrative management practices on personal, departmental, and business unit levels, with collaboration and understanding of common goals and reinforced by measurements and incentives to leverage the synergy of joint insights and efforts.

3. Foster a widespread intellectual asset management mentality to maximize the operational and strategic value of human capital (people's knowledge and their motivation to use and renew it), structural intellectual capital, and information capital.

4. Establish people-focused management and organization of knowledge-related work as a central condition to create and leverage capabilities and to provide competitive products and services in the global, knowledge-driven business environment.

Advanced enterprises manage the six major challenges successfully by pursuing these initiatives. As a result, the challenges — and ways to handle them competently — are becoming better understood, although most challenges are not known in advance: they are novel. In addition, information technology is becoming increasingly sophisticated and continues to expand its support of most areas of the enterprise, making the availability of appropriate information better and more timely. Still, the approaches and practices that vigilant organizations pursue are becoming ever more people-focused and rely on collaboration not only between people but also between organizational entities.

In philosophy, the new people-focus is quite different from the Taylorism era where the emphasis was on visible work and many workers were treated as replaceable "programmable automata." Now, the focus has shifted to "invisible" and hard-to-observe intellectual work that relies on independent initiatives, personal reasoning, and innovation. As the executive vice president of a large enterprise stated: "Previously, we were concerned with what we saw — work flows, information flows, how people worked with their hands and so on. Now, to be competitive, in addition, we must focus on how people work with their minds and how knowledge and understanding are created, flows, and utilized and how it is exchanged with outside parties. These are new challenges."

The new practices have been found to be very effective and focus on making individuals, teams, and groups work better — with better understanding and insights, greater proficiency and foresight, higher involvement and motivation, increased responsibility and versatility, improved innovation and renewal, and increased building and sharing of expertise to enable others and promote better practices. All these changes rely on excellent tacit and explicit personal knowledge and understandings and on competitive structural intellectual capital assets. Knowledge management becomes a critical foundation for the change, enabling the reinvention of the business by systematic knowledge support, maintenance, and renewal. Compared to past practices, advanced enterprises have, in effect, reinvented the way they now conduct business.

The story does not end there. Significant leadership is required to achieve the desired results. In addition, enterprises pursue and implement initiatives to create permanent practices for accountability and for monitoring short-term and long-term results, both accompanied by quick, flexible, and decisive retargeting when conditions change. Open-loop and "hopeful" operation in a changing and competitive world does not work (Sullivan & Harper 1997).

ENTERPRISE EFFECTIVENESS REQUIRES GOOD INTELLECTUAL CAPITAL ASSETS

The concept of intellectual capital (IC) is very important. IC in its many forms allows us to identify action-oriented and order-focused intellectual assets that are the main components that guide people and enterprise behaviors. Action-oriented IC assets consist of knowledge that people, organizations, and societies have about how to do things. Order-focused IC assets deal with how to categorize, organize, structure, and think about personal lives, businesses and other organizations, governments, and society in general in order to understand them, to position them to their greatest advantage, and so they can best fulfill their purpose.

From a static, "as-is" perspective, the enterprise IC assets are part of the intangible capital, which for a company, together with tangible capital, make up its "market value." Still, IC has a much greater importance when considered from a dynamic perspective — from the perspective of how well the enterprise will meet challenges as the world around it changes and therefore how well it will succeed and survive. IC assets, the intelligent capabilities, are needed to deal with new situations and problems in ways that keep the enterprise strong and prevent it from being vulnerable.

IC assets come in many forms. Personal IC assets consist of knowledge and understanding that a person possesses and owns in the forms of mental models, concepts, facts, rules, memories of incidents and situations, and many other manifestations. These assets include work-related personal relationships within or outside the organization. They can also be personal notes and other types of physical artifacts, including electronic documents not owned by the enterprise. Personal IC assets are the individual's property and form the foundation of each individual's expertise or competence — their ability to perform and act. Good and appropriate personal IC assets are necessary for any individual to act effectively. In addition, people must be motivated to use their expertise to deliver effective work. An aggregated structure of IC entities is presented in Figure 1-4, which is an adaptation and expansion of the Swedish financial company, Skandia's approach. There are many variants of IC considerations. Our purpose here is to introduce the general concept, and the interested reader might consult the extensive literature to learn more (Amidon 2003; Chatzkel 2002; Edvinsson 2002; Edvinsson & Malone 1997; Klein 1998; Roos *et al.* 1998; Stewart 1991, 1997, 2002b; Sveiby 1997).

The concept of IC and its categorizations allows us to identify the strengths and weaknesses of areas of understanding and action

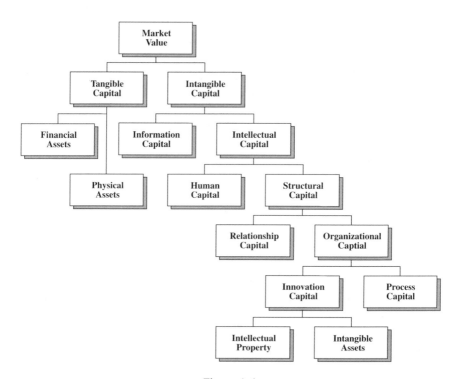

Figure 1-4

Normally, a company's market value reflects the values of its tangible and intangible capital. The effective-acting enterprise achieves its current and future performance by diligent application of personal and structural intellectual capital. Copyright © 1999 Knowledge Research Institute, Inc. Reproduced with permission.

capabilities. As indicated above, the IC concept is important in identifying the underlying knowledge support for current enterprise performance. However, it is more important as an indicator of the enterprise's future capabilities and potentials for success. A company has a good future potential when it has extensive IC assets consisting of human capital (employee expertise, relationships, competence, and motivation) and structural capital, which includes innovation capital (patents and R&D results, for example), process capital (such as manufacturing expertise), and relationship capital (loyal customers and suppliers and supportive employees and investors).

The connection between IC and business performance was explored and elucidated in the work started in the mid-1980s in Sweden by Karl-Erik Sveiby, Leif Edvinsson, and others. The Skandia Navigator resulted from that work and incorporated IC perspectives when evaluating the corporate potential and health (see Figure 1-5).[7] With such views, many firms and countries have audited their intellectual capital and use these insights to build new capabilities and competitiveness — mostly by strengthening personal IC assets through education and training but also by building structural IC. Notably, country IC audits have been performed by Australia, France, Israel, the Netherlands, Singapore, and the Nordic countries (Denmark, Finland, Iceland, Norway, and Sweden), among others, and are updated annually for most.

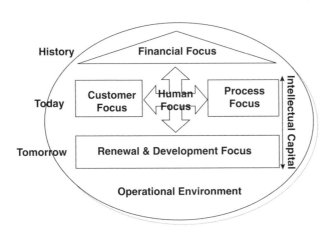

Figure 1-5
The Skandia Navigator. Copyright 1996 © Skandia Insurance Company, Ltd.

Examples of Structural Intellectual Capital

Figure 1-6 shows examples of structural IC assets for a typical enterprise (labeled Structural Knowledge Assets and SKAs in the figure). This illustration considers the structural knowledge assets to be part of the capabilities that people utilize to conduct work. It also considers feedback from customers and the outside world and learnings and innovations as part of these capabilities. Our view is that structural IC assets are continually created by conducting internal operations and daily work so as to be available for delivering better work in the future.

As indicated, the structural IC assets in part are embedded in the goods and services that the enterprise provides to its customers. They also include the practices and manners in which the company handles customers, suppliers, and other stakeholders. The IC assets contribute to the enterprise's capabilities to handle situations — to act — by making the IC asset capabilities available to the people who work for the enterprise. Hence, management and operating practices, systems and procedures, permissions and decision rights, and so on

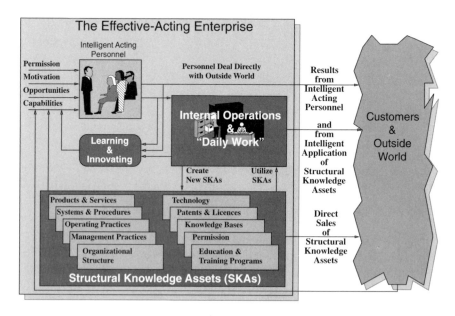

Figure 1-6

The effective-acting enterprise achieves its performance by diligent application of personal and structural intellectual capital assets. Copyright © 1995 Knowledge Research Institute, Inc. Reproduced with permission.

are all structural IC assets that the employees utilize in their jobs. The effectiveness of these IC assets determines the effectiveness of the resulting actions and hence the behavior and performance of the company.

Good IC assets, as suggested above and discussed in later chapters, are not sufficient to ensure enterprise effectiveness and durability in the present global competitive environment. In addition, appropriate work arrangements, supportive conditions, and a motivated workforce are necessary. By providing good leadership, senior and middle managers contribute importantly to how well people are willing and able to contribute to enterprise success.

The Role of Knowledge Workers

The function of personal knowledge, understanding, and judgments in achieving effective organizational performance is becoming clearer. Early on, managerial emphasis on work procedures and methods was placed on observable work. Later, it included the role of information and information flows, which are also observable. Now, focus is shifting to include knowledge. It has always been understood that know-how and expertise influence quality of work. However, the knowledge focus has tended to be centered on the individual's educational and training background and not on considerations of systematic perspectives for broader work processes or knowledge mechanisms within organizations. There has been little focus on invisible work, particularly on how workers think and utilize knowledge when performing tasks.

In the Tayloristic world of a century ago, the role of the worker was to execute work according to instructions and job descriptions. Work processes were considered to be definable and repeatable. For most, that has changed — and continues to change. Workers on all levels — managers, professionals, crafts workers, and "unskilled" workers — are all required to think independently to act effectively. They must respond to daily work challenges in ways that serve the enterprise, its customers, and themselves in the best way possible. Truly repetitive and routine work is increasingly automated, with the more demanding also including embedded artificial intelligence (AI) capabilities.

An example illustrates the new situation: Workers whom many consider to be semi-skilled, such as the room service personnel at Ritz-Carlton and Inter-Continental hotels, are increasingly expected to implement the corporate strategies of exceptionally friendly and effective service. They are asked to be on the outlook for problems and anomalies, to identify and to service special guest requests, and to recognize opportunities for improved and more effective ways of working and serving guests. Many of their challenges fall far outside conventional job descriptions for such positions, but the personnel is expected to identify the challenges and handle them quickly, competently, and innovatively. As a result of the success of this and similar actions in other areas, both hotel chains receive very high degrees of customer loyalty. The strategy has been implemented effectively.

Making the hotel model work requires good task knowledge. But people who do the detailed work must also have in-depth understanding of the enterprise's goals and intents and the broader knowledge and motivation to "think outside the box." They must use critical thinking and have personal motivation to exert the additional energy and take the next step. Perhaps more than anything else, they require the freedom to act and must understand that the guest-supportive actions are appreciated and rewarded by both management and the guests themselves. They must also understand that the better they perform their work, the better is the success of their organization and their own job security.

NOTES

1. As an example, in 2001, 70 percent of firms in the United States that exported goods and services had fewer than 20 employees.
2. "Taylorism" refers to the operation and management practices advocated by the father of scientific management, Frederick W. Taylor (1856–1915). A description of Taylorism may be found in Littler (1978). Taylor and Western practitioners of the rational approach to management, which were nearly all companies, are said to have promoted the view that workers should be told explicitly what to do and not be encouraged to use their own knowledge and ideas to change or improve work practices or work process. According to that view, workers who improve these areas on their own are counterproductive, and such worker involvements should be discouraged. According to Drucker (1993), common use of the term Taylorism is an incorrect interpretation of Taylor's personal work and philosophy. Taylor actually promoted worker participation and ownership — directions that were threatening to both management and

labor at the time, and he was vilified and intentionally misinterpreted —
resulting in the general misunderstanding.

3. For categorizations of knowledge and related intellectual capital assets, see Appendix C.

4. Nano-productivity refers to the productivity of a single job or position, often performed by a single person.

5. See Chapter 7.

6. See Chapter 2. An early indication of the importance of the intangible asset management mentality for managing intangible capital was stressed by Professor Baruch Lev (2001).

7. The Skandia Navigator is explained at <http://www.skandia.com/en/about/processes.shtml>.

2

THE EFFECTIVE ENTERPRISE

PREMISE 2-1: INDIVIDUAL ACTIONS LEAD TO OVERALL ENTERPRISE PERFORMANCE

Enterprise behavior is a result of the individual actions of its employees and the composite actions of its management teams and operating units. The enterprise's behavior is effective when most actions correctly implement its strategy and the desired goals are achieved and when the strategy reflects the enterprise's purpose, objectives, and intents. Success is achieved when its goals are appropriate and realistic and when they are reached and held over time.

PREMISE 2-2: EFFECTIVE ENTERPRISE BEHAVIOR LEADS TO SUCCESS

Effective enterprise behavior fulfills the enterprise's philosophy, intents, goals, and objectives. When these are appropriately defined to lead to enterprise success, attaining them leads to achieved success.

THE PROACTIVE AND DECISIVE COMPANY EXAMPLE

A steel mini-mill has practiced systematic and comprehensive knowledge management (KM) since its start-up in 1975. The company's senior managers do not think of their management philosophy and operating practices as KM, only as the most effective and appropriate approach to secure durable exceptional performance. Their business results, which they attribute to their knowledge- and people-focused approach, validate their beliefs. The

26

company's business and operational successes are exceptional. Let us consider some characteristics of their approach:

Management Philosophy

- The company's management pursues the hologram philosophy whereby each employee is a replica of the whole and understands management's visions and the company's daily business situation and long-term strategy. That allows employees to make independent decisions to implement corporate strategy, while taking into account short-term tradeoffs, broad business implications, and other consequences.
- The management recognizes that people are "incredibly smart and innovative" and perform to succeed when (a) given the opportunity to perform; (b) having sufficient job-related and general knowledge; (c) being provided with detailed up-to-date information on the plant's and company's performance and constraints; and (d) being accountable for their actions.
- The management believes that their employees must be better educated and have a better understanding of the operational, technical, and business aspects of operations than competitors. This is their basis for distributing decision making and enabling employees to act on their own.
- Collaboration is essential and reinforced. Employees are not judged on their individual performance; instead, they are judged on the performance of the whole team and the company as a whole.

Management Choices

- Decisions are delegated to the point-of-use to permit each operator to act immediately.
- The company's employees are salaried and divided into teams. Team leaders are rotated.
- There are no individual department bonuses. Twice-yearly profit sharing is distributed to all based on the total company's performance.
- There are no production quotas — only a stated desire to produce as much as possible at the highest quality required by the present market.

- Operations are closely integrated to break down barriers between departments.
- Adjacent operations report to the same general manager to strengthen integration.
- "Everyone participates in research." The company has no separate R&D function but is still performing extensive R&D. Senior operators and engineers collaborate on the research and development of new operations methods, new designs, etc. Teams are allowed to experiment with different operating conditions to test improvements.
- The company does not have a maintenance department per se. Operators are educated and expected to diagnose, troubleshoot, and repair the equipment. Maintenance people with special knowledge in electronics, computers, and so on, are part of operations.
- The company's plants are controlled by sophisticated process computers to reduce dependence on personnel for routine work and to achieve uniformity of operations.

Knowledge-Related Practices and Actions

- All employees are provided with competence to act independently, intelligently, and quickly — although collaboration is widely encouraged.
- Deliberate educational and knowledge distribution efforts ascertain that employees have access to the best possible knowledge available to handle situations.
- The company uses outside experts whenever possible and frequently surveys worldwide what others do. "Not Invented Here" syndromes are not prevalent. "We are not large enough to have in-house experts in most of the areas where we need expertise."
- Information on operating and technical performance is shared widely. Competitively sensitive information is controlled, but technical and operating information is made available to everyone. The performance of operations and potentials for improving performance (quality, throughput, energy consumption, etc.) are constant topics for discussion among operators at all levels.
- The company places extensive emphasis on education and provides education for high school equivalency for those without

diplomas. Education is provided for all in metallurgy, steel chemistry, metals processing, control, electronics, and other relevant technical areas, as well as in basic business principles, customer requirements, people skills, teamwork, and other subjects.

Resulting Behavioral and Cultural Traits

- All employees have a "can-do" mentality based on needs to pursue competence and innovation.
- Individuals are not afraid to ask others for inputs and expertise. The company maintains a "safe environment" culture.
- Peer pressure is very important to identify and weed out unwanted behavior.
- Management is careful to not blame individuals. Operating problems are examined to find what can be learned — if it is technical or human. If technical, solutions are sought and corrections implemented. If human, management explores how it can change the situation through its own behavior, education, staffing, or perhaps by changing the operation itself.

The Company's Business Results

Unless significant business results can be traced back to the way the company is managed, the management principles, corresponding practices, and actions will be without merit. However, for this company the results are significant.

- It is able to produce higher quality steel at lower costs than its competitors, and it is a preferred supplier for many very large customers.
- It uses less energy and time to melt and process steel than its competitors.
- Its plants are run with fewer operators than their competitors.
- The company is very profitable.

WHAT DOES IT MEAN THAT AN ENTERPRISE IS EFFECTIVE?

Fundamentally, an enterprise is effective when it is able to reach its goals and satisfy its objectives. Its goals and objectives must be realistic and reachable and in line with the enterprise's purpose. From more practical perspectives and in detail, for an enterprise to be effective requires that its functions be executed efficiently in close support of its intent and desired direction. It also requires that the enterprise innovate and renew itself from top to bottom.[1]

A basic goal of any enterprise — be it public or private — is to achieve its objectives. Ideally, this goal is best attained when all individual and aggregated actions are in full support of the desired direction. That ideal is not easily achieved; it may not even be possible. In reality, most actions result from decisions that are far from simple and straightforward. Complex conditions may lead to inappropriate choices. Conflicts between objectives require tradeoffs. Internal political pressures result in biased decisions. Lack of understanding — insufficient knowledge — leads to inappropriate evaluations of situations and impaired judgments of outcomes. Uncertainties from inadequate information must be addressed, and too often wrong actions are pursued by mistaken expectations.

Nevertheless, in this complex environment, it is important that each action contributes maximally to satisfy the enterprise goals. Actions must be effective relative to the desired objectives. Small individual actions aggregate into consolidated group and enterprise actions. For consolidated actions to provide the desired results, such as delivering valuable services to customers or creating high-quality products at reasonable cost, the smaller actions need to help achieve the desired enterprise goals. Ideally, all actions must deal appropriately and effectively with the conditions of the target situation — by making tradeoffs, avoiding undesirable biases, dealing with uncertainties, and so on.

The effective enterprise is an organization that acts intelligently in the present and is capable of dealing effectively with the challenges of the future. It meets its objectives by implementing its visions and strategies through the actions of individual employees and through its systems, policies, and organizational structure. It makes tradeoffs between short-term and long-term requirements, and it meets the objectives of both the enterprise itself and its stakeholders. Management teams of effective enterprises recognize that to be viable in the longer term, they must acknowledge that they have broad responsibilities. For many organizations, these responsibilities surpass conventional and narrow operating perspectives to include concerns for the environment, local and larger economies, society-at-large, and other stakeholders that are directly or indirectly affected by the enterprise's actions. The concerns also include attainment of the long-term objectives of the enterprise — the reasons for its existence. The breadth of responsibilities results from the understanding that the enterprise is an integrated element in the complex societal and environmental system and that the effects of its actions on other parts of the system will directly influence its medium and longer term viability. All parties are affected — owners, employees, customers, suppliers, society as a whole, and its physical environment — as well as the enterprise itself. The value of consistent effective behavior can be large. When employees — and the enterprise overall — do the right thing, the enterprise can tackle challenges with great effectiveness and enjoy success and durable viability.

Good Enterprise Performance Results from Effective Personal Actions

Effective behavior is important in all knowledge work. People tend to think of effective and intelligent performance as particularly important in high-level "valuable" problem-solving or decision-making situations like setting corporate strategy. However, effective behavior is equally, and often more, important on the factory floor and in detailed work throughout the enterprise. *Improving the quality of the myriad of "small" problem-solving situations in every employee's daily work culminates into a significant improvement in performance for the whole enterprise.* It makes the difference between a high-performing enterprise and a well-intending, but stumbling, organization. Enterprise strategy may be determined in the boardroom, but it is implemented mostly by the individual actions of employees throughout the organization. To implement the strategy appropriately requires shared understanding by employees on all levels beyond what currently is customary.

Enterprise behaviors take many forms. Top management actions are easiest to observe, be they approaches to mergers and acquisitions, handling problems such as product failures in the marketplace, or specific personnel policies such as retirement programs or stock purchase plans. However, other behaviors may actually be more important but are quite difficult to observe and characterize. They also may not be easy to modify or influence. Behaviors that are difficult to change include how individual customers are dealt with by customer interface employees, how quickly the organization can act to modify or develop new products and services when markets change or where new opportunities arise, and so on.

The enterprise is a collection of closely coupled systems in which the performance of each department or subsystem will affect the operations of other subsystems.[2] From strategic and enterprise performance points of view, the overall behavior of the enterprise determines its success. However, the overall performance is made up of the micro actions and performances of each department — the sales department, manufacturing department, R&D department, customer service department, etc. The actions and resulting performance of each department are again made up from the smaller nano actions and behaviors of individual people who hold positions within the departments. As indicated in Figure 2-1, the consolidated enterprise behavior, its overall performance, is the result of these countless nano and micro actions — the personal actions of everyone in the enterprise and anyone else who is acting on the enterprise's behalf. For the overall performance to be good, the actions by people must be good.

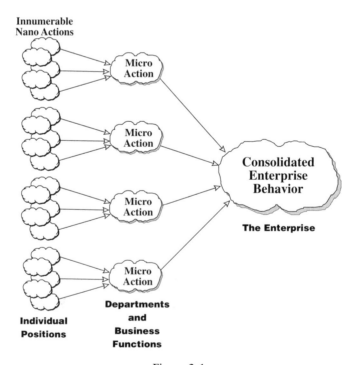

Figure 2-1
The effective-acting enterprise achieves its performance by diligent application of personal knowledge and structural intellectual capital assets. Copyright © 2000 Knowledge Research Institute, Inc. Reproduced with permission.

Effective Enterprises Rely on Broad and Deep Knowledge

Proactive managers emphasize that knowledge, particularly personal understanding of both work and enterprise intents, is the principal force behind the effective enterprise. Managers promote viability by developing, cumulating, and deploying competitive knowledge. They expect that these actions will foster proper and effortless handling of routine and simple tasks and that non-routine and complex tasks will be handled in a timely way and competently in the best interest of all parties. They believe that consistent effective behavior secures competitive leadership and the ability to pursue opportunities and render services that could not be delivered otherwise. For these reasons they choose to manage knowledge explicitly and systematically.

Overall enterprise performance — the degree to which enterprise objectives are fulfilled — is determined by the effectiveness of countless separate actions performed by individuals and groups — that is, how well regular situations and difficult challenges are handled. Organizational effectiveness is determined by many factors, the most important being the quality and availability of pertinent knowledge at points-of-action used to handle situations — that is, to make sense of information, innovate, decide what to do, act, and evaluate the implications of approaches and actions. Other factors, not covered in this book, include the mentalities and motivations of individuals and organizational characteristics that shape and channel individual actions into desirable and effective enterprise actions. In addition, many manage to create highly effective enterprises with low internal friction and self-energizing and rewarding work environments that operate with little wasted effort.

Important enterprise situations vary widely. Some work situations, such as fast, reliable, and error-free assembly, are well known and require routine, even automatized knowledge. Other work situational, such as project work to find solutions to stubborn operating problems, are complex and require extensive, at times abstract, knowledge and metaknowledge. Even in well-known routine cases, effective situation-handling involves many steps and requires specialized knowledge to support the primary situation-handling tasks of Sensemaking, Decision-Making/Problem-Solving, Implementation, and Monitoring as discussed in Chapter 5.

One important focus of this book deals with the relationship between knowledge and other intellectual capital (IC) assets and the situation-handling tasks and methods that people and organizations utilize to act effectively. Our purpose is to guide efforts to strengthen knowledge-related capabilities and to facilitate their use as they are built with the aid of deliberate and systematic management of knowledge-related practices and processes — that is, systematic and deliberate KM.

Similar steps are required for both simple and complex personal situation-handling cases and for organizational situation-handling. Many business problems are appreciably knowledge-related, as are many business opportunities. Unfortunately, there is a shortage of insights into business-related knowledge processes. The situation-handling model presented in Chapters 5 and 6 provides an aggregated framework to understand how to deal with knowledge-based activities. The model portrays processes associated with delivering competent work that is aligned with the enterprise's intents. It does not deal with learning or innovation mechanisms. Nor does it detail mechanisms within the primary tasks.

What Is Successful Enterprise Performance?

Traditionally in many people's minds, successful enterprise performance has been equated with good financial results. We take a different view. We adopt the view of many successful organizations and outstanding thinkers (de Geus 1997; Drucker 1999; Herzberg 2003; Mintzberg 2002, 2003; Pfeffer 2003). Good, successful performance focuses on the enterprise's capability to tackle and overcome challenges and both create and take proper advantage of opportunities while balancing a broad range of internal dilemmas or paradoxes, such as supporting all employees uniformly while at the same time fast-tracking promising leaders. It also includes financial health, which is a basic necessity. Behind this capability we find management leadership to guide and motivate the enterprise. We find strong intangible asset management mentality to create, maintain, and exploit intangible capital assets, particularly intellectual capital (IC) assets through deliberate and systematic KM. We also find widespread interests focused on deep engagement in work; broad, forward-looking critical thinking and situation-handling; a knowledgeable and well-informed workforce that participates in cooperation instead of politicking and competing; and an action-oriented, positive, and fear-free culture that focuses on achievement and progress instead of pursuing process issues and maintaining the status quo.

The successful and viable enterprise must continually satisfy its stakeholders, and it must treat its customers in such a manner that they will continue to demand its products rather than those of its competitors. The enterprise must deliver products and services with greater overall value than those available elsewhere and must provide them at attractive costs and with sufficient ease and support. To achieve this, the enterprise must deal effectively with present and future challenges. It must implement its visions and strategies through the personal actions that employees perform to operationalize enterprise strategy. That requires competent and well-informed employees and organizational actions guided by systems and procedures.

For many years, managers and academics have worked to develop theories and approaches to make private and public enterprises more effective. Conceptual frameworks outlining basic mechanisms have been created based on insights from management, economic, social, and cognitive sciences. Some advanced approaches focus on how knowledge is used to support actions that contribute to enterprise success. However, only recently has it been recognized how proactive organizations obtain practical experience with these methods to identify those that work in real life — in spite of many organizations that have pursued such practices for decades or even centuries (de Geus 1997).

External and Internal Enterprise Effectiveness

Enterprise effectiveness must be considered from two points of view: outside and inside. The *outside perspective* deals with effectiveness in the marketplace and relative to external stakeholders. Effectiveness can be measured by how well customers perceive that they are treated and by the value of the goods and services they receive, how good the financial performance is in the eyes of investors, the fulfillment of societal and environmental responsibilities, fairness in employee relations, and so on. The *inside perspective* deals with effectiveness within the enterprise itself — how well individual and aggregated actions are selected and shaped to fulfill enterprise objectives. Examples include the ability to create high-quality products, short time to market, good utilization of operating capital, efficient internal operations to reduce costs and deliver on time, fast widespread adoption of new and better operating practices and other valuable learnings, extensive building of new personal knowledge, and structural IC through creativity and innovation, workforce loyalty, satisfaction, and so on.

Success and Knowledge-Intensive Work

When actions work together to support enterprise objectives, the enterprise succeeds. Individual decisions, large and small, behind each action provide the desired effectiveness that leads to the proper result. In the aggregate, when decisions and resulting actions are made in support of the enterprise objectives, strategies, and visions — when they effectively support the desired enterprise direction — then the enterprise can be considered effective and can be expected to succeed.

There are other crucial aspects of effective behavior. One aspect deals with the effectiveness of networking among employees — and with outsiders — to collaborate to undertake joint actions in concert and aligned with common purpose. Another aspect deals with the issue of enterprise growth and renewal — positive change — by building enterprise intelligent capital through learning and innovation.

In our context, we consider work[3] to consist of active processes that generate valuable products and services through combinations or conversions of less valuable components, through outright creations, or through other actions. Most work of this kind is knowledge intensive in that the actions are governed by the application of knowledge and understanding — such as using mental reference models that give guidance by providing facts, rules, concepts, perspectives, goals, methodologies, models, or other kinds of action patterns. The quality of delivered work is largely a function of the applicability of the knowledge that has been applied. Appropriate knowledge is a necessary but not sufficient condition for effective work. Other factors also apply.

In business, knowledge-intensive work is conducted by people everywhere — in every department, in every function, at every organizational level. In addition, by embedding knowledge in inanimate agents, knowledge-intensive work is conducted by different functions such as automated systems and procedures, automatic control systems, and many kinds of machines and operating technology. *In short, knowledge-intensive work is the fundamental value-creating process of any organization or entity.*

The Importance of Information Technology

During the last decade, the perception was often that technology was central to success. However, the business world is increasingly realizing that the effectiveness of enterprises rests upon people. It is people's personal knowledge and IC assets — their expertise and motivation to be engaged in work — that are the distinguishing factors for success. Clearly, management and operational practices, financial assets, and physical assets such as production machinery, plants, distribution systems, and other capabilities are also important and necessary. Information technology (IT) and related technologies are significant, but secondary factors. They serve mostly as passive infrastructure and are not as central for competitive superiority as it was generally thought in the 1990s. This may change if IT becomes smarter and more sophisticated. Then IT will take on more active tasks, thus liberating people to pursue more complex challenges. However, making really smart systems outside the laboratory has proven more difficult than anticipated, and we can expect decades, possibly centuries, of development.

Productivity Is Not Always What We Expect!

Enterprise competitiveness is in part determined by its productivity — by its ability to bring added value to customers through products and services. Productivity is highly dependent on how smartly and effectively operations and interactions are performed and on how time and other resources are utilized to create and deliver high-quality results. Productivity is primarily a function of the application of available know-how — the understanding of what to do in every normal and expected situation and how to do it, as well as the competence required to handle more complex and novel situations. Know-how includes the effectiveness of work process arrangements, sophistication of work-related artifacts and technology, and work and operating practices (Sveiby & Lloyd 1987).

Most common measures of productivity are traditional performance measures for physical production systems. Productivity may be biased toward production of physical goods and delivery of revenue-bearing services when defined as a ratio of output divided by input. These metrics don't take into account key aspects of organizational performance, such as competitive differentiation, market share, completion of services and products on schedule, quality of services and products, or how well they fit with national goals. In addition, productivity gains typically are achieved with the support of other resource-consuming factors such as monetary capital and natural resources (Sardina & Vrat 1987). Knowledge work, because of its complex nature and the difficulties of isolating what the precise consequence of knowledge contributions is, has historically been excluded from productivity evaluation but has now become central in the knowledge era.

Different Kinds of Productivity (Wiig & Jooste 2003)

We must distinguish between different kinds of productivity. Economic theory refers to *macroproductivity* on national and global levels, *microproductivity* on business and institutional levels, and *nanoproductivity* on suborganizational levels such as the department or the productivity of an individual job or person (Thor 1988). We also distinguish between *performance* (or *material*) *productivity* and *economic* (or *financial*) *productivity* (Moore & Ross 1978). Both performance productivity and economic productivity are important for managing and analyzing enterprise success, but they can differ markedly, particularly in competitive situations. For example, if a company can now produce a specific type of machine with half the inputs needed earlier, performance microproductivity and performance nanoproductivity double. However, if competitors also improve their microproductivity and nanoproductivity performances to the same extent and everyone lowers their price to half of what it was, the economic microproductivity will not change. It may even be reduced. Every company will achieve progress, but the revenues for each unit of labor and resource utilization will remain the same as before. As a result, customers will benefit, but from a financial point of view, the company will not.

If the inputs and output quantity remain the same and the output quality, or the number of features or options increases, value creation and performance nanoproductivity will increase. If the enterprise can command a higher price for its outputs, the economic microproductivity will also rise. However, if competitors also raise quality and increase features and options, prices may remain stable, or drop, even though the value of what is being delivered to the customers has increased (assuming that they want and benefit from the improved quality, extra features, and options). So, while all participants are "more productive" from a performance point of view, the economic impacts will be far harder to measure or may not have changed at all. Better knowledge at the point-of-action — the workplace — makes it possible to deliver more with less or to provide higher quality outputs without increased efforts. Since competitors also strive to improve, the need to innovate faster than the competition is vitally important to maintain leadership.

Improvements in workplace operations and enterprise products and services through innovation and improved knowledge, understanding, and other intellectual capital (IC) assets normally lead to progress and performance productivity gains. But these gains may not provide increases in economic productivity if competitive or other mechanisms prevent organizations from realizing the economic benefits. Improving performance productivity without being able to realize economic gains is often the price of remaining competitive.

Improved application of personal or organizational knowledge does improve performance productivity. However, that may not translate into financial productivity! This explains why many attempts to link the success of KM initiatives to so-called hard numbers (typically, greater profits) do not take into account that people are thinking better, acting more effectively, and being more productive, just so the organization can remain competitive.

An additional, and unpleasant, aspect of progress and improved performance productivity is that frequently fewer people are required to provide the products and services demanded by the market. Better production machinery, infrastructure, systems, procedures, and so on may lead to layoffs and other kinds of staff reduction. Progress can therefore result in negative societal effects such as increased unemployment.

Value Creation and Productivity

Increased productivity — producing valuable results with fewer resources, producing higher value results with the same resources, or achieving a combination of the two — creates increased value for the enterprise. Most business leaders recognize that the ultimate basis for improving productivity consists of being able to make outstanding, knowledge-intensive decisions and innovations. They achieve this by applying quality IC assets to improve competitive positioning, product/service quality and features, and day-to-day product and service delivery.

Elapsed time of responding to customers to complete work and introduce new products into the market is an important aspect of productivity. Expedient handling of work — quick turnaround for client work, short time to market, and many more — improves performance and economic productivities on both the personal and organizational level. Reducing elapsed time requires innovation and task-related knowledge, often in many areas at the same time. It often requires extensive conceptual knowledge, such as script and schema knowledge and procedural metaknowledge.

With knowledge and other IC assets as the basic enablers of productivity, it again becomes necessary to manage them deliberately and effectively. The productivity gains required to remain viable become directly dependent upon effective and systematic KM.

A SYSTEMIC MODEL OF ENTERPRISE PERFORMANCE

As indicated earlier, all enterprises are collections of closely coupled subsystems in which the performance of each department or subsystem influences the operations of other subsystems and the overall enterprise. These influences travel along many pathways and have many different forms. As a result of the interconnectedness, the overall enterprise performance is affected by the distributed activities within every subsystem. For overall effective performance, the subsystems must be effective to provide the desired behaviors. A simplified model of systemic functions and connections within a commercial enterprise is shown in Figure 2-2. Four primary factors are indicated: Drivers, Enablers, Facilitators, and Mechanisms. Solid arrows indicate performance-influencing relationships. The figure provides a perspective of the role that IC assets play by enabling enterprise performance.

Drivers are the most important factors and provide impetus and energy to act. They provide goals, rationale, and intents for the enterprise and for people — the reasons for actions and criteria for performance. The drivers define the purpose and strategy for the enterprise.

The principal enablers of performance consist of knowledge, understanding, and other IC assets. Once the drivers provide the needs and goals for actions, enablers provide the means to establish the proper course, content, quality, and effectiveness of actions.

Facilitators consist of factors such as operating capital, relationship capital, and information capital. Facilitators provide resources to make actions easier — to reduce friction that works against actions. Information facilitates the ability to act by describing the contexts, circumstances, and particulars of situations that need handling.

Mechanisms consist of the functional elements that are manipulated — the processes that are operated to produce actions.

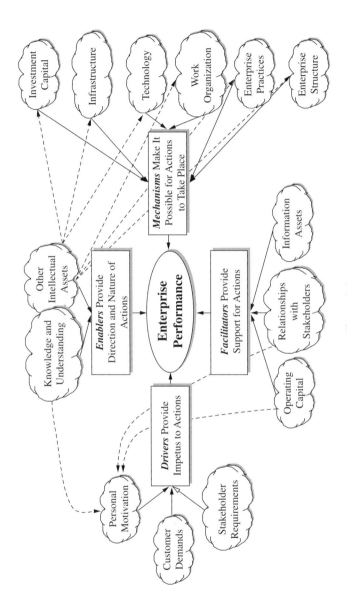

Figure 2-2

Drivers, enablers, facilitators, and mechanisms make the enterprise perform. Copyright © 1998 Knowledge Research Institute, Inc. Reproduced with permission.

Traditionally, principal attention and management efforts have been focused on mechanisms — the components of the system that implement actions determined by the drivers, enablers, and facilitators. Intensive analyses are often undertaken to find ways to make the mechanisms more effective — without regard to exploring which fundamental actions should be pursued to meet goals. The knowledge perspective makes it possible to shift the focus to components that determine the effectiveness of which actions should be pursued and how best to shape them given available understanding and resources — that is, not only how actions should be implemented.

Changing Enterprise Performance Takes Time

Given a systemic perspective of the enterprise, we also need to consider the dynamic nature of resulting performance after changes have been introduced in the primary or secondary factors. When any factor is changed, it may take considerable time before the new resulting enterprise performance levels are achieved. The model indicated in Figure 2-2 only indicates the different factors. It omits their dynamic and functional relationships.

Figure 2-3 provides a process perspective of the expected event chain from a change in a driver factor to a resulting enterprise performance. The example illustrates a change in an employee incentive program designed to improve motivation to share knowledge and thereby make a positive change in enterprise performance. However, the performance improvement from the incentive change will not happen immediately. It may take months, in some cases years, for the change to propagate through the different functions and departments within the enterprise before the improved performance is realized. Figure 2-3 depicts how the initial action changes effectiveness in the three subsequent areas of operations excellence, product leadership, and customer intimacy before resulting in improved enterprise performance (Treacy & Wieresma 1993). In the example, after the initial change it may take weeks or months before people become more knowledgeable — to the extent that they reduce operating costs and make better products and services. Additional time is required before these changes translate into increased demands in the marketplace and subsequently change profitability and viability.

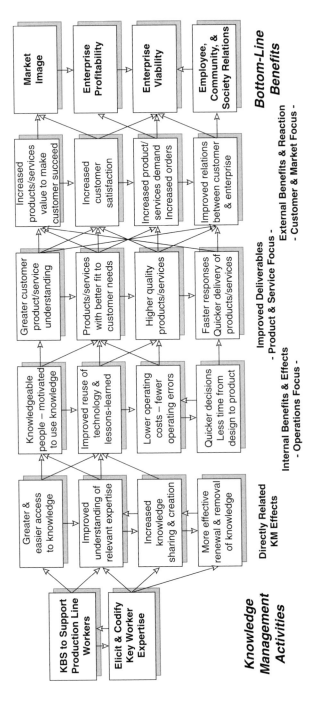

Figure 2-3

Enterprise performance results from changes that propagate through operational excellence, product leadership, and customer intimacy. Copyright © 1993 by Karl M. Wiig. Reproduced with permission.

Characteristics of the Effective Enterprise

Ideally, all enterprises should carry out their daily work exceptionally well. When they succeed in the short term, they should also, to the fullest extent possible, observe their goals and strategies to pursue longer-term opportunities and conquer or avoid threats. Such behavior will require management vision and considerable resources, infrastructure, and dedicated personnel. It is often anticipated and expected that all employees — and in the aggregate, the enterprise itself — always will act effectively, and "do the right thing." Everyone should make sense of challenges, find the best approaches to handle situations, anticipate outcomes, inform all concerned, implement decisions effectively, and so on. Unfortunately, few employees and enterprises, if any, live up to such expectations. Worse yet, only rarely is there an explicit and shared understanding among any of the enterprise's employees — or managers — of what "acting effectively" might mean in practice, although most would agree that such behavior would be highly beneficial. It also is difficult to determine what is required to make behavior more effective.

Enterprises are complex, and it is hard to manage the intangible and less visible functions associated with human intellectual work and application of structural intellectual capital. The complexity may appear deceptively simple since the operational and structural functions can only be partially observed and understood, and it is tempting to focus only on what is readily apparent — what is directly observable. Nonetheless, the interplay of individual factors cannot be reduced to the study of separate elements. The interrelatedness requires that the systemic effects be considered to the greatest extent possible.

The effective enterprise can be described by many observable characteristics such as:

Philosophy, Leadership, and Strategy
- The management and operating philosophy focus on creating environments and practices that promote the best possible performance.
- Top and middle management act as leaders and provide behavioral examples and role models and practice governance with integrity, purpose, and consistency.
- Rank-and-file employees are competent and effective leaders within their purviews.

- Goals and strategies are realistic, reachable, and competitive. The whole enterprise works to implement them.
- People at all levels share a common understanding of enterprise management and operating philosophy, purpose, strategy, and the general service paradigm.[4]
- Employees, departments, business units, and the overall enterprise deliver the desired service paradigms.

Resources and Efficiency

- The enterprise is well structured to allow its people, functions, and operations to implement strategy successfully.
- The enterprise has adequate financial, physical, personal knowledge, and structural IC resources.
- The enterprise utilizes its resources efficiently and minimizes waste in all forms.

Innovation, Quality, and Renewal

- The enterprise and its employees constantly innovate, renew, and maintain personal knowledge, IC assets, and other resources.
- Innovations and experiences are captured, communicated, and applied, and employees are recognized for their contributions.
- Everybody is motivated to perform their work competently, with appropriate task knowledge and metaknowledge to tackle work and challenges naturally and with relative ease.
- The enterprise regularly obtains outcome feedback on how well products and services perform — in the marketplace and within the enterprise — and uses these measures to monitor its performance.
- People consistently act in a timely fashion, and delays are rare.
- Employees consistently "close the loop" by communicating to the originators that messages or requests have been received, understood, and are being pursued.
- To minimize the risks of acting on inappropriate assumptions, employees clarify assumptions before proceeding.
- The enterprise creates, produces, and delivers superior products and services that match present and future market demands.
- Individuals, teams, units, and the enterprise itself deal competently with unexpected events, opportunities, and threats.

Motivation and Engagement
- Everybody understands what their role is in implementing enterprise strategy and why they personally benefit from making the strategy work.
- Employees are noticeably motivated and engaged in their work.
- Interpersonal work is performed through effective coordination, cooperation, and collaboration.
- Undesirable personal or systems behaviors are controlled.

Six Success Factors for the Effective Enterprise

Enterprise success depends on the interplay of many factors. Some are beyond influence or control by the enterprise. Others are associated with the strategic moves that its leaders pursue. Still others — particularly the six we consider here — are associated with how the enterprise arranges its internal affairs for operations and service delivery through initiatives, practices, and allocation of resources. Figure 2-4 provides an overview of a particular perspective of how enterprise performance is the result of management philosophies and practices, deliberate and systematic KM, allocation of resources, scoping of jobs, and assignment of employees. The six success factors affect the ability to handle situations to the best advantages for the enterprise, individual employees, and other stakeholders. Situation-handling is discussed in Chapter 5.

1. Management Philosophy and Practice
   A basic requirement for intelligent operation of the enterprise is a management philosophy that supports effective behavior of people and operational units. In particular, people will act effectively and responsibly when satisfied with their conditions, given the chance to contribute, and when they understand that it is in their interest. However, this perspective must be tempered with the realization that a few employees may have quite different personal agendas that are not in the enterprise's interest. These people must be managed differently.[5] In addition, a significant group of people — some organizations report 40 percent, others 60 percent — are reluctant to assume responsibility and prefer to work in supportive roles. However, they also

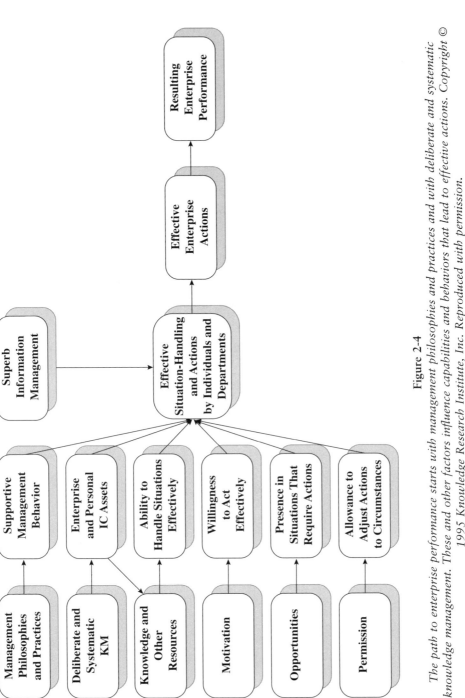

Figure 2-4

The path to enterprise performance starts with management philosophies and practices and with deliberate and systematic knowledge management. These and other factors influence capabilities and behaviors that lead to effective actions. Copyright © 1995 Knowledge Research Institute, Inc. Reproduced with permission.

need to be acknowledged and included when collaboration teams are structured and evaluated. In most instances, people who wish to act in support roles are crucial for performing the enterprise's basic work tasks.

Still, most people are eager to take on broader responsibilities that allow them to use their versatility, be more flexible, and adjust their work to facilitate the situation at hand. They frequently report greater job satisfaction and feelings of personal rewards as a result. Greater customer satisfaction, lower costs, reduced error rates, and increased preventions of mishaps are reported by enterprises that support employees to build knowledge and accept increased responsibilities in areas of competence. More importantly, the increased innovation that produces new approaches for enterprise strategies, tactics, and services is significant and leads to a considerable increase in structural intellectual capital.

Management philosophy must support changes in the enterprise culture, particularly through practices and incentives to approve and foster new behaviors that must become "the way things are done around here."

2. *Deliberate and Systematic Knowledge Management*

If we accept that it is correct that personal knowledge and structural IC assets in general are the most important factors behind enterprise success, then these assets must be managed diligently. These assets must be created, renewed, and exploited for the greatest benefits for all concerned by deliberate and systematic KM. That includes a widespread intellectual asset management mentality and culture, which we will discuss further below. The purpose of KM is the systematic, explicit, and deliberate building, renewal, and application of IC assets to maximize the enterprise's knowledge-related effectiveness and the returns from these assets.

3. *Knowledge and Other Resources*

Professional, craft, navigational knowledge, metaknowledge, information, and other necessary resources must be made available for employees to deliver quality work products that satisfy the requirements of the situation and the general service paradigm. Employees must possess requisite skills and attitudes and be supported in their ability to think critically and creatively by being provided with relevant metaknowledge. They must be provided with all other essential resources to handle situations appropriately.

4. *Motivation and Personal Energy*

Employees must be energized and motivated to be willing to act effectively and intelligently — "to do the right thing" — by knowing that they are provided with understanding and have emotional acceptance of how their actions will be of value to stakeholders, to the enterprise, and, most importantly, to themselves. In addition, they must have the secure understanding that "doing the right thing" can be accomplished with the available resources. Motivation is the most important and difficult factor to effectuate. It requires honest and ethical behavioral and communication approaches to create trust and goodwill that will be new to most organizations. As an example, Figure 2-5 indicates how appropriate management behavior generally can be expected to lead to high workplace respect, which is a precursor to positive workplace cooperation that results in achieving desired outcomes.

In addition, energy is a necessity for success — personal energy to pursue situation information, search and innovate aggressively to identify and create the best approaches to handle situations, act decisively, and monitor with strong leadership (Loehr & Schwartz 2003).

5. *Opportunities*

Employees must be placed in situations that require competent handling and offer them the opportunity to contribute and use their capabilities. Frequently, organizations fail to take advantage of the important expertise possessed by many of their employees and that results in less than desirable quality of work and unhappy employees who feel they are neglected. A totally different kind of opportunity that has resulted in highly valuable innovations is created when employees, as well as outsiders, are allowed to collaborate — or meet informally — to explore ideas and potentials for new approaches, solutions, and products and services. Valuable knowledge-related opportunities include:
— Opportunities to create and innovate.
— Opportunities to contribute and be recognized.
— Opportunities to perform and deliver value.
— Opportunities to learn, network, and share valuable knowledge.

Work flows must be organized to take advantage of people's capabilities and to exploit the potentials for innovation and application of diversity.

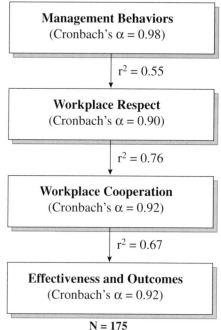

N = 175
The Management Effectiveness Model
"The primary effect of supervisory behaviors
is on workplace respect."

Figure 2-5
Supervisor behaviors significantly influence effectiveness and outcomes as
indicated by the management effectiveness model. © 2001 Wendell Brase and The
Regents of the University of California (Brase 2001).

6. Permission

Employees must be provided safe environments in which to do their work. Authority that matches their capabilities and expertise must be delegated to allow employees to provide them decision rights to adjust actions to correspond to the requirements of the situations they handle. They must be given permission to innovate, improvise, and "stretch" enterprise policies and practices beyond predetermined scopes and standards to serve the enterprise's and its stakeholders' best interest. They need to adjust actions given the enterprise's strategy, tactics, policies, and intents. At the same time, they must accept responsibility and accountability, act creatively and responsibly, and be accountable for their actions.

Six Behaviors of the Effective Enterprise

No matter how intelligent a leader's strategy for change, it will fail without the dedicated support of the rank and file. Winning that support often requires more effort than devising the strategy itself (Hymowitz 2002).

Effective and intelligent behavior is important in all knowledge work. People tend to think of such behavior as particularly important in "valuable" problem-solving or decision-making situations and other high-level tasks such as determining corporate strategy. However, contrary to that notion, intelligent behavior is equally — often more — important on the factory floor and in detailed work throughout the enterprise. As indicated earlier, most enterprise strategy is determined in the boardroom but is implemented by the individual actions of employees throughout the organization. Hence, improving the quality of the myriad of "small" decision-making and problem-solving situations that are part of every employee's daily work cumulates into significant improvements in knowledge worker performance for the whole enterprise. It makes the difference between a high-performing organization and a well-intending, but stumbling, organization.

Many researchers have studied the relationships between behavior in the workplace and enterprise performance. Wendell Brase identified relationships between management behaviors, workplace respect, workplace cooperation, and effectiveness and outcomes, as was indicated in Figure 2-5.

As for the success factors discussed previously, behaviors are functions of circumstances, traditions, availability of resources, and other factors. More importantly, they are also directly dependent upon what people know and believe and therefore are influenced by systematic KM. Among all the behaviors in the enterprise, six behaviors stand out:

1. *Ethical, Safe, and Approachable Behavior*
    Any enterprise that expects to survive over the long term needs to adopt a governance model that minimizes internal strife and countereffective behaviors. In the spirit of good senior management operating philosophy, everyone responsible should attempt to foster an ethical, safe, and approachable environment that supports effective situation-handling by

employees. Specific aspects of the corresponding behavior tend to be:

— Open, honest, and communicative to build solid understanding of issues with the security that there are no hidden agendas or other problem issues.
— Helpful and approachable managers and coworkers who all work to achieve enterprise success and viability.
— Managers acting as role models for personal attitudes, conducts, and leaders.
— Ethical and fair treatment in dealing with problems and opportunities.
— Trusting in the attitudes, mentality, and capabilities of managers and coworkers.
— Responsible and accountable for personal actions with tendencies to practice "The Buck Stops Here!" actions.

2. *Effectiveness-Seeking Behavior*

The enterprise continually works to renew and reinvent itself. It seeks to find the best and most effective approaches to operate and conduct business — within its internal operations and in all external relations. The employee effectiveness-seeking behaviors tend to be:

— Constantly learning and innovating with the goal of innovating faster and better than competitors — and not only learning faster than competitors.
— Implementing valuable innovations and exploiting IC assets quickly and wherever applicable.
— Delegating, collaborative, and trusting.
— Culturally supportive of strategy and mission.
— Goal oriented.
— Alert to advances among competitors and other parties.
— Considering many possible scenarios for future developments and challenges.

3. *Consistent and Durable Behavior*

In spite of the constant changes brought about by innovations and external changes, the effective enterprise is able to maintain a stable and reliable operation and uphold a solid reputation in the marketplace. It also emphasizes a healthy balance between short-term requirements and long-term viability. Specific aspects of this behavior tend to be:

— Focused on providing products and services that predictably and consistently increase market value and foster customer loyalties. Factors of product and service characteristics (in order of importance) are:[6]

— Consistent product quality and conformance to specifications
— Dependable delivery of products and services
— Product features — high-performance products
— Fast and reliable deliveries
— Low prices of goods and services
— Flexibility — new product introduction
— Flexibility — quick design changes by customer request
— Broad product line
— After-sales service
— Broad distribution
— Rapid volume change — support of just-in-time (JIT)
— Effective promotion and advertising

— Proactive and decisive to escape avoidable problems, exploit opportunities, and ensure competitive leadership.
— Fiscally conservative to ascertain that the enterprise consistently is financially healthy.
— Providing stable and predictable working conditions for employees throughout the enterprise regardless of necessary changes.
— Avoiding personnel layoffs and reducing personnel turnover to provide workforce security and trust, retain access to personal IC assets, and minimize personnel and hiring costs.

4. *Employee Engagement Behavior*

The degree to which employees are engaged in their work is repeatedly found to be a major factor associated with enterprise productivity.[7] In most organizations, people are deeply engaged in their work less than 20 percent of the time on the average. Instead of being deeply engaged, they perform much of their work by rote without examining what situations might require beyond what is normal. Desirable employee engagement behavior often reflects a deeper mentality and tends to be:

— Aware that they have the understanding to do things "right" — this awareness provides employees with the security and motivation to engage.
— Focused on "doing the right thing," particularly when it requires adjusting actions to different circumstances — instead of treating each situation as routine.

   — Considering the implementation of every task as an integral part of implementing enterprise strategy (remember the Ritz-Carlton and Inter-Continental hotel staffs in Chapter 1).

   — Quick to pursue critical thinking and other fundamental approaches in complicated and unusual situations.

   — Delivering "completed staff work." [8]

   — Practicing "closing the loop" by reporting back.

5. *Stakeholder Supportive Behavior*

    The outstanding enterprise knows its stakeholders and how they are valuable to the enterprise's performance and viability. The enterprise also understands its responsibilities toward the stakeholders — that it is relied upon to provide economic returns to owners, secure livelihoods to employees, provide the town or area where it operates with services, products, and economic support through its payroll and sourcing, and so on. The supportive behaviors tend to be:

   — Concerned with an understanding of stakeholders' needs, objectives, and welfare to fulfill them to the greatest extent possible and to build support and loyalty.

   — Responsible and accountable for actions that affect shareholders.

   — Socially oriented and understand that the enterprise has obligations and responsibilities toward its stakeholders and society in general.

   — Environmentally oriented by considering secondary and tertiary environmental effects from actions.

6. *Competitive Behavior*

    A significant behavior characteristic of the enterprise is its competitiveness — its ability to deliver competitive value and attract customers to choose its products and services over competing ones. Competitive behaviors take many forms and are driven by several underlying factors such as dealing competently with customers in friendly and efficient ways while maximizing both customers' and the enterprise's objectives. The behaviors involve individuals, teams, departments, and larger entities and tend to be:

   — Competitive in spirit with commonly shared desires "to be the best."

   — Competent, informed, efficient, expedient, reliable, responsible, quality conscious in all work and planning.

— Understanding of customers and their customers to be able to deliver products and services of greater value and cost effectiveness than their competitors.

— Advanced and leading — but practical, innovative, and curious about how things can be done better.

— Communicating competitive and other intelligence quickly and targeted together with critical evaluations of how reliable the intelligence is and what it might mean.

— Versatile, agile, and flexible, with the capabilities to quickly change directions when conditions warrant it.

— Bold, proactive, quick-acting, anticipatory, goal oriented, and farsighted, with wide horizons for the purpose of being better than competitors.

SUCCESSFUL PERFORMANCE IS DURABLE

The key to corporate longevity is to create a company that lives (i.e., learns and adapts), has a deep sense of self, and looks beyond the profit-driven economic model to invest in people and knowledge (de Geus 1997).

In his research Arie de Geus found that enterprises that have been successful over very long periods — more than a century — share four characteristics:

- **Conservatism in Financing** — that is, "The companies did not risk their capital gratuitously. They understood the meaning of money in an old-fashioned way; they knew the usefulness of spare cash in the kitty."
- **Sensitivity to the World Around Them** — that is, "They always seemed to excel at keeping the feelers out, staying attuned to whatever was going on. . . . they were good at learning and adapting."
- **Awareness of Their Identity** — that is, "No matter how broadly diversified the companies were, their employees all felt like parts of the whole. The feeling of belonging to an organization and identifying with its achievements is often dismissed as soft. But case histories repeatedly show that this sense of community is essential for long-term survival. Managers in the living companies we studied were chosen mostly from within, and all considered themselves to be stewards of the long-standing

enterprise. Their top priority was keeping the institution at least as healthy as it had been when they took over."

- **Tolerance of New Ideas** — that is, "The long-lived companies in our study tolerated activities in the margin: experiments and eccentricities that stretched their understanding. They recognized that new businesses may be entirely unrelated to existing businesses and that the act of starting a business need not be centrally controlled."

When an enterprise with broad internal capabilities consistently performs better than its competitors, it will endure the challenges of changed conditions and sustain its success. Commercial enterprises, and many public ones, are expected to continue to deliver value over long periods. Some public enterprises, such as organizations created to build a hydroelectric generating facility, may be expected to operate as long as their services are demanded; after that they may cease to exist. However, during their operating life, they are indeed expected to be effective. Commercial enterprises are most often expected to continue to deliver value in spite of changes in demands and market dynamics. Stakeholders of various kinds — capital providers ("owners"), employees, customers, supporting dependent public entities, and the society in which the company is located — expect to continue to receive benefits over the long haul.

A dominant perspective among employees, investor/owners, and societies is that enterprises are expected to deliver long-term value to all concerned parties from their operations. Only special-purpose organizations created to deliver one-time project results, or completing single tasks, fall outside these expectations. Such enterprises are still expected to be effective, albeit during a limited period. However, the long-term implications of their results may be more important than completing the project itself on budget and on schedule.

For companies worldwide, ownership valuation is often based on the expected future income stream, and this creates expectations for long-term performance. Nonetheless, expectations for some financial markets that base their judgments on quarterly results make the contrary seem to be the case. In these cases, prospects frequently are for short-term incomes to be dependable, and preferably increasing faster than general economic growth — and many seem to expect this growth to continue permanently. Clearly, on the average, that is impossible. Only a few unusual organizations have achieved such growth for extended periods.

The expectation for any successful enterprise, no matter the external conditions, is that its performance will be consistently strong and enduring and that the enterprise will exist in the long term without deterioration. Achieving such a feat requires that the enterprise consistently be operated effectively to achieve its goals — all around and in all its operational areas. It must also be able to create new directions and strategies when markets and conditions change, for some several times within a single year. However, as business statistics show, durable performance may be the exception. Average life expectancy for companies listed on the New York Stock Exchange is less than 30 years, and many are operated shamelessly or fraudulently to enrich top management or an inner circle without regard for other stakeholders (Kleiner 2003). Many companies go through a traditional life cycle, in the end becoming aging and doomed. Such a demise often results from avoidable management decisions and internal conditions that jeopardize effectiveness. As a result, few companies become centenarians. Also, many enterprises that have become large, such as GE and Alcoa in the United States, Mitsubishi in Japan, and many more have experienced periods of higher than normal successful operation and growth. However, the challenge is to make that performance last without disastrous downturns by maintaining enduring and consistent effectiveness. That requires management teams that have the enterprise's best interests at heart, by not being overly egotistic or narcissistic.

Sustained long-term viability and success in competitive environments require above-average — or even unusual — performance. In these environments, performance below some competitive threshold will lead to loss of market, customers, and profits, and will end in ultimate demise. However, some ineffective enterprises are able to continue operation in narrow market niches or geographical areas or in other areas with high cost of entry. These are exceptions, and the normal enterprise must exert considerable effort to be better than its average competitors to survive.

Durable successful performance depends on consistent and competitive effective behavior that rests on the enterprise's ability to learn and adapt quickly and innovate faster than its competitors. Such effective behavior can only be achieved when knowledge and other IC assets are managed systematically and deliberately and coordinated closely with current enterprise direction and intents.

Performance Is a Function of Many Factors Acting Simultaneously

Achieving durable enterprise success is never a question of executing a single function excellently or of having a single factor perform well. Instead, as indicated in Figure 2-6, long-term success is a result of many factors performing well in a balanced manner. The figure indicates 11 factors, some of which are interdependent. In reality, additional factors and mechanisms influence long-term

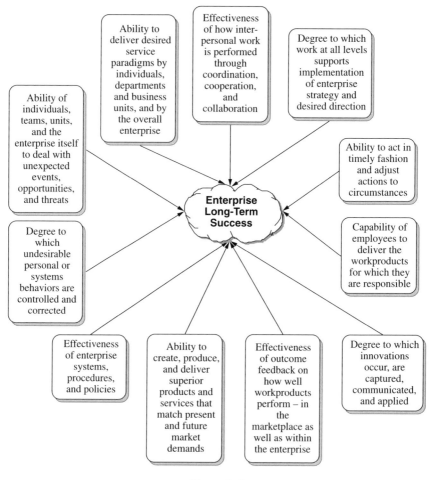

Figure 2-6

Long-term success is a function of many factors that work simultaneously to influence performance. Copyright © 2001 Knowledge Research Institute, Inc. Reproduced with permission.

success in very complex ways. The important factors tend to be different for different enterprises and external conditions.

THE INTELLECTUAL ASSET MANAGEMENT MENTALITY

"What's required is new accounting, a new measurement system which should be instituted internally within organizations. And we need a change in mentality" (Lev 2001).

A new, open, and positive culture tends to emerge when an enterprise builds and orchestrates an internal practice to deal systematically and deliberately with knowledge. In this environment, enterprises build and exploit IC assets, and people share insights and seek assistance from one another, ascertaining that they understand how best to implement enterprise strategy under a variety of conditions. Furthermore, people find it easy to open up and discuss difficult issues, emerging ideas, and tentative opportunities with one another. They are willing to take "mental" risks that would be unthinkable in more conventional environments. They seek collaboration to achieve better results quicker and are not afraid to build upon the ideas of others, nor to let others build on their own ideas. By opening up to new approaches and perspectives, and by building on the capabilities of others instead of only relying on their own, they in effect, expand their "action space."[9]

As people expand their action spaces and become more effective through collaboration, the whole enterprise improves. Complex tasks are addressed better and faster. More importantly in the longer run, innovations abound and make the enterprise more capable and able to engage in activities that previously were infeasible. People with intellectual asset management mentality:

- Believe that applied knowledge is a dominant factor of personal and enterprise effectiveness and growth.
- Ascertain that best available knowledge is applied.
- Assess knowledge needs, availabilities, and potentials to build or source knowledge.
- Build knowledge-related assets by investing wisely with longer term horizons in line with present and expected business directions.
- Organize work, knowledge location, and organizational structure to build and exploit personal and structural IC assets.
- Explore to improve work products and services.

- Apply knowledge as the main factor of personal and enterprise effectiveness and growth.
- Think in terms of threats, opportunities, weaknesses, strengths (TOWS) assessments of knowledge needs, availabilities, and potentials to build, source, or exploit IC assets.

Building and Exploiting Intellectual Capital Assets Are Important

KM practitioners and theoreticians are developing a new awareness of the need to change the KM focus and approach to a new generation of KM. The focus is shifting toward how KM can best support the desired enterprise strategy and performance and strengthen the ability of people to act in the interest of the enterprise. The approach is changing from technology and prescriptive methodologies to understanding how enterprise performance is shaped by people's actions supported by personal knowledge, IC assets, and additional resources. The new awareness emphasizes several points:

- The KM scope must not only be broadened to include operational considerations, but must also be collinear with the strategy, direction, and purpose of the enterprise, be it a company, city, region, or country.
- The KM scope must be broadened to focus on the tradeoffs that are required to secure long-term viability — constrained by the needs to secure short-term survival (to avoid bankruptcy, for example).
- The KM efforts must be self-sustaining and self-renewing. This requires that KM becomes an automatic, integral, and natural part of how everybody pursues "living the job."
- KM must be people-centric, not technology-centric, and encourage utilization of people-related mechanisms such as storytelling, communities of practice (CoP), social networking, and so on.
- Modern IT is vital, at the present primarily for automation and KM-infrastructure but later to include intelligent applications to offload reasoning and other mental tasks from knowledge workers.
- KM must be led by someone to conceptualize an integrated perspective of all KM elements into a greater and systematic whole and coordinate KM initiatives to ascertain that KM practices are

pursued and continue to be effectively supportive of the enterprise's desired direction. This role is needed to coordinate the many, often isolated, KM thrusts such as knowledge sharing, storytelling, communities of practice, knowledge harvesting, various IT-based KM capabilities and systems, and KM-friendly, culture-promoting efforts.

People Adopt New Mindsets!

Practitioners of deliberate and systematic KM develop widely shared mindsets across their organizations. They focus on two aspects:

1. The psychological, social, organizational, economic, and technical mechanisms that make knowledge and other IC assets strengthen operational and strategic situation-handling and the effectiveness of resulting actions and enterprise performance; and
2. How knowledge and other IC assets need to be managed from competitiveness, investment, and enterprise renewal points of points of view to support the enterprise and its stakeholders in both the short term and the long term.

These mindsets embrace proactive, exploratory, and innovative perspectives with notions of careful and responsible IC assets management. The mindsets are not prescriptive. Instead, they amount to a benevolent "Intellectual Capital Stewardship Mentality" (see Chapter 7), which brings constructive and actionable knowledge perspectives to everyday situations — automatically, easily, and naturally. The mentality is built by helping people in several ways. They develop understanding of options for developing, obtaining, and leveraging IC assets for everyday work. They are provided with role models to understand the advantages for themselves, their customers and stakeholders, and the enterprise. They build understanding and motivation to think and react in the new way.

In organizations that pursue deliberate and systematic KM, the mindsets have become a natural and automatized part of the daily "Living the Job" and have resulted in adopting new operational considerations as routine. People are directly concerned with how to build, acquire, and apply the best possible IC assets such as expertise by experimenting, teaching, collaborating, discussing with experts and peers, hiring, creating and using knowledge bases, computer models, and in numerous other ways. From strategic perspectives, it makes people consider options and tradeoffs for how to invest time, effort, and resources to build IC assets for future needs.

NOTES

1. It is important to keep in mind that "effectiveness" is not the same as "efficiency." We use these definitions: *effective* — producing a decided, decisive, or desired effect or result; *effectiveness* — the quality or degree of being *effective*; *efficient* — being productive without waste; *efficiency* — the quality or degree of being *efficient* (Merriam-Webster 1986).
2. Systematic approaches, when applied to societal processes, emphasize applying systems theory to deal with interconnectedness, effects over time, parallelisms, and nonlinear behaviors.
3. *Work*: (a) something produced or accomplished by effort, exertion, or exercise of skill; (b) something produced by creative talent or expenditure of creative effort (Merriam-Webster 1986).
4. Service paradigms describe how the enterprise, separate units, and people ideally should behave and do for external and internal customers and how everyone should appear to customers through their actions as explained in Chapter 7.
5. In the extreme, it should be remembered that a small percentage (~3–5 percent) of the general population have sociopathic tendencies. Many become part of the workforce, in some instances at all levels.
6. Adapted from the Boston University 1987 North American Manufacturing Futures Survey.
7. Philadelphia Human Resource Planning Group 2002.
8. Completed staff work is the study of a problem and presentation of a solution by a staff member in such form that all that remains to be done on the part of the recipient is to approve or disapprove the recommended action. ("Recommended action" must be emphasized since the more difficult the problem is, the more the tendency is to present the problem to the recipient in a piecemeal fashion.)
9. Action Space — the domain that lies within the boundaries or the constraints that circumscribe the outer limits of actions within which the person or enterprise operates comfortably (see Chapter 5).

3

ACTIONS ARE INITIATED BY KNOWLEDGEABLE PEOPLE: PEOPLE MAKE DECISIONS AND ACT USING DIFFERENT KINDS OF MENTAL FUNCTIONS

PREMISE 3-1: THE MACHINERY OF THE BRAIN METAPHOR IS A USEFUL BEGINNING

From external observations of behavior, goal-oriented human reasoning can in part be described as a sequence of separate tasks. These tasks receive *information* about some target situation and apply *knowledge* to reason about them from the perspectives of a set of *objectives*. The actual tasks and underlying mental mechanisms are not known or understood with any clarity. Such a description of human reasoning is similar to that of a "computing machine" and provides an initial information theory model.[1]

PREMISE 3-2: THE MIND-AS-MACHINE METAPHOR DOES NOT COVER EVERYTHING

As Lakoff (1987), and later Fauconnier and Turner (2002) and others point out, the mind-as-machine view does not support many observable operational functions that people perform with little effort — complex categorization being one. Also, recent research describes other human mental functions such as conceptual blending (Fauconnier & Turner 2002), which involve capabilities far beyond the realm of the mind-as-machine metaphor.

Whereas the human mind and its functions may be a mystery, we characterize part of its behavior by augmenting cognitive sciences and additional research results by borrowing from systems theory and other areas. Consequently, many constructs for knowledge, its acquisition and application, presented in this book may be artificial and even questionable. However, they serve to provide a knowledge-based framework suitable for practical business considerations.

THE PERSONAL REASONING EXAMPLE

Peter Jones, an experienced design engineer, was drawing up the specifications for an industrial heat exchanger. The problem was complicated with information describing physical space constraints and close exit temperature requirements over a wide operating range. Peter had designed similar exchangers before and knew immediately that the best solution would involve countercurrent flow with a particular geometric arrangement. Without thinking explicitly about it, he knew precisely how to detail calculations and how to use the computer analysis programs. In fact, he performed all initial specification tasks without giving conscious thought as to how to do it or what to do next. He had a well-established script in his mind that he operationalized and activated nonconsciously, once given the information describing the situation.

The technical specifications were easily done, and while working alone, Peter completed them in a few hours. Then came the complicated part — to design the specified capacity into a physical shape that would fit into the available space. This was a new challenge. Peter and two collaborators struggled for several days to solve the problem by trying different geometric configurations. At first, none seemed to work properly. The ones they could fit into the space posed impossible manufacturing problems. After several attempts, they remembered having seen an unusually shaped exchanger using uncommon materials which had the needed manufacturing flexibility while also having the required thermal and physical properties. By obtaining more information on the materials, the team finalized the design and submitted it to the shop to be built. After completing this project, Peter realized that using these materials would allow his company to make a new line of heat exchangers for uses that they previously had not been able to serve.

In performing his work, Peter drew on a wealth of personal knowledge. He possessed mental reference models as automatized tacit knowledge about creating heat exchanger specifications. Such work had over time become routine for him. He reasoned rapidly, intuitively, and accurately with concepts, scripts, and facts that represented his tacit understanding of the detailed scientific principles and engineering methods pertaining to heat exchanger design. In addition, Peter and his team used other, less automatized knowledge to explore design options for the physical configuration of the device. Part of this knowledge involved methodological metaknowledge to guide collaborative problem solving and the search for a workable solution.

HAVE WE MISUNDERSTOOD HOW PEOPLE THINK, MAKE DECISIONS, AND ACT?

We need to understand that people prefer to think, make decisions, and act in ways that are natural and convenient for them. They like to feel that any decision can be made and implemented in an easy, manageable, and acceptable manner and that it will be the "best way" to promote and secure their own success and the success of both the enterprise and customer. We also need to understand why people choose to not "do the right thing" — why they choose to pursue something that is less effective — or even the wrong thing. There are many reasons for such undesirable behavior. For example, people who do the wrong thing may find that doing what is right is too difficult and it is not natural. They may perceive that it is not "the way we do things here" or that it is counter to culture, practices, and peer acceptance. They may lack the motivation to exert themselves or may find that the psychological cost is too high. They may think that their personal goals are better served by following a different path, or they may not see any merit in doing the right thing. Or they may not possess the requisite knowledge to do the right thing.

As we pursue our objective of identifying how we might support successful personal and enterprise behavior, we need to identify counterproductive misconceptions and how they can be addressed. During the last several decades, most of us may indeed have misunderstood how people utilize and deal with knowledge to prepare themselves and to deliver competent work. We have misconceptions as to how people learn and build knowledge, and remember, reason, and apply knowledge to decide and carry out actions. In addition, we often do not have a clear understanding of how knowledge relates to performance and how different working conditions affect the knowledge-related effectiveness of work. We also may not realize the depth of knowledge required to deliver complex work. Some of these misconceptions clearly have resulted from our efforts to explain the functions of the human mind in terms of simple information processing or mind-as-machine models — only from the machinery of the brain perspectives. In reality, our brains — our minds — are much more complex and perform many functions of which we have little understanding. As Lakoff points out, categorization and creation of metaphors are part of these complex operations (Lakoff 1987). Fauconnier and Turner (2002) brought in many later findings that substantiate the limitations of the machinery metaphor.

As a result, our narrow perspective of how the human mind needs to be treated has led to problems. Many of our traditional practices and methods used to prepare and support workers with education and systems are less effective than they should be. Our work environments may also be found wanting by providing conditions that hamper the effective use of the available knowledge and intellectual capital (IC) assets. Major developments that cause us to revise our understandings include the following.

- *Most people remember concepts and "stories" easier than they remember "facts."* Businesses and educational institutions often prepare people by providing theoretical education and training that emphasize facts, details, and relatively mechanistic and concrete aspects of "this is how you do it" and "these are the facts." General understanding and underlying rationales are not provided as often as needed: the focus is on telling "how" and "what," not on "why." The ability to perform under nonstandard conditions and deal competently with complex work relies mostly on utilizing mental models at different levels of abstraction rather than on piecing together new approaches from basic principles and facts. Education that provides integration of many aspects of practical situations through hands-on and laboratory work, or even storytelling, alleviates this problem to some extent.[2] As work becomes more complex (as was illustrated in Figure 1-2), relevant stories may be encoded as mental models and provide procedural metaknowledge and generic abstractions as will be explained.
- *Decisions are nonconscious to a larger extent than we realized earlier.* When possible, people attempt to make decisions by repeating previous experiences — by doing what they know how to do and what appears most natural to them. The majority of daily decisions are based on utilizing tacit mental models to handle situations by "covert activation of biases related to previous emotional experiences of comparable situations." (Bechara *et al.*, 1997). A large aspect of competence relies on

this behavior and requires extensive, well-developed libraries of mental reference models.

- *People have different cognitive styles and "intelligences"* (Gardner 1983). When groups of people are educated and trained or provided with cognitive work supports based on a single model of cognitive functioning, the results are often disappointing across the enterprise. The problem is that people have differing abilities to assimilate and utilize provided information. To the extent practical, we must provide different modes of communication or staff positions with people whose cognitive style matches the type of work to be performed (Helander 1990).

- *Stress impairs retrieval from long-term memory.* People who are hurried, perform under pressure, feel threatened, uncomfortable, or angry, are constantly interrupted, or work in noisy environments experience a reduced ability to use all they know in their efforts to deliver work. People who are content, feel motivated, happy and relaxed, and work in pleasant and effective environments generally are able to deliver better quality work, and although they appear to be in stressful situations, they are able to work fast and to deeply engage themselves in what they do.

- *The impact of example behaviors and role models is more important than we recognize from our normal practices.* Many leaders tend to minimize communication between subordinates and rank-and-file. They often provide terse and ineffective communications to direct work and describe how they wish their employees to behave and perform. They may not act as role models or provide living examples. By neglecting to provide conceptual and explicit guidance, they make it difficult for other people to act in the desired manner since they have not understood in-depth what is desired. People are uncertain about how to operationalize the desired behaviors — they cannot copy example behavior since that is missing. People are not provided with motivation to copy their leaders' behaviors since those are behaviors they do not respect; they do not see that their leaders find it necessary to act in the desired way. Without leaders acting as role models, new criteria for performance and behavior do not become part of enterprise culture. As a result, people do not understand or feel motivated to act as the enterprise desires — although that would be most effective and valuable for themselves, the enterprise, and other stakeholders.

- *Knowledge required to deliver complex work may require greater mental capacities than most people can provide.* The complexity of modern work often requires greater knowledge than a single person has the opportunity to acquire. (Examples include delivering modern medical services, solving complex industrial and business problems, and creating social and economic legislation.) Such tasks must be performed by collaborative teams whose members are included to provide complementary expertise, and their work styles must become integrated with general operations practices.
- *Knowledge and information are fundamentally different in both nature and function.* The purpose of information is proper description, whereas the purpose of knowledge is effective action. Knowledge and information are not part of a continuum and need to be managed separately and diligently by separate disciplines (see further discussion later).

Figure 3-1 indicates the seven areas that new developments suggest we have misunderstood. We can improve how we prepare and support knowledge workers at all levels, make it easier for people to become motivated, and understand how to perform their work and manage knowledge better by focusing deliberately and separately on KM and information management.

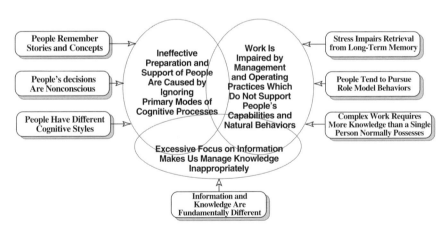

Figure 3-1

Seven areas of knowledge-related misconceptions that make workers less effective than we should accept. Copyright © 2002 Karl M. Wiig. Reproduced with permission.

Thinking, Reasoning, and Knowledge

Most people think of knowledge as a recipe — a defined procedure — for dealing with a concrete, well-defined situation. However, few situations are repeated; in their minute detail most situations are novel and need to be treated as such. Hence, knowledge needs to provide us with the capability — the understanding — that permits us to envision and operationalize possible ways of handling different situations and to judge and anticipate implications. Knowledge allows us to innovate, improvise, and adjust decisions and actions needed to serve each individual context while optimizing personal and enterprise goals and objectives. Our knowledge — such as scripts, schemata, and mental reference models — and mental capabilities provide us with the capability to work with a variety of situations. By utilizing conceptual blending, we generate new knowledge that takes us far beyond concepts and predefined methods and judgments, and allows us to create new concepts, metaconcepts, and mental models that often constitute innovative and novel situation-specific approaches.

Thinking takes many forms and serves many purposes. We think when we learn, when we generalize, when we retrieve memories, when we analyze and categorize, search for patterns, try to see similarities, identify associations, try to find additional instances, detect inconsistencies, reason consciously, decide what to do, handle situations and in many other endeavors. Gilhooly (1988, p. 1) explains that thinking involves:

> a set of processes whereby people assemble, use, and revise mental models. For example, thinking directed toward solving a problem may be regarded as exploring a mental model of the task to determine the course of action that should be the best (or at least satisfactory). A mental model often enables the thinker to go far beyond the perceptually available information and to anticipate outcomes of alternative actions without costly overt trial and error.

Gilhooly also suggests that "thinking is always occurring during periods of wakefulness, albeit often in a free-floating daydreaming fashion." Recent research, however, shows that much tacit thinking is also performed when we sleep and dream. We may actually even need sleep to organize and make sense of new knowledge and perspectives that we have obtained when awake.

Most important intellectual functions are tacit, unobservable, and take place when we dream and during other periods such as rapid eye movement (REM) sleep. As indicated, most of our thinking involves tacit reasoning. When we draw associations, try to remember, or assess outcomes from complex situations, we mostly perform these tasks nonconsciously. When knowledge workers mull over some conceptual material in their minds or when they internalize and organize newly acquired knowledge to build congruent understanding of their expertise and expand their associations, they may even appear to daydream or be totally inactive. Some managers have frowned on such behavior, considering these activities to be illegitimate and undesirable since they are not visibly involved in generating work products. Yet, these activities are absolutely necessary for the knowledge workers to solve hard problems, innovate, or internalize newly acquired knowledge to grow and develop, and thereby increase the organization's knowledge assets as well as their own.

An important type of thinking is *explicit reasoning*. It is of specific interest in the context of KM because it leads to conscious conclusions as part of decisions and other recognizable work products where the reasoning process can be inspected and verified. Other modes of thinking, however, may be more important because they are central both to knowledge creation and organization and to automatic or tacit knowledge work. We reason when we analyze a situation and when we arrive at conclusions, and that, typically, is the analysis result we are seeking. Johnson-Laird proposes that for the most part people reason without using "mental logic and formal rules of inference" (Johnson-Laird 1983). Instead, we reason with propositions, associations, and mental models embedded in our understanding of our natural language or other modes of reasoning. This may imply that much, if not most, of our reasoning is nonconscious and directed by immediate understanding, associative reasoning, pattern recognition, and other types of reasoning. A newer insight into these processes is explained by conceptual blending (Fauconnier & Turner 2002).

Our thinking processes and reasoning approaches are complex and governed by the knowledge we possess, our life's experiences, and the way our brains are organized and wired[3], by our individual aptitudes, cognitive styles, and dominant memory styles. Thinking is performed in different ways, using many mechanisms. When we mull over a particular situation, our thinking involves retrieval of episodes, specifics, and concepts that relate directly to or are associated with the situation. Our thinking process may also retrieve and examine more detailed and more abstract or aggregated concepts (*chunked concepts*; see Glossary) that relate to the central concepts. Furthermore, it may trigger issues (assisted by *priming*; see Glossary) that remind us, and permit retrieval, of relevant long-term memory items. And when we mull over something, our thinking will also rely on some of the reasoning strategies that are second nature for us. One aspect of KM deals with teaching new and more powerful reasoning strategies, such as critical thinking, in such ways that they become natural and automatic choices when it is appropriate to apply them.

When we read or listen to someone speak, we constantly think; that is, we process the incoming information stream both non-consciously and explicitly in working memories. This process is part of making sense of the information. A simplified example of this process is illustrated in Figure 3-2 for determining the meaning of the statement: "The sailboat sailed away" after we have first automatically parsed the sentence structure and verified that it is acceptable

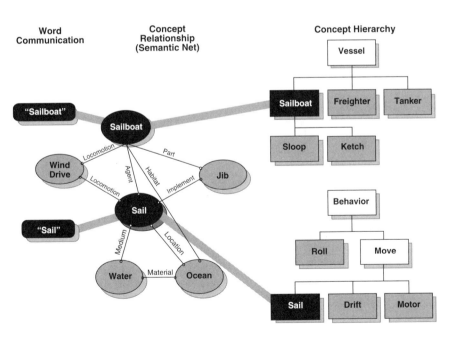

Figure 3-2
After a word communication ("The sailboat sailed away") is received, the mind may engage in complex processing that connects to prior associations (shown as a simplified semantic net) and concepts (shown as chunks in a concept hierarchy).
Copyright © 1993 Karl M. Wiig. Reproduced with permission.

from a syntax perspective and contains information that we understand and accept.

Associations and Biases Govern Our Actions

During the last part of the twentieth century, it was often accepted that decision making in general resulted from application of logical reasoning strategies (Janis 1989; Simon 1977). However, recent research shows that behavior using explicit application of logical strategies generally only applies to novices or people who struggle with complex or unfamiliar problems and engage in problem solving that requires conscious and structured synthesis and analysis (Janis 1989; Janis & Mann 1977; Simon 1977a, 1977b). Instead of our previous models, most reasoning is implicit or tacit, as Bechara *et al.* (1997) have demonstrated. People who make decisions in situations in which they are experienced use "covert activation of biases related to previous emotional [meaningful] experiences of comparable situations," in a process outlined in Figure 3-3. People use directly executable or adaptable examples of prior situations that they have

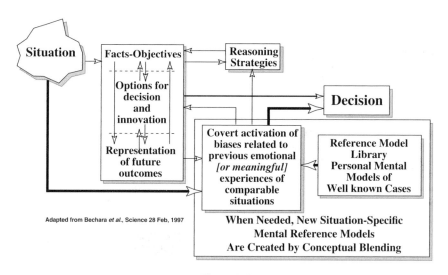

Figure 3-3
Decision-Making often depends on experience with comparable situations. In these cases, the dominant decision path bypasses explicit reasoning and proceeds directly to imitate past, known situation-handling. Copyright © 1997 Knowledge Research Institute, Inc. Reproduced with permission.

experienced, memorized, or learned about. They use mental reference models that in effect are tacit stories encoded at different levels of abstraction to respond to familiar situations by imitating previous behavior. That behavior might be a repetition of their own prior actions when the mental reference models reflect their own experience, or it might be an imitation of someone else's behavior when they reflect recounted stories.[4]

After a decision has been made, it will need to be implemented; that is, translated into action. Typically, many small decisions and actions are required to implement an observable and noticeable action, such as completing authorization of a commercial loan after the approval decision has been reached. All these small decisions also require mental reference models for their execution.[5]

Several issues have surfaced. One is the manner in which we intuitively rely on reference models to access and associate past experiences, behaviors, and understandings for how we choose to act in new situations. A major issue that occupies many researchers deals with the question, "Do people have free will?" (Wegner 2002). The question arises: "Are we indeed programmed to act in predestined ways as a result of our past experiences?" Important as such questions may be from philosophical points of view, they may not be of practical business interest and may fall outside our purview. Instead, we postulate that, by choice, we can build personal knowledge in the form of mental model libraries and other types of knowledge to suit particular purposes such as performing a certain type of work with greater expertise. We also believe that we can decide to use our knowledge according to our free will to maximize the effectiveness of our personal behaviors to serve the goals of the enterprise in which we are engaged, the stakeholders' goals, and our own objectives.

INFORMATION IS NOT KNOWLEDGE!

The Purpose of Knowledge Is Action; the Purpose of Information Is Description

When considering how knowledge affects personal decision making and reasoning, we need to understand what knowledge is and how it relates to information. We distinguish between *knowledge* and *information* by recognizing that they are fundamentally different. Information consists of data organized to characterize a particular situation, condition, context, challenge, or opportunity.

Knowledge consists of facts, perspectives and concepts, mental reference models, truths and beliefs, judgments and expectations, methodologies, and know-how. In part, knowledge also consists of understanding how to juxtapose and integrate seemingly isolated information items to develop new meanings — to create new insights with which to approach effective handling of the target situation.

We use information to describe and specify what things are. We use information to describe a situation and its context as they exist and develop. We use information in the form of data tables to describe everything from the physical characteristics of metals to today's and yesterday's stock market statistics and projections of its future performance. Clearly, much information is created by the application of knowledge to describe and explain. However, that does not make information knowledge.

We use knowledge to evaluate and handle situations, decide how we, for example, use physical tables, or assess how to trade our investment portfolio given stock market information. We use knowledge to assess, decide, problem-solve, plan, act, and monitor.

Actionable knowledge is possessed by humans as well as by other active entities (agents) such as process control computers that are programmed to take actions to manipulate process variables to achieve a desired performance. Actionable knowledge is used to receive information and to recognize and identify; analyze, interpret, and evaluate; synthesize and decide; plan, implement, monitor, adapt, and act. In other words, knowledge is used to reason to determine what a specific situation means, how it should be handled, and to carry out the resulting decision in action. In this context, knowledge serves two purposes: (1) methodological knowledge controls the reasoning process; (2) domain knowledge provides the content of reasoning. In addition, information is needed to describe the state of the situation that is the subject of reasoning.

Passive knowledge may exist in repositories — in systems and procedures, books, documents, databases, and in many other forms (see Chapter 1 and Figure 1-6). Structural IC consists mostly of passive knowledge except when embedded in active agents such as computer-based action systems. We use passive knowledge when it is obtained by an active agent and is operationalized. It can, for example, be operationalized and activated by a person who learns about it by reading a description of it, reasons with it, and acts on it. In a less obvious manner, it can be embedded in an organizational structure through specified systems and procedures that are operationalized by people observing managerial intents through their daily actions.

Knowledge is accumulated and integrated and held over time by receiving new information, using prior knowledge to interpret it and create hypotheses about its meaning, relevancy, and acceptability. If found "believable," the new knowledge can be accepted and internalized by establishing its relationship (associations) and deeper meanings relative to what already is known. This is the case with personal knowledge when the process takes place in a person's mind. It is also the case with creating structural IC (organizational knowledge) when knowledge is acquired and incorporated in repositories.

A brief, practical example portrays differences between information and knowledge. Consider the regular and supervisory control functions for an automated factory, as illustrated in Figure 3-4. In this system, information on the operating state of the process is obtained continuously by the computer. Knowledge from process experts is embedded in, and operationalized and activated by, the process control computer programs to automate operations. The experts provide personal knowledge and deep understanding of physical and operational principles and specific cases on how to deal both with routine and undesired operating situations. They pool their precise process knowledge with that of other experts, who have

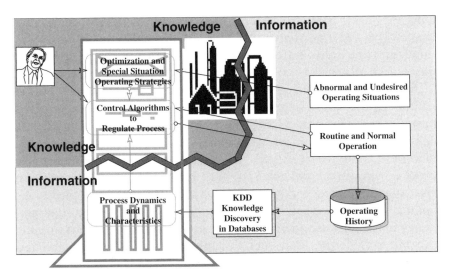

Figure 3-4
Differences between knowledge and information in process control computers.
Copyright © 1994 by Karl M. Wiig. Reproduced with permission.

embedded general knowledge on optimization and control principles in teaching materials, scientific papers, textbooks, and generic computer software used to generate the control algorithms. That knowledge is assembled by programmers and built into control programs.

The static and dynamic operating history of the process is analyzed by conventional, but sophisticated, statistical methods or advanced knowledge discovery in databases (KDD) to obtain data on selected process characteristics, including process dynamics. This historical knowledge becomes part of the control algorithms embedded in the control computer. Hence, the process control computer uses historical knowledge to regulate and control the process as a "business-as-usual" process. The computer cannot create new knowledge or innovate or improvise even when required.

On Information, Knowledge, and Discontinuity

To obtain perspectives on how we can manage knowledge or other kinds of intellectual capital assets — and appreciate that systematic KM must be different from how we manage information — we must define what we mean by the terms *information* and *knowledge*.

Our understanding of "knowledge" and "information" is principally different. At first, it may appear that they are part of a continuum from signals to data to information to knowledge and onwards and that they are all part of the same domain. However, when examining the nature of these conceptual constructs and the processes that create them, we find that undeniable discontinuities make information fundamentally different from knowledge. There are other differences as well, as will be discussed and indicated in Figure 3-5.

The discontinuity between information and knowledge is caused by using prior knowledge to create new knowledge from received information. The process by which we develop new knowledge is complex. The new inputs are compared to prior knowledge to determine and hypothesize if they are reasonable and acceptable. The process uses prior knowledge to make sense of the new information and, once accepted for inclusion, internalizes the new insights by linking with prior knowledge. To become knowledge, the new and accepted insights are internalized by establishing links with already existing knowledge, links that can range from firmly characterized relationships to vague associations. Hence, the new knowledge is as much a function of prior knowledge as it is of received inputs. A discontinuity is thus created between the received information inputs and the resulting new knowledge.

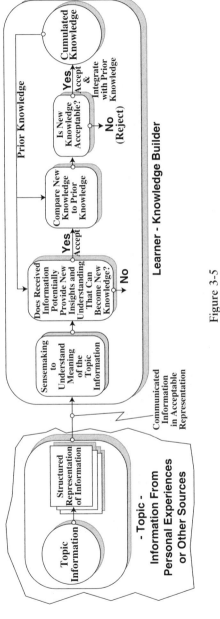

Figure 3-5

Illustration of a simplified knowledge creation model. Copyright © 1993 by Karl M. Wiig. Reproduced with permission.

Good Reasoning Matches Knowledge and Information

The goal of KM is to provide the best possible tacit and explicit knowledge to support and improve knowledgeable, competent decision making that will result in effective actions to fulfill enterprise and personal objectives. Without the systematic and deliberate development, renewal, and maintenance of knowledge and other IC assets, personal and enterprise effectiveness will suffer. Decision making/problem solving is normally followed by implemented actions and builds on application of knowledge assets matched with corresponding information assets. Matched knowledge and information make it possible for individuals, and the enterprise as a whole, to collaborate, understand interactions, make detailed and broad, effective decisions, and to implement them — all while pursuing goals.

As indicated in the simplified decision-making example of Figure 3-6, appropriately matched knowledge and information are required to decide and act effectively. The figure indicates the interdependence of knowledge and information for effective actions. Pertinent information about situations is required to describe conditions correctly, and competent knowledge is applied to interpret what situations mean and to decide how to handle them to the best advantage. Effective information management is required to provide the descriptions of the world needed to make sense and understand the situation. Hence, effective management relies extensively and separately on both KM and information management.

Figure 3-6 indicates knowledge assets and IC (intellectual capital) on the left side and information capital on the right side. It illustrates the separation of knowledge management of intellectual capital and information management of information capital to emphasize the need to manage both areas separately and competently in order to provide the assets needed for effective actions. The figure indicates paths of knowledge creation — *new knowledge* — that is, discoveries, innovations, and insights that pertain to new and original situations and conditions. It also identifies how *historic knowledge* can be obtained from knowledge discovery in databases (KDD); that is, knowledge and relationships that pertain to past, often sufficiently repetitive experiences that make machine learning possible.

In the enterprise, it is not practical to establish the details of knowledge and information for every important job function. That is feasible only for important and critical knowledge functions that are conducted by many people. Examples of such functions include

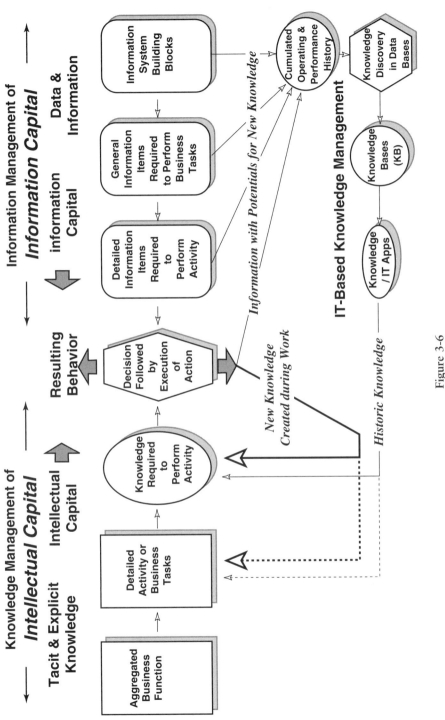

Figure 3-6

Intellectual capital (knowledge assets) matched with corresponding information capital provides the capability to act effectively.
Copyright © 1992 Karl M. Wiig. Reproduced with permission.

customer service functions, financial analysis functions, many project control functions, and hundreds of other examples. However, the model has proven a valuable tool for people who plan smaller activities and determine the resources required to collaborate, as well as people who are responsible for their own education and professional development.

Knowledgeable and Informed Decisions Deliver Performance

Operational performance depends directly on the merit of the underlying decisions and actions. *Effective actions rely on decisions that are both informed and knowledgeable.* As illustrated in Figure 3-7, decisions based on good information but little knowledge can be expected to be arbitrary and ineffective. Decisions based on excellent knowledge but little information can also be expected to be ineffective and often capricious as well. Sadly, often great emphasis is placed on ascertaining that actions are based on *informed decisions*, with less concern for ascertaining that they also are based on *knowledgeable decisions*.

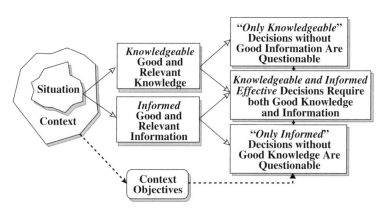

Figure 3-7
Three potential outcomes when decisions are both knowledgeable and informed — or only informed or knowledgeable. Copyright © 2001 Knowledge Research Institute, Inc. Reproduced with permission.

Goal-Directed Reasoning Relies on Goals, Information, and Knowledge

From a knowledge perspective, we are generally interested in aspects of human reasoning that lead to decisions and actions and that can be strengthened and be more effective with appropriate KM. Figure 3-8 illustrates a simplified financial planning situation where the financial planner's objective is to help the client make her own decisions on how to arrange her financial affairs. In this case, effective, goal-directed human reasoning requires (1) situation and context objectives to specify the goal-state and guide the reasoning direction, (2) information to describe the situation and its context, and (3) knowledge to direct and control the reasoning process by providing understanding of the situation and insights into how to reason about it. We need understanding of what is to be achieved and then knowledge and information to make the right things happen.

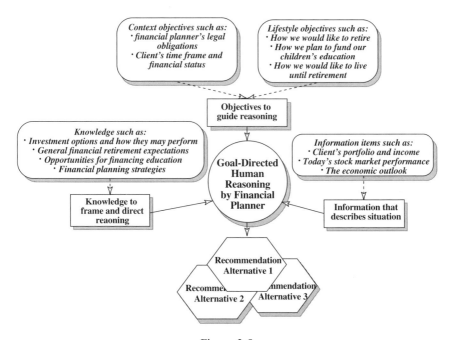

Figure 3-8

A competent financial planner utilizes goal-directed human reasoning to establish the best strategy for her client. Her task requires objectives to specify the goal-state, information to describe the situation, and knowledge to reason and act. Copyright © 2002 Knowledge Research Institute, Inc. Reproduced with permission.

The process shown in Figure 3-8 focuses on the financial planner's goal-directed reasoning to generate several recommended alternatives for the client to consider. However, the process does not stop there. The overall objective is to assist the client by also building sufficient understanding to make her own decisions on which alternatives to pursue. Hence, the second goal-directed reasoning, now by the client, is added to the process as illustrated schematically in Figure 3-9.

The objective of this example is to highlight some of the objectives, knowledge, and information-building blocks that are needed to support a relatively simple, but knowledge-intensive, process. Expert financial planners have a clear overview of the processes in which they are engaged. Less experts planners are often uncertain — even confused — about the elements and structure of the process.

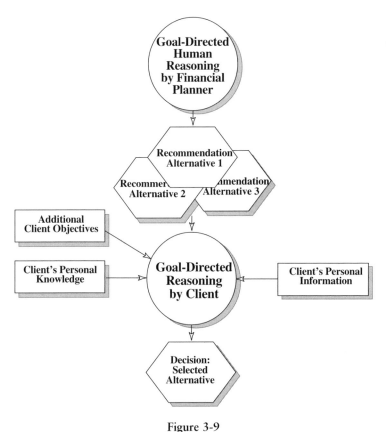

Figure 3-9
Clients make decisions based on the financial planner's recommendations. Copyright © 2002 Knowledge Research Institute, Inc. Reproduced with permission.

The importance of this example is to illustrate that knowledge-intensive processes such as financial planning can be illustrated and communicated to coworkers to help build mental reference models of the work they are to perform. Such models are also helpful to support knowledge mapping and explorations of how to improve work.

Personal Knowledge Is Built from Mental Models

We adopt the premise that operational knowledge is generally represented as mental models in our minds. Many of the mental models are also reference models. The mental models encode situations that we know from personal experiences, that we have learned from other sources, or that we have generated in our own minds from thought experiments and speculation, goal-oriented reasoning, or "just thinking" about something. Hence, mental models can reflect reality or imagined situations. Beyond mental models, we possess other kinds of mental constructs such as facts, perspectives, concepts, truths and beliefs, judgments and expectations, methodologies, and know-how.

Pursuant to our premise, much of our personal knowledge is created by assembling our understanding, insights, expectations, and preferred procedures into mental models (Johnson-Laird 1983, 1988; Johnson-Laird & Byrne 2000; Nadel 2003; Wilson & Keil 1999). We possess mental models on many levels of abstraction and in different domains. Some mental models, such as those that describe how we open a door or start a car, are concrete and may be deeply internalized and automatized to the extent that they have become tacit. Others consist of scripts that describe chains of tasks or events to form our expectations as to how situations may develop or which sequence of tasks we should follow to perform certain work. Still others are more general schemata or are based on metaknowledge as indicated in Figure 3-10 and discussed further in Appendix C.

People form lasting mental models that embody understanding of what the world is about, how it works, and what is normal and permissible behavior. As situations and episodes are observed or experienced, they are compared with existing mental models — prior knowledge. New mental models are formed, and prior models are reinforced, expanded, or revised. Daily life leads to an ever-expanding set of concepts, expectations, and responses in the form

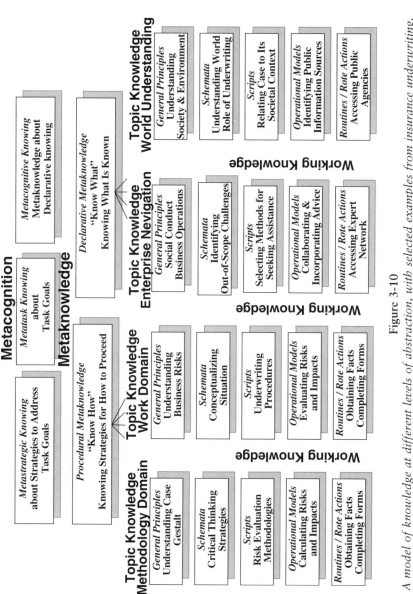

Figure 3-10

A model of knowledge at different levels of abstraction, with selected examples from insurance underwriting, and indicating the knowledge domains for methodology; primary work, enterprise navigation, and world understanding. Copyright © 2000 Knowledge Research Institute, Inc. Reproduced with permission.

of routines, scripts, and schemas to deal with the world. When a person repeatedly observes similar situations, such as the behavior of authority figures, the mental models of such situations are reinforced, and, very importantly, associations are constantly strengthened between the mental models of these situations and the responses that are observed as being typical. The mental models become mental reference models.

As we become more familiar with particular behaviors after repeated exposures, we find them to be more acceptable — even permissible and desirable — as responses to situation types in whose contexts they have been observed. Examples include how a store clerk deals with an angry customer, how an office worker chooses to participate in office gossip, how a loan officer handles a personal loan application with credit problems, and so on. The more familiar we are with a situation type (i.e., the stronger our associations are), the more automatic is our response. When associations are very strong, we tend to react without reflection. When a person meets with any situation, he relies on his library of mental reference models to interpret the situation and decide how to handle it. We hypothesize that the selection of the mental models that guide the situation is based primarily on the strength of associations; that is, the number and intensity of exposures to similar situations, real or fictitious. However, as may be apparent from earlier discussions, the situation-at-hand will be different in some respect from any previous situation, and therefore the mental reference models need to be modified, primarily by conceptual blending.

On Mental Models

Kenneth Craik (1943) suggested that the mind constructs "small-scale models" (mental models) of reality that it uses to anticipate events. It has since become evident that such mental models are also used to generate decisions and actions. People construct mental models from what they perceive or imagine or from readings and communications with people. Mental models may be visual images or abstract representations of situations. We use the broader representation of "mental models" to mean representations in the mind of situations, events, etc., that have been experienced or are learned from other sources. These are *real mental models*. We also include mental models that result from thought experiments and self-imagined situations. These are *imaginary mental models*, and may be untrue.

Mental model structures may be analogous to the structure of the situations that they represent, unlike, say, the abstract structure of logical equations used in formal rule theories. Many recent studies present experimental evidence that corroborates the predictions of the mental model theory of reasoning, while others suggest revisions and modifications to some of the theory's tenets to accommodate new data. Critics of the model theory include proponents of alternative theories such as deduction based on inference rules. The controversy about whether people reason by relying on models or on inference rules has led to better experiments and to developments of the mental model theory of thinking and reasoning in novel domains.

Many Mental Models Are Based on Metaknowledge

The role of metaknowledge in personal behavior is crucially important and provides the basis for many of our more abstract and general mental models.[6] However, metaknowledge often is neglected because its structure is elusive and tacit and because only within the last decade has its importance been widely explored and it is still not well known. As a result, for most people, the concept, nature, and roles of metaknowledge are in many cases misunderstood, generally unknown, or even considered irrelevant for practical purposes (Kuhn 2000).

Metaknowledge has often been considered to be limited to the knowledge a person has about the knowledge that he or she possesses. Metaknowledge may not be considered by itself. Instead, it may be oriented toward addressing challenges or tasks that have purposes and goals. As we now understand it, relationships between kinds of metastrategic knowing and two kinds of metaknowledge are indicated in Figure 3-10 and are explained further in Appendix C. On the highest abstraction level, metaknowledge consists of *metacognition*, which Kuhn (2000) indicated can be divided into:

- *Metastrategic knowing*, which provides strategies to address task goals.
- *Metatask knowing*, which provides specifics on the task goals themselves.
- *Metacognitive knowing*, which is metaknowledge about declarative knowing.

On the lowest abstraction level, *metaknowledge* can be divided into:

- *Procedural metaknowledge*, which is about know-how and strategies for how to proceed toward the task goal.
- *Declarative metaknowledge*, which is about know-what and knowing what is known.

People build metaknowledge automatically in their minds without being aware of it (by implicit learning), but part of metaknowledge can also be taught explicitly, and this has important practical implications. For example, by learning about procedural metaknowledge, a person can build mental models of different methodological approaches suitable for different types of problems. The relationships between metaknowledge and topic knowledge — as we understand it at present — are indicated in Figure 3-10 with selected knowledge examples from insurance industry topics. Some important aspects are that metaknowledge-based mental models:

- Provide people with tacit mental strategy models for procedural (methodological) and declarative (topic) knowledge.
- Provide greater work effectiveness by leading to:
  — Greater innovation and creativity by providing powerful strategies and broad and abstract perspectives that allow development of new patterns.
  — Increased ability to "go straight for the goal" and "do the right thing the first time" instead of procrastinating or making errors.
  — Better understanding of, and ability to exploit, the processes in which they are engaged.
  — Fewer false steps.
- Help people to be aware of the intellectual processes in which they are engaged and of alternative strategies that may be better.
- Make people explicitly cognizant of how they think — and may allow themselves to think — when engaged in situation-handling under many different conditions.

The Importance of Metacognition

The importance of metacognition and metaknowledge is beyond doubt. Unfortunately, however, their importance for acquiring new knowledge takes place in ways that are not readily apparent.

Metacognition is particularly important for planning and monitoring (see Chapter 5), as indicated by Kuhn (2000, p. 178):

> The [metacognition] model makes it clear why efforts to induce change directly at the performance level have only limited success, indicated by failures of a newly acquired strategy to transfer to new . . . contexts. Strategy training may appear successful, but if nothing has been done to influence the meta-level, the new behavior will quickly disappear once the instructional context is withdrawn and individuals resume [prior] meta-level management of their own behavior.

The importance of metacognition for both planning and monitoring the whole process of situation-handling is further emphasized by Kuhn's statements (p. 179), that:

> The meta-level directs the application of strategies, but feedback from this application is directed back to the meta-level. This feedback leads to enhanced meta-level awareness of the goal and the extent to which it is being met by different strategies, as well as enhanced awareness and understanding of the strategies themselves, including their power and limitations.

When allowed to develop metaknowledge on creative and critical thinking and on knowing what is known, knowledge workers at all levels increase their effectiveness and ability to develop and take advantage of improved topic or subject knowledge. Metaknowledge is important for areas as disparate as situation-handling (including problem-solving and decision-making), systems thinking, dealing with interpersonal situations, and technical work topics, and may include techniques such as topic-, methodology-, and structure-related conceptual maps. Competent people benefit from having practical and pertinent metaknowledge about topics such as what in general is and is not known. They must also develop or be provided with knowledge of what they know and how to think critically and be innovative; that is, they need metaknowledge, and they need to engage in metacognitive reasoning to understand how and why they can perform better and why that will serve themselves and the organization well. Deep internalization of metaknowledge through repeated exposure or effective teaching leads metaknowledge to become a natural extension of a person's operational repertoire.

Adoption of general critical thinking as a natural approach to problem solving is one example.

The Importance of Implicit Learning

As indicated earlier, *implicit learning* provides an important learning mode (Cleeremans 2003). People often do not know they are learning implicitly when they tackle slightly different problems, perform work in a different way, or observe something that is unfamiliar. When encountering interesting or otherwise noteworthy situations, people learn implicitly from the experience. Such learnings may be captured in "raw form" in episodic memory but are frequently processed further to derive an understanding of what they mean. Implicit learning becomes particularly prevalent when we repeatedly experience the same situation over and over again, or experience different situations that are similar to some degree. In these cases, we nonconsciously develop new insights and ideas, and we even see possibilities for innovation based on greater understanding of underlying patterns and other aspects of the material. Even when learning consciously (as when being taught), we are not aware of how we implicitly develop important insights beyond the explicit information we receive. Another important aspect of implicit learning is the role it plays in building metaknowledge and metacognitive capabilities.

The Personal and Enterprise Knowledge Evolution Cycle

One model for building personal knowledge is indicated in Figure 3-11. New insights, ideas, and innovations begin their life as glimpses — tacit, subliminal, vulnerable, and hard-to-explain knowledge. When the ideas are better established, they become idealistic and uncritical visions or paradigms that point to opportunities, but they are not ready to be defended or used. Later, the new knowledge may be systematized as different abstractions as metaknowledge, general principles, schemata, scripts, methodologies, or operational models — and perhaps as theoretical knowledge. After practical use and testing, it is ready to become pragmatic decision making and factual knowledge. After steady and long-term use, the knowledge is internalized and automatized to become automatic routine working knowledge that we apply naturally and often without being aware of it.

The model of the personal knowledge evolution cycle model presented here has five stages that depict how knowledge, as it matures

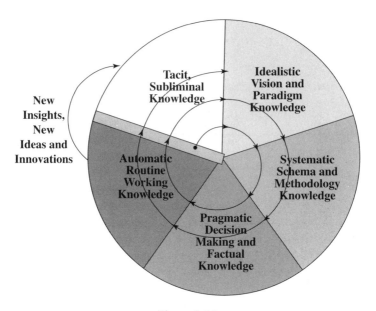

Figure 3-11
Personal knowledge development as a general evolution cycle. Copyright © 1995 Knowledge Research Institute, Inc. Reproduced with permission.

and becomes better established in a person's mind, migrates from barely perceived ideas or notions to be better understood and useful. The five stages are as follows.

- **Tacit Subliminal Knowledge.** This knowledge is mostly non-conscious and is not well understood. It is often the first glimpse we have of a new concept.
- **Idealistic Vision and Paradigm Knowledge.** Part of this knowledge is well known to us and explicit — we work consciously with it. Much of it — our visions and mental models — is not well known; it is tacit, and it is accessible only nonconsciously.
- **Systematic Schema and Reference Methodology Knowledge.** Our knowledge of underlying systems, general principles, and problem-solving strategies is, to a large extent, explicit and mostly well known to us.
- **Pragmatic Decision-Making and Factual Knowledge.** Decision-making knowledge is practical and mostly explicit. It supports everyday work and decisions, is well known, and is used consciously.

- **Automatic Routine Working Knowledge.** We know this knowledge so well that we have automated it. Most has become tacit — we use it to perform tasks automatically — without conscious reasoning.

One role of person-focused KM is to facilitate and, at times, to accelerate the maturation of knowledge to the point that it can be applied to deliver competent work. As we will discuss in Chapter 7, deliberate and systematic — comprehensive — KM does not mean autocratic top-down determination of which knowledge must be created, transferred, and utilized to be competent to perform desired work. Instead, it means the creation of a knowledge-vigilant personal mentality and corporate culture perhaps guided from the top and also strongly motivated by rank-and-file. Each individual and each department adopt the mentality as part of daily work, continually looking out for the knowledge perspective to ascertain that appropriate expertise and understanding are brought to bear to deliver the desired work. The comprehensive KM culture also recognizes a particular aspect of personal behavior. This aspect deals with the realization that many individuals deliver outstanding work in unusual situations without having extensive topic knowledge. Instead, they have strong metaknowledge that provides capabilities to make sense of novel situations and create effective approaches to handle them.

We use conceptual knowledge-level categories to indicate how individuals hold specific knowledge items. Later, we will see how that may affect the individual's capabilities to learn, innovate, make decisions, and perform regular knowledge work. It may also affect how individuals are able to collaborate and work with others who do not hold comparable knowledge on equal levels. People may hold the same general knowledge at different levels. Hence, a beginner underwriter for group health may hold knowledge on developing a proposal to a large service organization as *idealistic* knowledge. The underwriter expert with whom the beginner works may hold the same knowledge (judgments, regulatory aspects, and particulars on contract opportunities), but as more internalized *pragmatic* knowledge. Finally, an unusual underwriting master may hold this knowledge as *automatic* knowledge.

The models that comprehensive KM practices often use to structure their activities and priorities include the enterprise knowledge evolution cycle indicated in Figure 3-12, which also considers five stages:

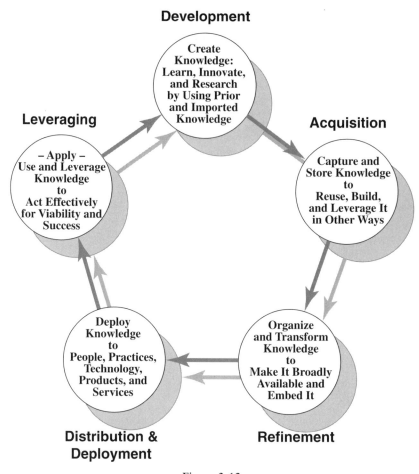

Figure 3-12
Enterprise knowledge development evolution cycle. Copyright © 1995
Knowledge Research Institute, Inc. Reproduced with permission.

- **Knowledge Development.** Knowledge is developed through learning, innovation, creativity, and importation from outside.
- **Knowledge Acquisition.** Knowledge is captured and retained for use and further treatment.
- **Knowledge Refinement.** Knowledge is organized, transformed, or included in written material, knowledge bases, and so on to make it available to be useful.
- **Knowledge Distribution and Deployment.** Knowledge is distributed to points-of-action (PoAs) through education, training

programs, automated knowledge-based systems, expert networks, to name a few — to people, practices, embedded in technology and procedures, etc.

- **Knowledge Leveraging.** Knowledge is applied or otherwise
  leveraged. By using (applying) knowledge, it becomes the basis
  for further learning and innovation as explained by other
  mechanisms.

The importance of the enterprise knowledge cycle becomes evident
when people within the enterprise consider when and where to build
and exploit structural IC. This is part of the intangible asset management mentality as emphasized by Lev (2001) and discussed in
Chapter 7.

THE NEED TO INCREASE PEOPLE'S KNOWLEDGE

Knowledge Required to Act Effectively

Leaders of effective enterprises understand that all employees, at
every level, must possess broad knowledge to address their work
challenges competently. Broad knowledge is needed to deliver competent and effective work and to innovate. It includes directly work-
related professional and craft knowledge, organizational navigational
knowledge, and understanding of enterprise goals, objectives, and
functions. It also includes practical and pertinent metaknowledge
such as critical thinking and other procedural and task-related goals
and about what is and is not known. In addition, people need to be
emotionally engaged to apply their knowledge by delivering the work
required. It is not enough to have intellectual and practical understanding and to know the value of delivering quality work for stakeholders, the enterprise, and themselves.

Work-domain topic knowledge and general world knowledge (i.e.,
managerial, professional, and craft knowledge) allow people to
gather appropriate information, understand and evaluate, explore
and innovate, decide how to handle the situation, project and judge
acceptability of potential outcomes, and implement selected actions
effectively. Innate personal capabilities — attitudes — clearly provide
a basis for acting effectively, but without specific work and general
knowledge and skills, people cannot attain the necessary practical
and subject-specific proficiency needed to fulfill expectations. Better
knowledge normally improves the quality of work by supporting

"smart working" rather than "hard working" — for both individuals and organizations.

Good managers make quick decisions based on established judgments while considering broad implications and the novelty of the situation at hand. Such behavioral models must remain our ideal. Managers — and every employee with any level of responsibility, including factory floor workers — must be provided with awareness to consider broad consequences of their decisions — upstream, downstream, adjacent operations, over the longer term, and while taking into account how relevant stakeholders are affected. As achieved by the proactive and decisive company example in Chapter 2, workers must be provided with an understanding of what is expected of them. They must be provided with clear communication of their role in implementing enterprise strategy, objectives, and direction, and they must be able to explore what it will mean for them personally, in order to build operational mental models and understanding. They must also understand the nature of the services they are asked to provide, sometimes expressed in the form of service paradigms (Chapter 7). These communications and discussions can be conducted through "knowledge cafés," "town meetings," or similar processes as discussed in Appendix B.

In routine work, topic knowledge is very important and can also be used as a basis for automation. When work becomes more complex, the availability of topic knowledge is more limited; it is impossible to provide appropriate "how-to" topic knowledge for all conceivable possibilities. In these situations, metaknowledge becomes progressively more important as work complexity increases, as indicated in Figure 3-13.

With improved knowledge, people know better what to do and how to do it. They must be provided with knowledge of what they know and how to think critically and be innovative. That is, they need metaknowledge, and they need to engage in metacognitive reasoning. Then they will know *why* they can do it better and *why* it will serve themselves and the organizations well. These are basic reasons why the major purpose of KM is to make the enterprise intelligent-acting by facilitating the creation, accumulation, deployment, and use of quality knowledge.

There is one problematic issue, however. People tend to make single-criterion decisions. That is, normally people are not prepared to deal with multiple-criteria decisions and do not intuitively understand how to make decisions that require them to balance several criteria or objectives simultaneously. Since that is the case, it is no

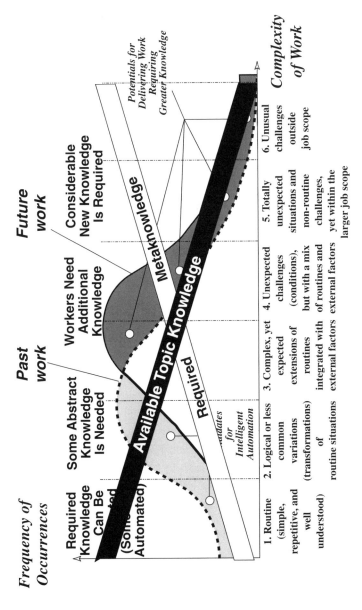

Figure 3-13

Topic knowledge has greater applicability in routine work, while metaknowledge is more important when work is complex. Copyright © 1998 by Karl M. Wiig. Reproduced with permission.

mystery that managers may ask to "just keep it simple, stupid!" (the so-called KISS principle) and why monetary measures often become the only criterion for selecting the desired action.

Examples of Approaches to Develop Mental Models in People

Many important approaches are available for helping people build work-related libraries of mental models. Following are examples that pertain to building mental models for domain topic content and methodological strategies at abstraction levels ranging from concrete to script to schema to metaknowledge.

- **Knowledge Sharing by Storytelling** has always been part of individual and societal transfer and sharing of concepts, principles, judgments, beliefs, traditions, and other insights. Stories are also used to communicate operational and methodological knowledge. Industry and business storytelling is part of everyday knowledge sharing among collaborators, communities of practice, and most other parties. Whereas the stories themselves may be explicit and part of structural IC assets, effective storytelling allows listeners to internalize messages and build personal mental models of value for future considerations and actions.[7]

- **Business Simulations** are increasingly used by business schools to teach graduate students models and implications of organization management. They are also important tools to assist managers, supervisors, and line personnel gain insights into how to handle various business situations that they may encounter. Business operations at every level are challenging and always raise a question of exercising critical thinking and integrative skills and making well-judged tradeoffs between multiple objectives. Everybody recognizes these requirements for senior management. However, to a surprising extent, these requirements are also for assembly workers, cafeteria personnel, and the company's sanitation people.

  Developing the mental models needed for integrative and objectives tradeoff considerations and actions is considered difficult and low priority and is often neglected, with the result that workers — particularly at the lower levels of the enterprise — are often ineffective. Whereas people may know the details, they lack the integrating mental models. We find that targeted and simple business and operations simulations and games prove to be ideal learning environments to remedy these problems.

- **Aircraft Simulators** allow pilots to learn to handle a wide variety of challenges. Repeated exposure to both routine and unexpected situations lets pilots internalize — and to some extent automatize — mental models for how to handle the diversity of situations. For pilots the tacit automaticity is important since many demanding flight events happen quickly and cannot be handled consciously. In addition, handling events nonconsciously and automatically reduces the mental burden on conscious working memory, which may be needed for other purposes during problem events.

- **Apprenticing, Learning on the Job, and Shadowing** have been well established aids over the centuries to help people build competence for specific jobs. However, the notion that the resulting competence rests on libraries of mental models has not been understood until recently. By being part of the daily and varied operations over long periods of time and by being able to absorb, internalize, explore, and perform work themselves, they build extensive and directly applicable mental models. However, they may only be prepared to deal with business-as-usual, since their experience mostly relates to past and present practices. At times, people who learn on the job will mainly build knowledge of "that is the way it is" and have limited understanding of the underlying mechanisms making them vulnerable when confronted with novel challenges.

  One aspect of learning on the job involves a coach who shows an apprentice how to perform a task and then lets the apprentice perform the same task himself. In this process, the apprentice internalizes the procedure as an operational mental model, often tacitly.

- **e-Learning** has become an important tool for education. It is available anywhere, anytime, and at relatively low cost. When the e-based material is complemented with human coaching, retention is reported to be very good. e-learning systems are effective tools for building mental models when they include case stories, topic-focused games, and simulations. In addition, these systems also need to provide basic supporting knowledge elements such as concepts, principles, methods, and facts.

When teaching with stories, simulations, or games, it is important that recipients have sufficient background and prior knowledge to categorize the particulars and significance that are communicated. For example, in business simulations, before a person can benefit from a realistic scenario that asks her to operate a company in a competitive environment, she needs to possess rudimentary understanding of accounting, taxation, marketing, and so on. The better her knowledge of the details of business, the more she will benefit from the simulation. A large number of detailed general business processes, principles, and facts can be taught with stories, games, and simulations. Examples include balance sheets, taxation considerations, accounting procedures, production management, personnel management, customer relations, and logistics, just to name a few. Stories can also be used to teach highly specific tasks such as maintenance and diagnostics of specialized equipment.

The importance of a business simulation game compared to storytelling lies in the learner's opportunity to participate actively in an evolving situation over a period of time — often days (Oliva 2003). Learners need to internalize how to assess situations, project implications, and see the results from the actions they select. Stories, on the other hand, impart descriptions to relatively passive audiences who may, or may not, grasp the importance of the points of the story. Stories also provide relatively short exposures compared to the longer duration and deeper engagement of the simulation games. However, stories provide many advantages. They are low cost; they are quick and can facilitate exposure to many different conditions and scenarios; and they can be made very interesting and, therefore, can be quite memorable. Simulations and stories are still less effective than the many options for learning on the job, but they provide greater opportunities for exposures to many different contexts and varieties of situations.

NOTES

1. A fundamental assumption of cognitive science has been that the mind/brain is a "computational device" (Wilson & Keil 1999, p. 527). Many of the basic perspectives used in this and my earlier books were initially motivated by Dean Wooldridge in his 1963 book *The Machinery of the Brain* and have generally been substantiated by later research. However, from other perspectives it is becoming quite clear that the mind/brain functions are complex beyond any known computers.

2. Not all attempts to provide integrated understanding are successful. The case story educational method pursued at many business schools has come under criticism from proponents of integrative management because the case stories are often not interdisciplinary. They mostly provide integration within single disciplines such as finance, human resources, logistics, and information systems, instead of also addressing the interrelatedness of all these areas within the real world of the functional enterprise.

3. Each person's brain develops different neural connections — it rewires itself — as new experiences, understandings, etc., are internalized. Also, as people gain expertise, different parts of the brain are developed and may even increase in extent (Schwartz & Begley 2002).

4. Little (some say nothing) is known about how knowledge is encoded in our minds. Therefore, many knowledge characteristics discussed in this book may represent speculative, qualitative, illustrative, and operational aspects of knowledge based on system science models and lack foundation in reality.

5. We are indebted to Argyris and Schön (1974) for introducing their theories of action with the view that people have mental maps — mental reference models — with regard to how to act in situations.

6. The concept of metaknowledge is also well known in artificial intelligence but is different from personal metaknowledge, which is discussed here.

7. See Denning (2000), Kotter and Cohen (2002), Ready (2002), Snowden (2000), Solomon (2000), and Wright (2000).

4

MENTAL AND STRUCTURAL REFERENCE MODELS

PREMISE 4-1: PEOPLE IMITATE PRIOR BEHAVIORS

When people make sense of situations, make decisions, act to implement decisions, and monitor the acceptability of their work, they will, to the largest extent possible, imitate something that is previously known to them. In particular, people think and act by adapting, operationalizing, and executing mental reference models — scripts, schemata, abstract generalizations, and metaknowledge — of memorized approaches according to which they can handle the current situation and context naturally and feel comfortable about their approach. People prefer to act in ways that are easy and have low psychological costs.

PREMISE 4-2: ORGANIZATIONS RE-ENACT PAST PRACTICES

Organizations strive to provide stable and comprehensive operating environments with practices that will ensure effective and beneficial handling of all normal and many less normal situations. To that end, they attempt to encode best practices and structural intellectual capital assets into systems and procedures for broad use, instill appropriate "this is how we do it here" thinking into its culture and leadership, and teach desired behaviors to employees at all levels. Organizations prefer to choose practices that are effective by being resource efficient, delivering quality results, and creating good value, while at the same time providing easy-to-manage operations that are readily acceptable to employees.

THE PERSONAL MEMORY EXAMPLE

Shawn is an experienced shipping dispatcher for ChemCo, a bulk chemical producer. She has recently been transferred from

Dispatching to Shipment Planning where she generates the short-term shipping schedule. Much of what she knows from dispatching is of direct use to her in the new position. However, there are new considerations and requirements with which she is unfamiliar and that she needs to learn — and learn quickly.

A week into her new position, after Shawn has generated her first short-term schedule, a large high-priority order comes in and requires that she reschedule immediately to get the shipment out as early as possible. The material is in inventory, but the trucks needed are already committed for other shipments. Although the problem is similar to dispatch situations with which she is very familiar, short-term scheduling introduces additional considerations. Shawn must identify which other shipments would be candidates for delays if she were to free up the trucks needed. She works with Sales to determine problems and relative priorities of potentially delayed shipments. She works with Production to explore possible manufacturing impacts. As she does this, she also searches for possibilities for subcontracting shipments to outside truckers.

While she assesses ChemCo's options, Shawn, with the help of her manager and colleagues in the other departments, weighs the advantages, costs, and issues associated with the options of delaying shipments and buying outside trucking services. Many factors need to be considered. Delaying shipments in most cases impacts customer relations. Delaying shipments also postpones revenues and at times creates manufacturing, inventory, and storage problems. It is also more costly to use outside trucking than ChemCo's own trucks.

All of this is new territory for Shawn, but she learns fast and her manager is of great help in guiding her along. Sally, Shawn's manager, does not work directly with Shawn to show her in detail how to deal with the issues. Instead, Sally tells stories about how she pursued similar problems in the past. She also tells Shawn what to watch out for and what impacts the scheduling decisions might have on departments, operations, customers, and on ChemCo overall. She tells Shawn with whom to network — who her good friends are in Sales, Production, Marketing, and Contracting. Sally's stories also include examples of situations and indicate how it all fits together. Without being directly aware of it, Sally helps Shawn develop an integrated understanding of how to deal with a whole range of issues from both an overall perspective and a detailed approach.

During this experience, Shawn automatically builds a library of mental reference models that she can use to tackle this kind of situation in the future.

Mental Model Preview

As indicated in Premise 4-1 and earlier in Chapter 3, when people make decisions, they tend to the largest extent possible to rely on prior experiences. They adapt and execute reference models that make it possible to imitate prior successful behavior — or, in the words of Bechara *et al.* (1997, p 129): "[They carry out] covert activation of biases related to previous emotional experiences of comparable situations."

People and organizations build and remember large collections — "libraries" — of behavior patterns that are formed from experiences and internalized by positive or negative feedback and reinforcement. Many patterns are also built from the experiences of others, such as when companies obtain descriptions and understandings of best practices from other parties. People and organizations react alike in that they will repeat behaviors that were successful and reinforced positively. They will avoid behaviors remembered as unsuccessful. Personal and organizational behavioral patterns often represent memorized chains of separate expected situations and actions, each being an expected outcome or a response to handle a situation within a particular context.

For similar problems, the context often makes a difference. For example, within the same enterprise, there may be one policy (or pattern) for handling a dissatisfied large repeat customer who has received a major shipment later than expected. This customer may receive top priority for the next shipment and even compensation for estimated loss. The policy may include procedures for estimating loss and for assessing other aspects needed to handle the situation. Another, less accommodating policy may be in effect for handling the same kind of problem for smaller occasional customers and may not include any special favors.

Personal Reference Models

"Give me an example that I can adapt to fit my problem!" This is a statement that is expressed by many people when they encounter a new situation. They are seeking a reference model to aid them to handle the situation easily and effectively.

As we discuss in the next chapter, in situation-handling mental models are used as references to past experiences — hence the term *mental reference models*. Mental models appear to exist at different levels of abstraction and maturity. Some refer directly to experiences with past situations and only consist of encoded sensory data and may be located in episodic memory. Generally, such episodic models are characterizations of scenes, events, or other observations, and what they mean has not been interpreted. That is, features, mechanisms, principles, and implications or consequences inherent in episodic experiences have not been extracted, reflected upon, or thought through; therefore, what we may understand from these episodes has not been derived or be available in our minds. Alongside with the levels of abstractions for mental models that we discussed in Chapter 3, people also appear to build conceptual hierarchies for reference models. When we observe how people apply and use their mental reference models, we can observe that the models provide behavioral guidance on four conceptual levels as indicated in Figure 4-1.

Other mental models whose meanings have been interpreted may reside in whole or in part in semantic or procedural memories. Their meanings are internalized and have to some extent been integrated with other mental objects after conscious or nonconscious analysis and interpretation to create understandings. We tend to analyze and mull over the meanings of mental models that are interesting or notable in some manner such as methodological models and models of educational stories.

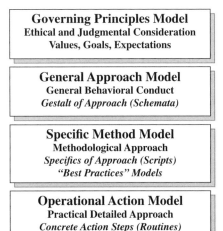

Figure 4-1
People possess mental reference models on several conceptual levels. Copyright © 2000 Knowledge Research Institute, Inc. Reproduced with permission.

For our purposes, we believe that the memory location of mental models and their characteristics are not important. In our context, what is important is that, in addition to other mental constructs, mental models are present and vary in function, specificity, and depth and are used as references for situation-handling and other mental tasks. It is also important to know that we can help people build libraries of mental reference models by learning on the job and general education and by providing them with stories and anecdotes — such as stories portraying the handling of concrete and specific situations and stories illustrating general principles. The degree to which general stories and case histories are memorized and internalized is a direct function of how important or interesting they are to the receiver. Dull events and stories that illustrate the obvious are not remembered well, although they may continue to reside uninterpreted in episodic memory. Another approach to building tacit mental models occurs through implicit learning as indicated in Chapter 3.

There are competing theories for how people store, recall, and reason with mental models and other knowledge. In this book, we presume that people engage in a combination of model reasoning and deductive-inductive-abductive reasoning.[1] We also adopt the operational view that different and distinct short-term and long-term memory functions serve specific and dedicated purposes. Given these premises and other insights, we consider the mental models that a person possesses to be primarily tacit and represented in the mind in different ways governed by the nature of both the situation being modeled and the particular person's memory and thinking style. For example, the mental reference model for how to drive from one location to another may include many scenes that are structurally encoded as visual features combined with a script of where to turn at specific times or scenes. For others, the mental model of the same route may consist of street name anchored scripts.

Another example may be a set of mental reference models for how to evaluate a commercial loan application. Such a situation includes a number of individual concepts such as creditworthiness, payment history, and business outlook, each having separate reference models for how to gather information and how to assess indicators/measures/attainments of the concepts, and so on. In addition, there will be reference models for how to consolidate the individual dimensions into a cohesive overall evaluation.

By being tacit, mental reference models reside in nonconscious long-term memory and are recalled "on command" from working memory as part of the priming process. As we discuss in the next chapter, that may happen as part of sensemaking, when a person receives, structures, and organizes information about a situation before making sense of it. Her priming memory employs pattern matching and metaphoric reasoning to cause past knowledge of similar and relevant situations to be recalled from long-term memory, typically in terms of mental reference models. In sensemaking, we can think of these models as being part of the person's situational awareness capability. Much of our reasoning is qualitative and probabilistic and is influenced by what we know about the context and by our values and biases. This, we believe, is the general mechanism by which relevant mental reference models are recalled and utilized for the subtasks associated with this task. An illustration of how we may envision some of the functional entities of the human memory system is shown in Figure 4-2 and is explained further in Appendix C.

Reference Models Are Stories!

Stories provide the basic structure and often the origin of mental reference models. Social scientists have long understood the importance of stories, which have been the basis for transmitting cultural insights in most societies. Recent cognitive science insights into decision making give direct indications that encoded stories have direct relations to many types of mental models on the personal level. There is also an emerging realization that stories play important roles in capturing, retaining, and utilizing operational and theoretical knowledge in business. The importance, roles, and nature of stories in business have recently been treated by Denning (2000), Kotter and Cohen (2002), Ready (2002), Snowden (2000), and Wright (2000). This realization has significance for many aspects of KM — such as which methods are effective for sharing knowledge within communities of practice, how one should acquire and institutionalize personal knowledge into structural intellectual capital (IC), how effective education should be performed, and what is needed to conduct knowledge diagnostics effectively.

Mental reference models are typically represented by encoded procedural or cause-and-effect constructs from stories that have been distilled to extract salient relationships, features, and patterns. These characteristics are combined in our minds and are remembered,

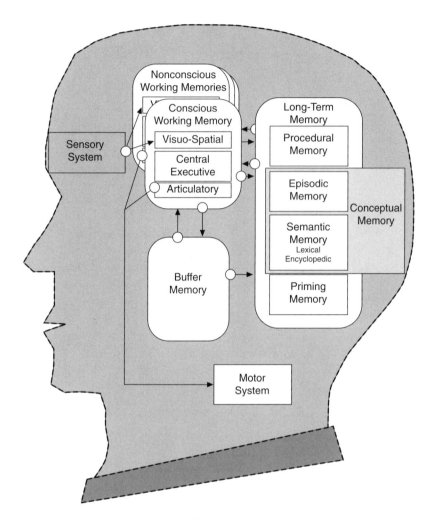

Figure 4-2
*Conceptual model of the human memory system. Copyright © 1993 by Karl M.
Wiig. Reproduced with permission.*

perhaps as a unit, or more likely in ways that we might represent by
chunked hierarchies or semantic nets.

Most people seem to find it easier to remember complicated relationships and conditions when they are presented, integrated, and
structured in the form of stories. The stories provide both a context
and a framework. It is more difficult to remember isolated knowledge items such as principles or rules. As a result, it is more likely
that people remember personal experiences as static events or as
evolving situations — as stories.

For the most part, people cannot recall all the stories in their memory on demand. Most stories are tacit and normally unavailable to conscious thought. However, given a particular situation, priming memory brings relevant stories to bear, either as conscious thought or as tacit patterns used to guide automatic actions. We use pattern recognition and other reasoning strategies to recall memories that resemble the situations at hand. In this way, as is discussed in the next chapter, people use mentally encoded stories automatically and nonconsciously to handle situations as part of their Situational Awareness, Action Space and Innovation, Execution Capability, and Governance Competence.

WHY ARE STORIES IMPORTANT?

Stories come in many forms. They may be verbal tales of events that have happened and may be presented linearly in time. They may be descriptions of separate actors and entities and their relations to one another. Some stories may never be verbalized. They may be tacit, as when a master shows an apprentice how to perform a particular task without explaining anything. Stories may be drawings of mechanical designs or diagrams of computer programs. They may be pictures, even artworks such as paintings of medieval boar hunts or an Australian aborigine's illustration of the importance and propagation of knowledge within his society. Stories do not require depiction of dynamic evolution, although many imply or make explicit progression over time. Most stories illustrate causal chains: "This is what was done and that is what happened," often with associated explanations of why the consequence happened. Other stories may be static descriptions of situations, such as an illustration of the positions of opposing forces on a battlefield or a description of the current state of an ecological system. In all cases, stories describe, and by their descriptions they provide categorizations, structure, and frameworks that, when believed and internalized by recipients, allow the building of understanding and mental models.

It Is Always Hard to Grasp the Whole Coherently

Stories are important for building context-specific personal mental models. In general, synthesizing isolated knowledge objects into new cohesive patterns or contextual models without being given a framework for structure is an innovative and creative act that often is difficult to perform and perform well. Whereas we may know all the individual knowledge objects that may apply to deal with a situation — principles, theories, concepts, particulars, and other matters — it requires complex synthesis and originality to integrate them into a new and effective mental framework that will be appropriate for handling the situation.

That is why it is hard for a mechanical engineering graduate who knows all the theoretical principles and basic engineering practices to create the design of a working machine before he has formed a "story" — a congruent model — in his mind of how all the elements fit together. It is much easier to be told a story that provides a structure into which the weave can be created for the specific purpose and be memorized as a routine, operational model, script, schema, or generalized pattern, depending on the level of abstraction with which he will work. From a connectionist principle, this involves conceptual blending of the story with his prior knowledge to create a new mental space that is applicable for his purpose (Fauconnier & Turner 2002).

As people gain deep understanding of how to handle complicated situations effectively in the form of internally consistent stories and mental models, they tend to internalize the approaches to handle such situations as "second nature." In these cases, people will automatically choose such "natural" approaches since they are easy (they know well how to perform them), they are acceptable, and they are executed at low psychological costs.

In our minds, we often link isolated knowledge objects with other knowledge objects to form understandings of relationships, implications, and other combination characteristics. We synthesize to create a weave — a mental model, a story-like construct for a particular context. To serve this purpose, mental models take many forms and may be encoded descriptions of a static scene, a dynamic episode, a complex situation, and so on. Stories have significance for many aspects of KM — such as how knowledge is shared among people, how knowledge is acquired and institutionalized, how education is performed, and how knowledge diagnostics is conducted.

Stories are important when illustrating and communicating specifics of a context. From a wider perspective, they are even more important when providing deep insights into culture, folklore, and ideologies — even religion — through their underlying meanings. Many stories are metaphors that provide partial, but important, understanding of complex aspects of approved and accepted behaviors, societal aspects, and life in general.

Stories Are Unsurpassed for Effective Communication

In many societies stories are listened to time and again, and the mental models are internalized, becoming stronger and better understood with each repetition. They build the mental models that become part of what is firmly believed. This is also why we often say: "Oh — I should have known that" when we discover or are told about an overlooked aspect of a situation with which we are well acquainted. In these cases we may know all the details but have not been able to envision all implications or consequences. The power of stories is evident in such cases as how to diagnose and correct problems of a particular machine by delineating specific aspects and relationships — some as being important and others of less importance. The story not only provides us with a categorized structure, but it also identifies major issues and ways of approaching the situation.

Personal experiences of many kinds are encountered or communicated effectively from one person to another in the form of stories. People use stories to recount how to handle complicated problem situations, take advantage of opportunities, deal with dilemmas, observe moral and ethical principles, avoid conflicts, and many other aspects of business, social, and personal life. Stories are also used to communicate how to apply methodologies and practices to deal with a host of small and large challenges including Problem-Solving and Implementation of large projects. As is well known, stories are useful for communication of metaknowledge and metaphors.

Denning (2000) reminds us about the importance of using stories in the effort to change enterprises. His experiences in the World Bank deal with considerations that are of great importance in enterprise communication (Denning 2000). He emphasizes two important aspects in enterprise communication. (1) Storytelling is highly effective for sharing perspectives among employees throughout the enterprise. From effective knowledge management perspectives, stories that provide shared understanding among employees is a major success factor for competitive enterprise performance. (2) Storytelling has great value for transfer of visions. In such cases, uses of real, but simplified, stories can make key individuals throughout an enterprise build visions when understanding how selected principles and concepts should be considered for different contexts. Denning explains how the use of expertly crafted stories can make people exclaim: "That principle also pertains to my operation!" even though the story illustrates a different context. These stories must, Denning explains, be crystal clear and must spell out the nature and function of the target principles. They must not be too detailed because that empha-sizes the story's original context and hence will detract from the transfer of vision.

We Rely on Stories to Tackle New Problems

When faced with new challenges, relevant stories often help us create mental models that let us tackle the task effectively. Consider Alice, an insurance underwriter, who is asked to produce an insur-ance policy quote for a retail business in a socioeconomic area with which she has no prior experience. She knows risk analysis tech-niques and methods, and general business risks, and she has good general knowledge of the retail business, though not of this particu-lar kind. Alice knows all the principles and theory. However, she does not know how her knowledge objects, other mental models, and con-siderations should be applied to the specific retail business in the par-ticular geographic location.

Her coworker Jean has worked with a similar case before and tells stories of how she approached that situation. In relating the stories — and there are several — Jean points out that she also made misjudgments and tells the reasons for those and how she corrected for them. As a result, Alice is able to weave together a cohesive model of the approach she will use to handle the situation — to interpret the business and situational information, build the problem-specific methodology for analysis, problem-solve the insurance quote, and create the proposal details — all within the company's guidelines and intent and to the satisfaction of her own professional judgment.

Stories Help Us Learn Better

Stories often assist us in learning and are used in effective educa-tional settings by complementing the teaching of theory, principles, and other topic-related knowledge objects. Students are helped by following and understanding stories, engaging in conceptual blend-ing to tie mental objects together, and creating new ones. In this way, they make new mental spaces as coherent wholes in their minds by understanding new concepts, how individual objects fit with one another, and how build expectations for evolving scripts and the like. Good stories let us integrate and create coherent and harmonious mental models so that we can understand relationships and make sense of the whole.

Instead of describing the synthesized characteristics of complex matters, people find it easy to use stories to describe concrete situations and events. For example, stories are useful when the point they are making and which they want others to understand is abstract, such as when emphasizing the general nature of the potentially undesirable consequences of unethical acts. People find it much more difficult to make explicit the general and abstract principles and lessons that underlie the story's moral or teachings. Difficult as it is, that step is at times necessary to help recipients identify and focus on the general idea and build the intended understanding — the intended knowledge. It appears that the most effective approach to transfer deep concepts is storytelling followed by discussion and dialogue about what the story tells.

As an example of an effective use of a story from enterprise education, let us visit a class in papermaking for operator trainees. The small class had learned about all the parts of the paper manufacturing process from chipper, digester, bleaching plant, refiners, the paper machine with its head box to presses, felts, dryers, calenders, spools, and all other objects. The teacher covered designs, construction, individual functions, and principles of operation, but the trainees still had problems understanding how everything fit functionally and operationally together in detail, although they understood the general flow of materials through the process. The teacher then told a "story" by following one piece of wood from the point where it entered the chipper, was transformed into pulp and fine cellulose fibers, before entering the paper machine and in the end emerging as high-quality paper after calendering. As he told the story, he indicated how the piece of material that started as a wood chip was gradually transformed to paper and how it was beneficially or adversely affected by proper and improper operation of the equipment. As a result, after the story had been told, each student was able to build coherent mental models of the whole process and develop a mental framework for how to operate the different areas of the papermaking process.

Stories and Mental Simulations

When making nonroutine decisions,[2] Klein (1998 and 2002) explains that we may perform quick mental simulations to ascertain that a potential decision candidate will perform acceptably. Mental simulations allow us to imagine the consequences of operationalizing potential decisions and can be compared to dynamic, step-by-step mental visualizations of what we may expect if we proceed. If we possess a story-related mental reference model that is sufficiently relevant to the target situation, we perform the mental simulation by tacitly adjusting the model to the new context and we operationalize and activate it as a thought experiment to generate an envisioned outcome. If we do not have a prior mental model, we perform the mental simulation by synthesizing a new mental model story that should make sense in the new context. We create the story by envisioning how individual aspects of the situation might be combined and how they will perform within the mental scenario. In effect, in a short time — Klein indicates often in a few seconds — we have created and tested a new mental model that is added to our library.

Figure 4-3 outlines a model of the role of mental simulation when operationalizing general knowledge to create an operational model

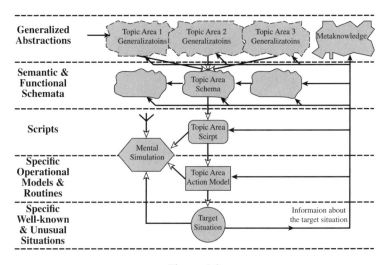

Figure 4-3

The role of mental simulation in a model for operationalizing general knowledge to serve a particular nonroutine and complex situation. Copyright © 1999 by Knowledge Research Institute, Inc. Reproduced with permission.

to address a nonroutine target situation. We assume that the person will use his general knowledge and will draw upon conceptual knowledge in the form of mental models of generalized abstractions, schemata, and scripts to create an operational model that is then activated to handle the situation.

For most complex situations, people will draw upon mental models from many topic domains to incorporate different perspectives that need to be blended to make a coherent picture. Decisions of this kind are often based on expectations and the strength of associations, rather than on a systematic decision-making process. Klein (1998 and 2002) provides extensive discussion on how people make decisions in real situations. These findings, by themselves, have strong implications for how we prepare people to continue learning and for how we assist them to perform work more effectively. In particular, we need to provide people with the kinds of knowledge that will facilitate their best performance — the highest degree of effective intelligent-acting possible. However, as indicated previously, most people have problems with dealing competently with making multicriteria decisions — particularly when there are uncertainties involved, which always seems to be the case.

As an illustration of intuitive or nonconscious decision making, consider that I am driving my car on a winding mountain road, another car passes me, and at the same time an oncoming car appears. I am faced with a situation where I must address a complex problem quickly. I must consider how people (in the other cars) are likely to react under such circumstances; what may be physically possible given the speed of the cars; the road surface; the terrain on the side of the road; the driving characteristics of my own car; and my own driving skills. Several generalized abstractions, schemata, and scripts may be involved in my thinking within a time span of a second or so. I may use metaknowledge (knowledge about what and how I know) to decide how to handle the situation. I may retrieve a mental model script from memory and use that as a basis for generating a new, situation-specific script, with a resulting operational model used to perform a mental simulation — if I have time before I need to act — to ascertain that my potential action will satisfice[3] the situation. As indicated in Figure 4-3, mental simulation involves exploring if the operational or action model will provide a satisficing solution by using expectations and perspectives from internalized conceptual knowledge. If the simulation results are unacceptable, the topic script and its resulting action model are modified and the simulation is repeated.

Organizational Reference Models

Management of any operation, be it a large enterprise or a small team, is always difficult. Any such operation is a dynamic and continuously changing socioeconomic system with multiple objectives and tradeoffs, conflicts and shortages of time, attention, and other resources. In addition, any operation and situation is connected to multiple external entities. Within the enterprise, there are connections to other departments and operations. Externally, there are connections to customers, suppliers, owners, and other stakeholders. In this "mess," we still need to manage our operations to achieve the best possible performance relative to all relevant objectives. It is impossible for even the best manager to arrive at decisions and approaches from first principles and "scratch" to deal with the challenges. Instead, operation and performance of enterprises to a large extent depend on prior experience in the forms of structural reference models to provide guidance for all kinds of challenges. They benefit from utilizing reference models in a number of ways. Reference models allow enterprises to repeat best practices that have proven successful in the past, particularly when they were also supported by, and in concert with, management philosophy, operational practices, and culture.

Some reference models that people share are culturally embedded as stories or conventions that describe "this is the way we do it here." Others are included in the enterprise's structural intellectual capital in the form of practices, systems, procedures, enterprise policies, and the manner in which the enterprise and its work processes are organized.

In the enterprise, many structural reference models perform functions that are of crucial importance in that they provide the framework for standard and uniform behavior that will result in non-chaotic, orderly, and manageable operations. Examples of some functions provided by organizational reference models include guidance to

- Outline expected and desired personal conduct (such as providing behavioral models for how to live the performance paradigm).
- Provide approaches to handle a wide variety of problem situations, many of which occur only rarely and therefore cannot be expected to be well known by the people who are expected to deal with the problem.

- Provide standardized approaches to handle routine business problems.

In numerous enterprises, many organizational reference models are automated in computer-based performance support systems (PSS) or other types of work aids. Some of these can include large libraries with thousands of reference models and have extensive reasoning capabilities to aid operations quickly and reliably.[4]

Leaders Create Powerful Reference Models

Managers and influential people at all levels of the enterprise wield enormous power (Anonymous 1998). Because of people's natural tendencies to copy and mimic the behaviors, perspectives, and values of others, the managers set examples — good and bad — that are imitated and followed by people around them. Hence, much too often without being aware of it, they directly affect the attitudes, mentalities, and culture within their operations. Tacit behavior by management automatically becomes a guideline for the rank-and-file for permissible behavior, desired practices, and practical demonstrations of the enterprise's intent.

It follows that, in any enterprise, the daily behavior of its leaders creates important reference models. Since people try to be like their leaders and use them as role models, all leaders need to provide living examples for governance, ethics, operational philosophies, practices, and for how to deal with each other, customers, suppliers, problems, and the enterprise in general. As indicated in Chapter 3, people behave and act by "covert activation of biases related to previous emotional experiences of comparable situations." There is no escape for leaders who automatically will act out their mental models (Bechara *et al.* 1997). Their examples will be replicated by the mental reference models they build in their coworkers' minds as they observe the leaders' behaviors and engage in tacit implicit learning. Their attitudes will be copied; their mentalities will be imitated; and their ways of handling problems will be emulated. Top leaders, to a large extent, function as organizational reference models that often are emulated throughout the enterprise by managers, professionals, and other people.

Some important examples of areas where leaders become role models include how customers, suppliers, and employees are treated and what level of emphasis should be placed on short-term profits and on "meeting the numbers" balanced against long-term objectives, on willingness to experiment, on attitudes toward taking risks, and so on. A particular area of the importance of leadership guidance relates to attitudes toward resolution of tradeoffs and dilemmas where conflicting objectives lead to difficult situations. An important example here is how the enterprise should deal with damage control when unanticipated problems occur.

If any member of the top management team exhibits unethical behavior, someone within the organization will surely copy it. Similarly, if any pacesetters exhibit sloppy behavior in any way, that too will be copied. One might argue that corporate and public leaders have obligations to behave ethically and effectively, and their examples will be copied liberally by others, who then by their individual behaviors will make the enterprise behave likewise. Since we expect ethical and effective behaviors from these enterprises, their leaders — often tacitly and without awareness — are instrumental in creating the enterprise behaviors.

NOTES

1. Within the discipline of psychology, the debate on how people reason is still ongoing, although it appears that most researchers conclude that people employ many different strategies with which they reason.
2. Our perspective is that decisions imply action that is intended to change the state of the target situation over time (or, on occasion, nearly at once) and lead to the desired outcome. Decision–action–change–outcome implies a dynamic system (the "situation") with inputs (action) and outputs (outcome).
3. When a decision maker looks for an option that is just "good enough" s/he "satisfices." Simon (1945) introduced the concept of satisficing to characterize the expedient behavior of decision makers who stop short of finding the best solution that fulfills all criteria to the best degree. This notion contrasts Collins' (2001) notion of always needing to do the very best to succeed.
4. Performance support systems cover many functions such as "Lessons Learned Systems" and, when intelligent, often utilize technologies such as automated case-based reasoning. See, for example, Wiig (1995) and Weber *et al.* (2001).

5

A Knowledge Model for Personal Situation-Handling

Premise 5-1: Situation-Handling Requires Action

People are required to act in all kinds of situations — large and small. Whenever changes are needed, they will be achieved through actions. Actions are required even in simple situations to keep balance when walking, purchase food for dinner, copy a letter, write a business report, close a sale, deal with customer problems, create new products, and so on. The actions that are required depend upon the situation, its context and objectives, the person's understanding of the situation, and the person's capabilities. Actions always require energy or resources to be implemented. Energy may be physical energy or mental energy — at a psychological cost. Resources may be financial or physical assets or personal, organizational, or societal resources such as time, attention, or other intangible assets. To handle the situation, action is always required.

Premise 5-2: Good Situation-Handling Is the Result of Effective Actions

Good situation-handling by people implies that the resulting personal performance will be good. Personal situation-handling performance results from the quality of personal actions. When personal actions are effective — that is, when they are based on appropriate understanding of the situation and its context and directed to maximize relevant personal, enterprise, and other objectives within the contextual constraints — then cumulated personal performances leading to enterprise performance will be good.

117

Personal Situation-Handling:
A Customer Service Example

Susan Stark, a customer service manager, is informed that a key customer returned a recently shipped high-technology instrument, indicating that it did not work correctly. From additional information and previous experience, Susan quickly recognizes that the instrument indeed has quality problems. She needs to decide how to deal with it in a manner that is practical and provides effective support of the enterprise's intent and strategy and at the same time satisfies her personal performance goals.

Susan handles this situation tacitly and rapidly; she does not need to explore it extensively or consult with others. Three immediate action-options come to mind: (1) cancel the sale and let the customer place a new purchase order when a new instrument is needed; (2) repair the returned instrument and send it back to the customer; or (3) manufacture and deliver a new, problem-free instrument as soon as possible. In turn, she tacitly and automatically performs quick mental simulations to explore the acceptability of each outcome. By examining what she is about to do from the perspective of her enterprise's intents — its strategy — and her personal attitudes for how business should be conducted, she immediately rejects choices (1) and (2) and decides that the company's best approach is to manufacture a new item as fast as possible. She implements her decision by ordering and expediting the building of the new instrument. Furthermore, she decides to inform the customer personally of what her company will do to correct the problem. Parts of this situation-handling process are outlined in Figure 5-1.

Introduction to Personal Situation-Handling

The handling of situations is at the center of all life, of all work, and of all progress. Our world is dynamic with constant changes, both beneficial and detrimental. In this environment of change with its opportunities, problems, and issues, interventions in the form of actions are required whenever expected outcomes of undisturbed situations fall short of desired goals.

It is generally accepted that good knowledge produces good enterprise performance and that better knowledge leads to even better performance. Exactly how this happens is normally not specified or explored, and most knowledge management (KM) efforts

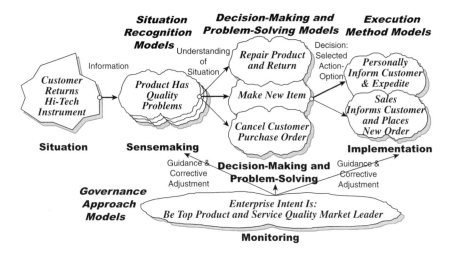

Figure 5-1

Situation-handling by a manager who decides how to handle the return of a high-technology instrument by a customer. Copyright © 2001 Knowledge Research Institute, Inc. Reproduced with permission.

are conducted without considering the underlying knowledge processes that utilize the knowledge to generate operational and strategic behaviors and performances. That is almost as detrimental as flying blind and, not surprisingly, has led to many KM failures. This book's purpose is to outline some of the mechanisms and processes in which people and organizations engage as part of work. To handle situations, people obtain information about situations, use knowledge to perceive what they are about, decide how to handle them, and implement appropriate actions while attempting to maximize their own and their enterprise's interests (Suchman 1995).

Actions of any kind result from decisions that may range from automatized and tacit to deliberate and explicit.[1] Decisions to act are based on the nature and requirements of the situation at hand, the applicability and quality of available knowledge, the ability to implement them, and many other factors. Quality and appropriate availability of information is one factor. To better understand some of these processes, decision making has been studied and described by many authors, particularly during the last 50 years. However, much of that work has not had the benefit of the recent research in cognitive science. In addition, making the decision is only one of several tasks that people perform when confronted with situations that require interventions or lead to other actions, including internal adaptation or problem avoidance such as outright flight.

The General Context

We assume that work and most other endeavors generally consist of a process whereby a person receives information about a situation, identifies what it is about and how it will evolve relative to what is desired, finds ways to deal with it to bring the situation closer to desired objectives, and ascertains that it is done satisfactorily. In most cases, however, the situation is ongoing and is subject to repeated or continuous information gathering: Sensemaking, Decision-Making, and Implementation of actions. When dealing with situations in which people make decisions that result in actions, we say that they engage in *situation-handling*. In all areas of life, situation-handling is important. During a normal workday, people engage in hundreds or even thousands of small, individual situation-handling episodes. Most such episodes are personal, nonconscious (tacit), and automatic and require a few seconds, others require more work, and still others require extensive teamwork and collaboration and can have long durations. Clearly, in order to achieve high-grade enterprise performance, these individual personal situation-handling episodes must be as effective as possible. Separately, they must be effective, and in the aggregate they still must be effective. The latter requirement immediately brings to the fore the need for appropriate enterprise practices as well as organization systems and procedures that promote and take advantage of the effective consolidation of good individual actions, as discussed in the next chapter.

From a KM perspective, understanding of personal and organizational situation-handling, including Decision-Making/Problem-Solving, is important to manage knowledge successfully. This understanding requires insights into areas as diverse as situation-handling practices, cognitive sciences, knowledge transfer methods, microeconomics, management principles, and supporting information technology. Such insights are required to diagnose knowledge-related operations that will help determine drivers and conditions, conceptualize KM initiatives, implement capabilities, and assess and monitor utilization of knowledge-related resources and practices. Frequently, acquiring the requisite understanding of knowledge-related mechanisms on the personal and organizational level takes KM professionals into new fields and requires them to view work and operations from perspectives that may be new to most of them.

What constitutes a *situation*, however, is far from clear, particularly when it is incipient with an almost undetectable start or evolves over time as most situations tend to do (Stafford 2002). It may be difficult to identify the beginning of a situation or even determine when it has ended. Most situations are quite dynamic and fluid and can change substantially over time as results of internal dynamics or external actions. Other situations may consist of a single occurrence. Still others may comprise a sequence of events separated in time, such as when an insurance underwriter is working a case in small time chunks whenever new information arrives, until a final action is implemented. Or a situation may consist of a condition that changes dynamically over time and is handled repeatedly until no more attention is required — such as driving a car from home to work (Garvin & Roberto 2001). For example, medical situations may follow such a pattern when a physician diagnoses a patient, who subsequently receives a series of treatments to gradually become better. Many other, often complex, business situations also follow this pattern. Other examples include handling prolonged negotiations of labor contracts, research and development to create a new manufacturing process, or the process of developing a customer relationship in the commercial loan business.

Within the enterprise, business functions consist of interconnected dynamic systems or processes of many types that are similar in nature to other processes within the world in general. Most processes can be manipulated or influenced by external action; some, when tightly organized, can be made to follow intended patterns in general and then can even be controlled to some extent. Examples are oppressively controlled dictatorships. However, in business, the dynamic behavior of individuals, departments, and the enterprise itself will generate changing conditions — situations and events — that directly or indirectly affect finances, products, services, people, departments, enterprises, customers, other stakeholders, and so on. Thus, these behaviors may require attention to make their performance acceptable. These situations need to be managed by initiating interventions — actions — to change or manipulate them to modify their behaviors and outcomes. They can be handled to fulfill personal or enterprise goals and objectives.

A person handles situations by identifying what they are about, by making decisions about what to do with them, by implementing the decisions — the selected actions — and by monitoring what is happening, explicitly or implicitly. As situations evolve, Sensemaking will be repeated, and new action-options will be developed and executed — at times before implementation of prior actions is completed or their final effects are known. The handling of these situations becomes an exercise in "steering" very complicated and dynamic problems, often with insufficient information and understanding. Nevertheless, such situations must be handled. They often can be handled better with improved understanding of the situation-handling process, which provides insights into which situation-handling tasks may be improved with the available knowledge, information, and resources.

As discussed further in the next section, situations that involve regular work can vary considerably from simple routine to highly complex. *We argue that more complex work generally is of greater importance by creating greater value.* It therefore becomes important to facilitate competence development in people who are asked to deal with these situations. They need good and pertinent knowledge, not only within their conventional work domain, but also within broader domains to understand how their actions affect — or are affected by — adjacent and up- and downstream processes or functions and external entities. They need broad perspectives, good world knowledge, and methodological skills to innovate and envision options and implications.

THE KNOWLEDGE-BASED SITUATION-HANDLING MODEL

The knowledge model for situation-handling is based on an information processing paradigm and is constructed in good "engineering fashion" by combining and integrating building blocks borrowed from many areas. It rests on perspectives from cognitive science, systems science, management science, information theory, and other areas, such as long-time experiences with intellectual and manual work. In the personal domain, the model is a vast simplification and idealization of the real and complex mental processes about which our understanding is still rudimentary. For organizations and computer-automated situation-handling functions, it is still simplified but more realistic. In particular, this model addresses processes associated with delivering competent work. Hence, the model does not deal explicitly with learning or innovation mechanisms or the detailed mechanisms and processes within its four primary tasks.

We argue here that knowledge is the key factor in effective situation-handling. People use their knowledge to handle situations more or less effectively to satisfy enterprise goals, to gain personal advantage, and to satisfy many other purposes. They may attempt to control, influence, or change the situation outright when that is possible, adapt to it when it is not, or pursue a combination of adaptation and external change — interventions — to move conditions in the desired direction. We divide situation-handling into four primary tasks: (1) Sensemaking; (2) Decision-Making/Problem-Solving; (3) Implementation; and (4) Monitoring. A schematic overview of the relationships between these four tasks is indicated in Figure 5-2. This figure also indicates some connecting variables and paths along which information and knowledge enter the process. In addition, it presents the "functional proficiencies" needed to operationalize each primary task: *Situational Awareness; Action Space* and *Innovation Capability; Execution Capability;* and *Governance Competence* and *Perspectives.* The degree of usefulness attained by the functional proficiencies is highly dependent upon the extent and quality of knowledge and expertise that people possess or is otherwise made available to tackle the tasks. If knowledge is limited or competence is reduced, the functional proficiencies become constraints that will reduce the effectiveness of the overall situation handling. If knowledge is improved and expanded, the functional proficiencies will provide opportunities to improve current performance or even make it possible to pursue new strategies.

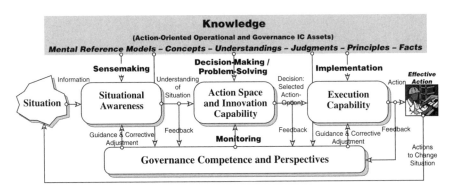

Figure 5-2

The personal Situation-Handling model — from situation information and Sensemaking to implemented effective action. Copyright © 2001 Knowledge Research Institute, Inc. Reproduced with permission.

In this model, the concept of *Situational Awareness* originated with the evaluation and characterization of fighter pilot competences and behaviors (Wickens 2002). The concept of *Action Space* was introduced to us through the work of Dr. Ragnhild Sohlberg of Norsk Hydro. The work on tacit and explicit decision making that supports the following discussions is reported by many researchers, including Bechara *et al.* (1997), Damasio (1994, 1999, 2003), Glimcher (2003), Janis (1989), Klein (1998, 2002), and Simon (1976, 1977). Beyond these contributions, the large body of research provides foundations for understanding many aspects of knowing, learning, decision making/problem solving, innovation, and creativity. For current perspectives on mental functions, see Bereiter (2002) and Fauconnier and Turner (2002). For a brief, excellent, and readable overview of tacit decision making and associated processes, see Stewart (2002a). Given these and other sources, we can explain the four primary tasks and their functional proficiencies. It also helps us to realize that in the past we misunderstood how people handle situations and make decisions. We once believed that decision making is a rational and mostly conscious set of deliberations. These generally held misconceptions have misled — and still mislead — the development of many KM-related management practices with results that at times are quite disappointing.

For the newer perspectives, many researchers have contributed greatly to this field. See, for example, Anderson (1981, 1983), Baddeley (1992a, 1992b), Boden (1990), Damasio (1994, 1999, 2003), Gazzaniga (2000), Halpern (1989), Ivry and Robertson (1998), Janis (1989), Johnson-Laird (1983), Kahneman, Slovic, and Tversky (1982), Krogh *et al.* (2000), Lakoff (1987), Lowen (1982), Neves and Anderson (1981), Pinker (1997), Polanyi (1966), Posner (1989), Schön (1983, 1987), and Singley and Anderson (1989).

Figure 5-2 introduces the notion that knowledge in various forms directly influences the performance of the primary tasks by enabling the functional proficiencies. From a knowledge perspective of situation-handling operations, we are particularly interested in the roles that mental reference models have in increasing the effectiveness and performance of each primary task.

As indicated, situations are rarely single events. Instead, they are often ongoing situations that require repeated attention and multiple actions. In general, situations are dynamic and can change substantially over time, caused by internal dynamics and external actions. From the decision maker's point of view, a situation may appear to evolve, for example, as a result of obtaining additional information about a business opportunity. It could also be as a result of the situation itself changing — by external events, by itself, or by being changed by the actions executed to manage it. New information, new considerations, and new actions need to be pursued to manage it. Figure 5-3 illustrates some of the complex interactions associated with handling ongoing situations in greater detail than Figure 5-2.

The Customer Service Example Revisited

In light of the situation-handling model, let us examine what Susan does in our earlier example. She uses her prior knowledge, which she has stored in her mind as tacit mental reference models and other types of knowledge. Using her mental Situation Recognition reference models, which are part of her Situational Awareness functional proficiency to make sense of the situation, she understands the situation to be almost routine. Since she thinks she understands the situation, she applies her mental Decision-Making/Problem-Solving

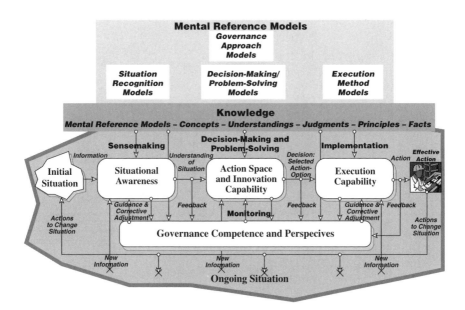

Figure 5-3
The personal Situation-Handling model becomes more complicated with additional tasks in an ongoing situation. Copyright © 2002 Knowledge Research Institute, Inc. Reproduced with permission.

reference models, which are part of her Action Space and Innovation Capability, and she makes the decision automatically and rapidly, within about 6 seconds — even though she needs to engage in "multi-stage Decision-Making."[2]

As part of the Decision-Making task, she performs mental simulations guided by Monitoring and her mental Governing Approach reference models (see the following section on topic domain knowledge). It is this process that led her to reject the first two action-options because they satisfied neither her company's intents nor her own criteria for how to treat clients. She implements her decision routinely by being highly familiar with corporate practices, systems, and procedures and by having good networking contacts with the people in manufacturing. Part of this knowledge she possesses as Execution Method reference models included in her Execution Capability.

Throughout, the manner in which Susan performs her Sensemaking, Decision-Making/Problem-Solving, and Implementation tasks is supervised by her Monitoring task and her Governance Competence and Perspectives functional proficiency — particularly her mental Governance Approach reference models. This executive function operates in the background — mostly nonconsciously and automatically — and provides objectives and guidance to influence the way she interprets information, makes decisions, chooses action-options, and implements the desired actions. As a result, her overall situation-handling supported the enterprise intent for how to deal with important customers. The corporate situation-handling is rapid, routine, and flexible, and falls in line with implementing the enterprise strategy and also satisfies Susan's own professional values.

THE FOUR SITUATION-HANDLING TASKS

The four primary situation-handling tasks work together to comprise an integrated system with operations that are partly sequential and partly executed in parallel. For personal situation-handling, the operations are normally executed tacitly within a person's mind. Within an organization, the operations may be executed explicitly by a person, different individuals, teams, departments, or even highly automated systems such as an automatic credit checking system for credit cards. The operations progress from initial observation of the situation and its context to execution of the selected action — or actions — intended to change the situation outcome to best fulfill the context and situation objectives.

The degree to which situation-handling provides a valid treatment of the target situation is influenced by numerous factors. Many of these factors can in turn be influenced to improve sensemaking performance in specific situations or in general. Tables 5-1 and 5-3 to 5-5 provide examples of positive and negative conditions that affect the primary tasks of situation-handling.

Sensemaking and *Situational Awareness*

The purpose of Sensemaking is to create an understanding of what a situation "is about" — what it means, how important it is, and, for Decision-Making/Problem-Solving purposes, to determine how familiar the decision maker is with that type of situation.

Sensemaking is one of the most important and perhaps one of the most ignored aspects of work. Before a person can handle a task, tackle a challenge, or deal with a situation, he needs to identify the circumstances — the normal characteristics, problems, and general context. Unless both the target situation and its context are properly understood, the situation-handling is liable to be handled unsatisfactorily. The resulting decisions and action-options may become ineffective and arbitrary because of misunderstanding or even capricious because of preconceived biases.

Given its importance in business in Decision-Making/Problem-Solving in general, and from our perspective on how people can and need to act effectively, it is remarkable that Sensemaking is not treated comprehensively — at times not at all — by cognitive scientists and others concerned with how people think and behave. The topic is not found in recent cognitive sciences encyclopedias (Nadel 2003; Wilson and Keil 1999). Instead, Sensemaking is found to be an important technical concept in artificial intelligence (AI) and computer sciences. Some researchers consider Sensemaking to be an ongoing activity that deals with a person's attempts to understand her environment in general. In this book, we take a different view similar to that required for situational awareness. We use the term to mean making sense of a particular situation, and we understand it within a specific context and deal effectively with it.

Sensemaking

Sensemaking is the first task of situation-handling, and this is where analysis and reasoning to understand the situation take place. From a somewhat different perspective than the one we pursue here,

Weick (1995) treated Sensemaking in general and specifically within the organization. Lakoff (1987) explained that, to provide a foundation for discrimination of what is important and what is not, Sensemaking builds on extensive categorization of the important aspects of the target situation.

The cognitive processes by which a person observes and forms an understanding of a situation — be it static or dynamic — are complicated. The processes proceed through sequential steps and iterations as relevant information about the situation is gathered, analyzed, and interpreted. The Sensemaking task relies on Situation Recognition Model knowledge as discussed later in this chapter. Additional forms of knowledge are also used. These, as indicated in Appendix C, include facts, concepts, rules, and expectations. Personal Situation Recognition models are primarily mental reference models that exist in the minds of people at different conceptual levels as was discussed in Chapter 4. The models can be highly concrete (though, at the same time, both automatized and tacit) for routine tasks, more generalized operational models for familiar but less automatized tasks, or generalized scripts and schemata for broader or less familiar tasks. More general reference models are also possessed as metaknowledge — either procedural or declarative metaknowledge. These models provide abstract strategies, features, and structures applicable to the domain and serve as the basis for operationalization in the new context.

Many factors can affect Sensemaking , some positively and others negatively, as indicated in Table 5-1. Attention is an important factor that determines the degree to which situations are observed and prioritized (Davenport & Beck 2001). Lack of attention may even lead to important information — or whole situations — being overlooked or ignored. Also, the person or the enterprise may refuse to accept information that describes a situation. That may happen when information is considered to be unbelievable for some reason, or if it describes a threatening situation that the person wants to avoid and may therefore tacitly ignore (Sherman & Cohen 2002). Sensemaking also involves the "leaping to conclusions" problems: the person prematurely and erroneously assumes that the target situation fits a previously known pattern when that is not the case.

Situational Awareness

Situational Awareness is the functional proficiency that helps a person become aware and make sense of a situation. Any time a

Table 5-1

Examples of conditions that improve or impede Sensemaking.

Examples of Conditions that Affect *Sensemaking*

Conditions	Positive Influences	Negative Influences
Expertise and Generic Knowledge	In less known or unfamiliar situations having broad generic knowledge consisting of scripts, schemata, and procedural and declarative metaknowledge — Provides capability to understand complex or novel situations.	Having strong expertise in narrow areas — Can make the person miscategorize situations as belonging to types she is familiar with when that is not the case.
Specific Knowledge in Well-Known Situations	Possessing practical experience consisting of routine and operational mental models that cover broad ranges of typical cases — Provides ability to correctly make sense of large numbers of situations.	Good theoretical but lack of practical experience — Leads to lack of real-world understanding and inhibits a person's general ability to correctly identify and make sense of situations.
Bias and Belief	Lacking subjective bias that influences perspectives or misdirects attention — Leads to ability to correctly understand unusual situations.	Believing that a situation is different from what it actually is — or believing that some types of situations cannot occur — Leads to misclassifying — even ignoring important situations.
Information	Obtaining good and timely information that describes the situation accurately and as completely as possible — Leads to ability to understand situations properly.	Received information that is incomplete, biased, corrupted, delayed, etc. — Prevents appropriate Sensemaking and may lead to misunderstanding of the situation.

(Continued)

Table 5-1
(Continued)

Examples of Conditions that Affect *Sensemaking*

Conditions	Positive Influences	Negative Influences
Ability to Analyze	Increased ability to analyze situations given critical thinking skills, knowledge, and other resources — Leads to better and quicker understanding of broad ranges of situations.	Reduced ability to make sense of the situation due to lack of knowledge, resources, etc. — Leads to misclassifying or even ignoring important situations.
Preoccupation and Lack of Attention	People who pay attention and are not preoccupied — Tend to understand situations faster and with greater situation awareness.	If people are preoccupied or have misplaced attention — They misunderstand or even overlook important situations, at least initially.
Time	Given enough time to digest and understand the given information about the situation — Leads to better sensemaking in complex situations.	Lack of time to project importance and consequences of the situation should it be allowed to evolve on its own — Leads to misclassifying — even ignoring important situations.
Fast Changing Conditions	Situations that change quickly — Require people with great familiarity and situational awareness skills to make sense and understand the situations.	When a situation is changing too fast to make sense of its current state — Leads to conditions where it is either too late to handle the situation or a new and different state emerges that requires different handling.

person encounters a situation, no matter how insignificant and minute, he observes it by obtaining information about it and proceeds to understand it by decoding, analyzing, interpreting, and accepting it as being believable. These tasks are largely performed tacitly. In some cases he uses specific and detailed knowledge about similar situations to make sense of the situation from the accepted information.[3] In other general or less known cases he uses more abstract knowledge. He normally will already have an understanding of the general context. That is often part of his work environment and general role. During the Sensemaking task, he uses his a priori Situational Awareness capability to understand the target situation. The quality and proficiency of his Situational Awareness determine the extent to which the current situation, its context and environment, are first observed and then perceived and the accuracy with which the resulting perception — the understanding of the situation — mirrors reality. Without appropriate Situational Awareness, he does not have sufficient understanding of the situation and its context and cannot make proper sense of it. Inadequate Situational Awareness limits the ability both to observe and to perceive the situation adequately, and in such cases becomes a Sensemaking constraint.

In organizations, the corresponding structural knowledge is manifested in many ways — it can consist of shared beliefs, stories, or even embedded knowledge in practices and organized systems and procedures. In some enterprises, these models can be reference cases embedded in work-aids such as automated case-based reasoning (CBR) systems and other kinds of intelligent systems. The structural reference models can also be embedded in operational and management practices as well as in systems and procedures.

Decision-Making/Problem-Solving and *Action Space and Innovation Capability*

Decision-Making

Decision-Making — the identification and specification of what to do given a situation and its context — is one of the most important activities in which people can engage. Many researchers have contributed to this field over the years. However, only recently have the roles of knowledge and expertise in Decision-Making become better understood and more explicit as a result of work in cognitive sciences, psychology, knowledge management, and related fields. Decision-Making, as we perceive it, covers three functional task paths: (1) simple decision making, (2) complex decision making, and (3) novel problem solving.

When the situation is first understood, it is possible to determine how it should be handled. Well understood situations can be handled directly with single-stage Decision-Making. This mode may at times involve the quick mental simulations to evaluate potential alternatives. Well understood situations can be handled directly with single-stage Decision-Making. More complex situations will need multistage complex Decision-Making or even novel Problem-Solving. Multistage Decision-Making/Problem-Solving typically requires iterative handling, with additional information gathering and sensemaking. Decision-Making theories and practices have been treated extensively by others and should be consulted by the interested reader in works by Bechara *et al.* (1997), Glimcher (2003), Hammon *et al.* (1999), Janis (1989), Janis and Mann (1977), Keeney and Raiffa (1976), Klein (1998, 2002), Simon (1976, 1977a), Sowell (1980), and Wiig (1993).

Most situations that people encounter during the workday are familiar to them and handled with tacit single-stage Decision-Making. In these cases people have prior understanding which they possess in their minds as task-specific mental templates or reference models that they operationalize to arrive at action-options that they can carry out. They may often be unaware that they make these decisions.

To make these tacit decisions, people use approaches such as qualitative or fuzzy pattern recognition and metaphoric reasoning to locate and apply the mental reference models and other mental objects that are most similar to the situation at hand. For well-known situations, the mental models are likely to describe routine and concrete tasks and may be activated by direct execution. Less known situations will not correspond directly to past experiences, and mental models — when any exist — may be possessed at higher abstraction levels as scripts, schemata, or metaknowledge. In these cases, which are the norm for intellectual work, the new situations are handled and decisions are made. Actions are implemented by adapting and operationalizing the reference models that most closely resemble the new conditions or can be expected to lead to useful approaches to the target situation. The resulting operational models are then activated to perform the intended actions. Adaptation and operationalization are often tacit when a person works alone. Only for more vexing and high importance situations may the process become explicit and conscious, particularly when engaging in teamwork and collaboration. These steps often require conceptual blending and may lead to creative innovation and valuable solutions. For a person with narrow and mostly concrete and detailed knowledge, innovative adaptation is difficult. Curious people with broad knowledge, understanding of general principles, and open minds with flexible Action Spaces are often able to innovate better. The conceptual blending involved in adaptation and operationalization often is a creative process that leads to novel and innovative solutions. *This, we argue, is an important form of innovation and creativity.*

We can illustrate four levels of situation understanding with corresponding Decision-Making/Problem-Solving modes as indicated in Table 5-2. When novel or less known situations are encountered, they may need to be handled differently, as indicated in Figures 5-4 and 5-5. Conditions that affect Decision-Making/Problem-Solving effectiveness are shown in Table 5-3.

Single-Stage and Multistage Decision-Making

The function of the Decision-Making/Problem-Solving task is to determine or create and select appropriate action-options to be implemented. The functional task path that is pursued depends upon the decision maker's familiarity with the situation at hand and its importance. As indicated in Figure 5-5, the functional task path may be single stage for simple Decision-Making when the decision maker possesses concrete mental model templates to deal with familiar situations. In less well-known situations, she is likely to engage in multistage complex Decision-Making or even novel Problem-Solving. For situations that are perceived to involve conditions beyond her or the organization's operational experience and knowledge, it may not be possible to make single-stage decisions to determine how it should be handled. In these instances, deciding the desired action cannot be determined by regular, simple Decision-Making by operationalizing previous experiences memorized as mental reference models or templates. Instead, the desired action must be determined through more innovative and complex multistage Decision-Making or Problem-Solving processes.

Table 5-2
Situation Understanding governs the mode of Decision-Making/
Problem-Solving; that is, how the tasks are performed and which kinds of mental
reference models are used.

Situation Understanding Categories	Dominant Decision-Making/Problem-Solving Mode	
Situation is unimportant	No Decision, No Action Needed	
Situation is too difficult to handle	Decision: No Action Possible	
Situation is routine and well known		***Simple Decision-Making***
	Mental Models Used	■ Concrete situation-specific Decision-Making reference models with close correspondence to the situations-at-hand
	Tasks Performed	■ Reference models are operationalized tacitly and executed automatically to generate desired action-options
Situation is generally known and follows scripts and abstract patterns		***Complex Decision-Making***
	Mental Models Used	■ Primarily abstract situation-specific and methodological Decision-Making reference models (scripts, schemata, metaknowledge) ■ Concrete situation-specific Decision-Making reference models all with characteristics similar to situations-at-hand
	Tasks Performed	■ Reference models are operationalized and executed consciously (at times tacitly) to generate desired action-options
Situation is insufficiently known or novel but is still considered to be important		***Novel Problem-Solving***
	Mental Models Used	■ Concrete situation-specific Decision-Making reference models all with characteristics similar to situations-at-hand ■ Abstract and generalized methodological and situation-specific Problem-Solving reference models (metaknowledge, scripts, schemata)
	Tasks Performed	■ Methodological reference models guide Problem-Solving process tacitly for smaller and simpler situations and consciously for complex teamwork situations ■ All reference models are operationalized and executed to generate desired action-options

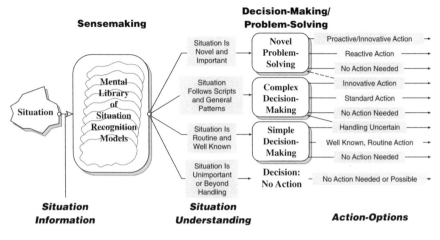

Figure 5-4

Situation understanding categories govern the nature of Decision-Making/Problem-Solving and the type of the selected action-options. Copyright © 2002 Knowledge Research Institute, Inc. Reproduced with permission.

Mental Simulations

Klein (1998, pp. 45–74) points out that in multistage Decision-Making and personal Problem-Solving, the acceptability of the potential action-option is tested through "mental simulation" that can be more or less tacit. Mental simulation involves exploring whether the operational or action model will provide a satisficing solution by using expectations and perspectives from internalized conceptual knowledge (Simon 1945). In mental simulation, if an action-option is foreseen to lead to unacceptable consequences, alternative approaches are generated from relevant mental models and tested by projecting expected performance until an acceptable action-option is obtained. This can be a quick and simple conceptual blending process, with one or a few iterations completed in seconds. For difficult situations, the process to find an acceptable action-option may require elaborate and conscious multistage Problem-Solving that can involve teamwork over long periods of time.

Problem-Solving

Along with regular Decision-Making, Problem-Solving may be one — or perhaps the most — important activity within the agile and proactive enterprise. Problem-Solving is the process that allows a

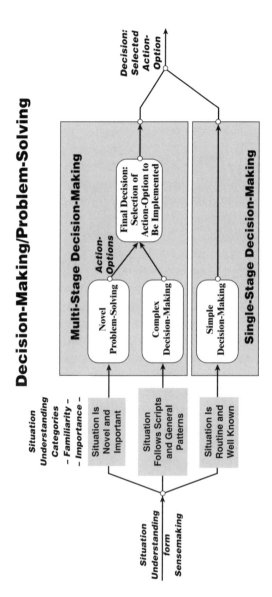

Figure 5-5

In familiar situations, selecting the action-option to be implemented is performed by simple, single-stage Decision-Making. In more complex and important cases, the final decision is obtained by multistage Decision-Making or Problem-Solving. Copyright © 2002 Knowledge Research Institute, Inc. Reproduced with permission.

Table 5-3

Examples of conditions that improve or impede Decision-Making/Problem-Solving.

Examples of Conditions that Affect Decision-Making/Problem-Solving

Conditions	Positive Influences	Negative Influences
Understanding Enterprise Strategy	Understanding enterprise strategy — Facilitates rank and file to make decisions that serve to implement enterprise strategy.	Not understanding strategy properly — Leads to inability to implement enterprise strategy.
General Understanding of First and Higher Order Goals, etc.	Understanding immediate (first order) intents, goals, objectives, priorities, and enterprise long-term and stakeholder (higher order) intents, goals, objectives, priorities — Leads to creation and selection of more relevant and appropriate action-options.	Lack of general understanding of first and higher order pursuits — Leads to creation and selection of ineffective and often wrong action-options that may conflict with enterprise strategy and intents.
Possessing Task-Specific and Operational Knowledge	Good task-specific and operational knowledge in the forms of extensive libraries of mental models, etc. — Leads to handling wide ranges of routine decisions with single-stage Decision-Making.	Inadequate task-specific and operational knowledge — Even with good situation understanding, leads to multi-stage Decision-Making or Problem-Solving when not needed.
Possessing Theoretical and Metaknowledge	Good abstract (theoretical) knowledge and metaknowledge — Leads to ability to effective handling of complex and novel situations.	Lacking abstract knowledge and metaknowledge — Leads to decision rigidity and inability to handle complex and novel situations.

(Continued)

Table 5-3
(Continued)

Examples of Conditions that Affect *Decision-Making/Problem-Solving*

Conditions	Positive Influences	Negative Influences
Knowing Implementation Constraints	Understanding potential implementation constraints and other conditions that might inhibit implementation — Leads to action-options that will be easier to implement.	By not understanding Implementation constraints — Decision Maker will unwittingly create and select impractical action-options with undesirable results.
Access to Resources	Access to expert networks, communications, and other resources — Leads to creation and selection of better action-options, particularly for complex and novel situations.	Lack of access to resources — Leads to limited ability to gather information, to obtain expert assistance, etc. and ultimately leads to ineffective action-options.
Action Space	Large Action Space — Leads to very effective action-options that shortcut conventions, etc.	Large or unconstrained Action Space — Leads to creating and selecting action options beyond permissible boundaries.
Innovation Capability	Good Innovation Capability — Leads to effective action-options by "thinking outside the box" and being willing to be curious and innovate.	Limited Innovation Capability — Leads to action-options that are conventional, constrained, and repetition of past practices.
Poor Situation Understanding	Ability to acquire better information and repeat Sensemaking — May improve situation understanding.	Acting upon poor or inaccurate situation understanding — Leads to creation and selection of undesirable action-options.

person or team to find desirable action-options to handle novel and complex situations in ways that will benefit all stakeholders. As such, innovative Problem-Solving is required in difficult high-value-added situations with considerable importance. This has been widely recognized, and Problem-Solving principles and methods are treated by many researchers and practitioners. Interested readers should consult their works (Ackoff 1978; De Bono 2000; Gilhooly 1988; Schön 1983, 1987). In addition, many sources in society provide advice on Problem-Solving and handling of dilemmas. Such sources include parental guidance, role models, cultural storytelling, religious texts, laws and legal principles, and cultural rules for good conduct.

As indicated, rapid Decision-Making and Implementation of routine actions cannot handle less well understood situations effectively and instead require creative Problem-Solving as part of multistage Decision-Making. Because these situations are not well known, reference models (such as patterns or templates) for desired actions may not exist, thereby requiring Problem-Solving. Good Problem-Solving uses methodological mental models to guide the process and often relies on extensive application of personal critical thinking and conceptual blending as part of "intuition." For situations that are quite unfamiliar or unknown, the best reference models may consist of methodological metaknowledge. For situations that have just some similarity with prior experiences, the applicable mental models may consist of scripts and schemata.

In all cases, good Problem-Solving requires curiosity, flexible perspectives, and broad understanding of the general context. That includes good topic domain knowledge, knowledge of adjacent domains, world knowledge, and metaknowledge to support regular work and innovation effectively. Deficiencies in either knowledge domain often will result in repeating trivial and reactive actions, whereas innovative and proactive actions bring about more desirable outcomes. *Finding good and effective solutions to complex and less understood situations is of great worth to any enterprise. Hence, Problem-Solving often becomes a major value-creation activity for which we need to prepare deliberately and systematically. However, few do.*

In difficult situations, Problem-Solving often becomes an iterative process that may include additional Sensemaking. For example, decision makers may need to return to the situation several times to obtain more information leading to a better understanding. During this process, it is frequently found that the situation itself, or the perception of it, may be changing, further complicating the

Problem-Solving task. To address these challenges, Decision-Making/ Problem-Solving tasks rely largely on knowledge in the form of Decision-Making models and Problem-Solving models.

Action Space

Given an understanding of the situation, a person's ability to make decisions about how to handle it is guided by her Action Space and Innovation Capability. The Action Space denotes the realm — the "space" — within which the person is competent, willing, comfortable, or otherwise prepared to make decisions and act. The Action Space is not a passive domain with fixed boundaries. It is formed by curiosity and by the creative capabilities, methodologies and personal attitudes, mentalities, and motivations that allow people to perform regular tasks and consider novel actions and to innovate within the boundaries of what they find permissible and acceptable. A person's Action Space is closely related to what she considers permissible within her constraints. Consequently, much is reflected in her Governance Competence and Perspectives with their goals, values, permissions, and constraints.

A competent person will understand the context of new and slightly different situations and will readily initiate and pursue options, innovating within his Action Space and Innovation Capability. However, he may be uncomfortable and unwilling to consider actions outside this domain, which can sometimes prevent effective behavior. On the other hand, an unwillingness to step outside the action space can also prevent undesirable actions and in the aggregate will render the enterprise behavior uniform and better organized. Many enterprise management teams tend to limit their employees' Action Spaces for precisely that reason.

For an undesirable example of a constrained Action Space, consider Ian, an assembly worker who experienced consistent problems when using parts supplied by another department. He thought that the problems might lie with the parts themselves which did not fit properly when they were incorporated into the assembly. As a result of the reigning culture, Ian was not comfortable with diagnosing the situation by himself. Hence, following accepted procedures, he reported the issue to his supervisor, who then handled the issue "by the book" by treating the problem in the proper channels. This resulted in considerable delay and costly production upsets. This episode was representative of many persistent problems within the plant.

Later, as part of initiating new procedures with greater responsibilities and freedom, Ian and his coworkers received additional education. They were given more complete contextual knowledge to increase their competence, motivation, authority, and independence. Ian and his colleagues in turn developed expanded Action Spaces and Innovation Capabilities. Ian now feels comfortable about analyzing and diagnosing similar situations and, when needed, contacts the other departments directly without going through channels. That fixes problems quickly and productively without delay and without added supervisory overhead.

This is one example from a company that was plagued by production delays and other operational problems. After analysis and examination of best practices in other companies, assembly workers and companion groups received additional training and were given broader operating scope with greater responsibilities to alleviate problems of this kind.

Unfortunately, personal and organizational constraints often cause better and more effective actions to fall outside the workers' Situational Awareness and their Action Space and Innovation Capability. That hinders effective Sensemaking and Decision-Making/Problem-Solving and impacts enterprise performance. Similar constraints exist in the other capability areas and limit the situation-handling effectiveness, thereby contributing to impaired enterprise performance.

Innovation Capability

The act of personal innovation involves bringing together mental constructs, such as concepts and mental models in ways that are novel. Innovation and deep expertise are capabilities that we use to integrate and engage in conceptual blending. These traits are not preprogrammed functions that consist of operationalizing or executing prior knowledge as a "mind-as-container" model might suggest. Instead, they represent a unique human aptitude. As discussed by Fauconnier and Turner, innovation is often an implicit mental function that involves conceptual blending — the powerful capability that is exclusively human and that allows new juxtapositions of mental constructs (such as mental models) when motivated by new contexts and situations (Fauconnier & Turner 2002).

Innovation Capability denotes the degree to which a person's attitude, motivation, and knowledge inspire her to pursue creation and search for novel and more effective alternatives (Boden 1990, 1994;

De Bono 1978, 1992; Halpern 1989). With a broader perspective, she may also innovate by pursuing double-loop learning (Argyris & Schön 1974). By being curious and innovative, she invents opportunities that may not be obvious, and she reframes, generates, and tests solutions to better attain enterprise goals as well as her personal objectives. When engaging in simple Decision-Making, she may allow herself to experiment by tacitly infusing her routine reference models with new ideas or with ideas from other, similar situations. She may use the opportunity to speculate and generate new perspectives on how her work might be done better. In these cases, the competent person engages in double-loop learning and applies critical thinking.

The extent and effectiveness of Action Space and Innovation Capability are functions of personal knowledge and mental capabilities that integrate knowledge objects and mental constructs, or engage a person in conceptual blending. As such, the effectiveness of those functions is determined by what the person knows and understands about how to handle related situations, the way she understands them, and how far she is willing to go to ascertain that the best decision option is determined. These proficiencies are functions of personal energy, attention, curiosity, attitudes, emotions, motivation, and available resources, along with understanding of the authority and permissions delegated by the enterprise. When the functional proficiencies are more limited than the scope of the person's work responsibilities requires, the Action Space and Innovation Capability will reduce her operational effectiveness and therefore become constraints on effective decision making. Conversely, when we can assist people to expand their Action Space and Innovation Capability competently, new opportunities will emerge for improved performance and new strategic options.

Implementation and *Execution Capability*

Implementation of decisions is a major problem in enterprises as well as in all walks of life. The expected results from first-class decisions, excellent strategies, and good intentions are frequently not realized because action-options were not implemented appropriately or even at all (Bossidy & Charan 2002; Flood *et al.* 2000). Frequently, personal and enterprise Execution Capability are inadequate and hinder timely and effective implementation of desired courses of action, resulting in many failed business ventures.

Implementation

Once a decision is made or selected, it must be implemented or executed since in any effective enterprise, good decisions are expected to result in useful actions. If decisions are not properly acted upon and implemented, Decision-Making/Problem-Solving become hypothetical exercises of no consequence; they are wasted efforts. Implementation effectiveness depends upon the Execution Capability, which relies upon the specific knowledge needed to understand the decision and its intents, general concrete and abstract knowledge of how to implement actions implied by the decision, availability of resources, and many other factors. The effective performance of the Implementation task relies on knowledge in the form of Execution Method models, other types of intellectual capital (IC) assets, and general resources (Edvinsson & Malone 1997; Stewart 2002b; Sveiby 1997). In the organizational domain, whereas most actions are small, implementation may involve large and complicated efforts that require extensive support from specialized and competent personnel, systems, and other resources.

An area of typical problems is the conceptual gap between Decision-Making/Problem-Solving and Implementation. When action-options are implemented — even when they are performed by the same person who made the decision — the decision maker may not have the understanding or the correct memory of the foundations that underpin the action-option. Hence, when the real-world details of Implementation result in conditions different from those presumed during Decision-Making/Problem-Solving, it is necessary to improvise in ways that still implement the decision intent. Without proper consideration of the concepts and intents, the implementation will in some way be inappropriate. This is a general problem for large enterprise decisions as well.

Execution Capability

Excellence of Implementation depends upon good Execution Capability and can be improved significantly by targeted training. In many instances, good decisions are not implemented as intended because of limited personal or organizational Execution Capability, which then becomes a constraint. For the myriad of small action-options that people implement every day as part of normal work, the Execution Capability is determined by the person's general competence. Hence, on the assembly line, decisions to perform minor adjustments and repairs are almost automatic for the competent worker. Similarly, an experienced insurance adjustor who surveys a damaged building makes and tacitly implements numerous decisions on what to look for, assesses the damage, estimates the repair or replacement costs, and so on. The success of Implementation and the effectiveness of Execution Capability rely on many factors as indicated in Table 5-4.

For larger decisions and action-options in the enterprise setting, good personal Execution Capability, in addition to functional expertise, also requires good social and communication skills. People with leadership qualities have greater success in seeing that their decisions and recommendations are implemented. Implementing most larger action-options requires resources such as budgets, management attention, personnel, and time. When personal decisions result in team or group implementation (such as a manager making a decision that is intended to be implemented by a department), the reasons and underlying premises for the decision and the associated action-options need to be communicated extensively. As indicated, people who participate in implementing the decisions must have tacit and intuitive understanding of the decisions. Unless they understand, they will not be able to incorporate the desired action-options in their tacit Decision-Making activities.

The execution capability must also include features to suppress bad decisions. If an action-option is determined to work against the intent of the enterprise or otherwise is found to be unsound, it should be stopped. In many instances, situation-handling should be repeated.

Monitoring and Governance Competence and Perspectives

Monitoring

Situation-handling is overseen from start to finish by the executive Monitoring task. Monitoring is about pursuing desired directions and accountability of actions. Based on values, beliefs, principles, goals, and other objectives, Monitoring provides guidance for interpretations, decisions, and actions and delivers corrective adjustments to the other tasks as required. Monitoring provides goals, objectives,

Table 5-4

Examples of conditions that improve or impede Implementation.

Examples of Conditions that Affect Implementation

Conditions	Positive Influences	Negative Influences
Conceptual Transfer	When action-option details, reasons, and flexibilities are understood by those who will implement a decision — The decision success is improved.	Insufficient transfer of concepts, expected outcomes, etc. behind a chosen decision — Leads to inability to implement the action-option as envisioned and intended.
Communication	Good communication, such as face-to-face discussions and other personal involvement by the decision maker — Assures good Implementation.	Superficial briefings, messages via e-mails or written materials and other cursory communications — Invites arbitrary and inappropriate Implementation.
Resources	Adequate monetary, staff and other resources — Are requirements for good Implementation.	Lack of vital resources — May lead to Implementation delays, problems, even canceling.
Personal Incentives	Implementers who understand how they benefit from successful Implementation — Will ascertain action-options success.	When implementers do not understand how they benefit — Implementation success is threatened.
Decision Maker Style	Decision makers who are engaged in Implementation, directly or indirectly — Ensure successful action-option Implementation.	When the decision maker is detached or emotionally removed from Implementation — Implementation effectivity will be reduced.
Decision Alignment with Strategy	Decisions that are aligned with strategy — Will generally receive enterprise support and commitment.	Decisions that do not support or are counter to enterprise strategy — Will — and should — not be implemented.

and intents to project implications and different perspectives for the processes and results from the other three tasks.

Monitoring relies on regular feedback from the Sensemaking, Decision-Making/Problem-Solving, and Implementation tasks. This executive function oversees and participates continuously in setting the directions and framing of the other tasks. It is engaged from the beginning and throughout the process, and not just after a task has finished. For the most part, monitoring on the personal level occurs tacitly within the knowledge worker's mind. As situation-handling progresses, Sensemaking, Decision-Making/Problem-Solving, and Implementation are all monitored to ensure that the performances of these tasks are acceptable to the enterprise goals and objectives as the person understands them. Hence, the effectiveness of Monitoring becomes a function of how well they have been communicated and how well the person has assimilated them. The success of Monitoring relies on many factors as indicated by the examples in Table 5-5.

Table 5-5
Examples of conditions that improve or impede Monitoring.

Examples of Conditions that Affect *Monitoring*

Conditions	Positive Influences	Negative Influences
Understand Enterprise Strategy	When enterprise strategy is understood — Monitoring of situation-handling tasks provides effective guidance and corrections.	Badly understood enterprise strategy — Leads to ineffective Monitoring and insufficient situation-handling guidance.
Personal Attitude	Positive, inquisitive, and action-oriented attitude — Leads to aggressive situation-handling with thorough treatment of all tasks.	*Laissez-faire* attitude — Leads to ineffective Monitoring by paying little attention to oversight.
General Knowledge	Broad knowledge — Provides good and bad implications of many potential situation-handling directions.	Narrow knowledge — Limits the ability to envision consequences and hence leads to ineffective Monitoring.

Governance Competence and Perspectives

The effectiveness of the Monitoring task is both enhanced and limited by the Governance Competence and Perspectives proficiency, which provides the ability to assess the performance of the primary tasks and gives guidance and corrective adjustments if needed. The knowledge behind Governance Competence and Perspectives consists of understanding enterprise strategies and intents and what the person may do to assist in their implementation as long as it is in her own interest. The knowledge also consists of understanding what the person would like to do and see happen to promote his own career and job security — including ethical and professional principles and allegiances. The knowledge also includes perceptions of cultural driving forces, peer and management pressures, and similar factors that influence behavior. These knowledge areas are possessed in the form of mental models, mental spaces, and other types of mental constructs.

The person's attitudes and ways of behaving are also important aspects of personal Governance Competence and Perspectives. The person's curiosity, aggressiveness, willingness to persevere, analytical tendencies, ability to envision future implications and scenarios, all directly affect the executive influences that Monitoring exerts through guidance and corrective adjustments to the other tasks.

Whereas Figure 5-2 makes implicit reference to the kinds of knowledge needed for situation-handling, it does not include the meta-monitoring functions that oversee and gauge the performance of all four tasks, including Monitoring itself. Meta-monitoring includes functions that may intervene in or change the situation-handling process structure or principles. In the same manner as for the other tasks, the Monitoring task relies on model knowledge in the form of Governance Approach Models as described in the next section.

THE EXPERT AND THE NOVICE: WHEN SITUATIONS ARE NOT AS FIRST BELIEVED

Sensemaking must always be open to the possibility that the situation might not be what it seems. The expert is often the expert because he can recognize that a situation needs to be handled differently than the routine approach apparent at first. He quickly senses the necessity to consider other alternatives instead of correcting a wrong approach later when a mistake has become apparent.

Recognition of deviations from the expected is particularly important in evolving situations. Situations that change over time are initially difficult to understand. In those cases, when they are misunderstood and handled accordingly, it eventually becomes apparent that the first approach does not work. A new approach is needed.

The recognition that the situation is different is determined by Sensemaking. The acknowledgment that "it does not work" is recognized and accepted by Monitoring. And this is where expertise becomes important. The expert is quick to perceive the reality of the situation, to recognize and accept the new circumstances, and to remedy the condition by changing direction before the initial misconception has become too costly.

The danger for the novice is to come to the situation with a narrow and preconceived outlook and a favored approach. The novice will sense and interpret the situation to fit his a priori perspective and will deal with the situation as if his understanding were correct. Later, when things go wrong, the novice in his Sensemaking will be slow to recognize his misconception, and his Monitoring function will be hesitant to accept that his understanding and approach are wrong, do not work, and that a new direction needs to be pursued.

We argue that expert behavior is as important for enterprises as it is for people and that the enterprises that succeed are the enterprises with good Sensemaking and Monitoring expertise.

STORY-BASED MODELS PROVIDE SITUATION-HANDLING KNOWLEDGE

People use qualitative pattern recognition and metaphoric reasoning to locate and apply the mental reference models and other mental spaces and constructs that are most similar to the situation at hand. For well-known situations, the mental models are likely to be tacit templates that describe routine and concrete tasks. These may be operationalized tacitly by direct execution. Less known situations will not correspond directly to past ones. Hence, related mental models and constructs — if any exist — may describe general patterns or templates and be possessed at higher abstraction levels as concepts, scripts, schemata, or metaknowledge. In these cases, which are typical, the new situations are handled — decisions are made by conceptual blending to adapt the reference models that most closely resemble the new conditions.

The new constructs can then be operationalized. Adaptation and operationalization are often tacit when a person works alone. Only for more vexing and high-importance situations may the process become explicit and conscious, particularly when engaging in teamwork and collaboration. For a person with narrow and mostly concrete and detailed knowledge, innovative adaptation is difficult. People with broad knowledge and understanding of general principles typically innovate better. The conceptual blending involved in adaptation and operationalization often is a creative process that leads to novel and innovative solutions. This, we argue, is an important form of innovation and creativity.

Topic Domain Knowledge

In order to handle situations competently, people need good *topic domain knowledge* — knowledge about job-related tasks — to deal effectively and competently with work. When a person has extensive knowledge, he is able to routinely perform many tasks. However, as we have repeatedly emphasized, work is not always simple, routine, and repetitive. Most workers need to deal with tasks that range in complexity from logical extensions and less common variations of routine situations, all the way to unusual challenges outside the scope of their normal jobs.[4] With the increasing job complexity created by globalization and general progress and sophistication, it is inappropriate, and even impossible, to provide people with advance topic domain knowledge covering every possible situation. Instead, to help people become effective in personal complex Decision-Making and novel Problem-Solving, they need to build — through acquisition or creation — more abstract topic knowledge consisting of scripts, schemata, metaknowledge, and other mental constructs. In addition, for team or conscious situation-handling, people can also be given opportunities to acquire just-in-time knowledge when available (Davenport & Glaser 2002).

Letting people build abstract scripts, schemata, and metaknowledge relevant to the topic domain prepares them to tackle more complex work with deeper understanding in areas relevant to their work. Broad knowledge supports the human ability to engage in the conceptual blending and integration of pertinent concepts, mental models, and perspectives needed to address new challenges. Such knowledge becomes more general as the abstraction level increases from routines to operational mental models, scripts, schemata, and general principles. A further step is to engage people in situations that let them build metaknowledge, especially procedural meta-knowledge and declarative metaknowledge which allow them to tackle very general situations and problems.

The Mental Reference Models in Situation-Handling

As indicated, people possess most situation-handling knowledge in the form of mental reference models. In addition, they possess and use knowledge in many other forms such as facts, concepts, and expectations. Organizations have similar reference models but in the form of structural IC assets. From the perspective of situation-handling, we divide reference models into four types:

- **Situation Recognition Models** are used for Sensemaking and provide characterizations of memorized events. These models are recalled through processes such as priming when situations comparable to previous experiences are perceived. People possess large libraries with tens of thousands of Situation Recognition models that incorporate encoded information of situations they have encountered or learned about.

  A major problem with Situation Recognition models is that they, for the most part, represent past experiences or expected circumstances. If the person is not alert to new challenges, new, unexpected, and important situations may go unrecognized. Such situations may not be noticed unless more abstract knowledge is available to recognize general patterns. To provide better understanding, organizations may use work-specific simulations and games, scenario planning, and other methods to develop Situation Recognition models for less frequent and novel conditions.

- **Decision-Making/Problem-Solving Models.** This mental library of reference models covers a large domain of alternatives for how to handle a variety of conditions and guides Decision-Making/Problem-Solving. The models range from quite concrete action models to abstract schemata and metaknowledge models. They include a wide range from simple rules for handling routine and well-known situations by rote, to procedures for more complex Decision-Making which may need the creation of innovative actions, to methodologies and procedures for novel Problem-Solving. Selection of the mental models that will be called into action depends on the particular level of situation familiarity and understanding that resulted from Sensemaking.

The mental reference models for Decision-Making/Problem-Solving, particularly for more complex situations, are often broad and abstract and need integration and operationalizing to become applicable for the target situations. Good decisions require broad perspectives, including assessments of potential implications, and therefore must deal with uncertainties and approximate (fuzzy) reasoning.

■ **Execution Method Models** are used for Implementation and provide guides to implement the desired action generated by Decision-Making/Problem-Solving. Many of these models reflect the detailed requirements of Implementation and are therefore complicated. They may take into account tradeoffs between available resources and decision objectives. Some also include aspects for how to deal with constraints or problems of different kinds. Others may deal with principles or practical project management. All seem to provide dynamic perspectives on the evolving Implementation process.

Mental reference models for effective Implementation are in general more detailed and less abstract than those for Decision-Making/Problem-Solving. In part, that is caused by the need to pay attention to details to ascertain that the decisions are executed appropriately. Another aspect points to the goal-oriented mindset required for successful Implementation, particularly on the organizational level, where implementers need to control progress, motivate team members, run interference, and secure resources and replan when required.

■ **Governance Approach Models** are used for Monitoring and provide both principles and guides for evaluating the situation-handling progress. These models contain goals and objectives for the particular situation that is handled. They also contain expectations and meta-methods for performing Sensemaking, Decision-Making/Problem-Solving, and Implementation of desired actions. Beyond this, we find meta-monitoring models that govern the monitoring process itself — for example, models to guide how a person reflects and learns from handling situations. These models may primarily be tacit understandings of what is expected and allowed and which consequences are acceptable. One important aspect of these models is the degree to which they relate the target situation to the enterprise's intents and practices. They also provide perspectives on how to consider target situations.

In addition to these mental reference models, people possess knowledge in many other forms — often as complements to the mental reference models. Different knowledge forms are indicated in Appendix C.

Understanding Adjacent Operations

Anyone who works within an organization understands the potential value of knowing what happens around their own position or function — upstream, downstream, and in adjacent departments and operations. Understanding how their own operating area relates to other functional areas makes it possible to understand how "my function" is affected by those functions that provide inputs to "me" and how "I" affect those who receive my function's work products, be they chemical flows, manufactured parts, completed clerical work, sales orders, decisions on how to handle competitive information, or any other work product.

Situation-handling effectiveness may be improved in many ways. For example, by understanding adjacent operations, workers can interpret the implications of what happens elsewhere and take advantage of positive developments or take preventive actions when problems arise.

If there are problems within their own function, workers can forewarn those who may be affected. They can also innovate with insight — for example, create deliverables (work products) that are better suited to effective operations elsewhere, improve communications, and create valuable network contacts to deal with future challenges. The list goes on and on with numerous benefits.

The Relevance of General and World Knowledge

General knowledge — both generic and a specific understanding of society, business, science, and so on — is important for effective situation-handling for many reasons. Of particular importance is the role of general knowledge in identifying and understanding the overall context in which the target situation is positioned. Comprehension of the situational context provides insights into overall goals and objectives and such aspects as potential flexibility for dealing with the situation to provide the most effective action-options.

Other reasons for the importance of general knowledge include the broadened abilities to create more innovative action-options and to project potential consequences and implications over wider domains and longer time frames. General knowledge also improves abilities such as "thinking outside the box" and understanding such as how to address situation-handling which have dilemmas associated with multiple stakeholders who have conflicting objectives. In addition, world knowledge provides direct and practical insights into the conditions of particular situations from extra-enterprise perspectives, thus permitting more robust and effective situation-handling.

General and world knowledge consists in part of mental reference models. That knowledge is augmented with other mental constructs, such as proxy beliefs and values, which are of some interest because to a large degree they affect personal motivation and perspectives.[5] More importantly, general and world knowledge also includes the personal capability to perform conceptual blending — to combine abstractions and practical understanding in new ways to find creative and innovative solutions to challenges.

NOTES

1. Most tacit decision-actions are automatized, whereas others require conscious processing. Collins and Kusch (1998) characterize automatized and nonconscious decision-actions as *mimeomorphic actions* that are executed automatically. They characterize deliberate and explicit decision-actions as *polymorphic actions* that deviate from the routine and are adapted consciously or semiconsciously to the situation and context.

2. For routine and many non-routine situations, decision making based on tacit mental models takes on the average 6 seconds as discussed by Klein (1998, 2002).

3. The process of receiving and accepting information is itself complex and relies on effective handling of subtasks that range from obtaining information, sensing data, decoding data to build information, analyzing information, comparing information with what can be expected, determining information reliability to accept/reject information, and so on.

4. Figure 1-2 identified six categories of work complexity from routine to novel challenges: (1) routine situations (simple, repetitive, and well understood situations); (2) logical but less common variations (transformations) of routine situations; (3) complex, yet expected, extensions of routines integrated with external factors; (4) unexpected challenges (conditions), but with a mix of routines and external factors; (5) totally

unexpected situations and non-routine challenges, yet within the larger job scope; and (6) unusual challenges outside job scope.

5. Proxy beliefs and values: We use both basic and fundamental work-related beliefs and values to generate a priori judgments and we use "proxy beliefs" in reasoning situations to analyze if a hypothetical condition will be acceptable. We first generate proxy beliefs associated with existing situations or potential scenarios by using our mental models to project what we believe the outcomes will be. Then we compare the believed outcomes with the values that we hold for those kinds of situations, and we immediately associate the value judgment of the outcomes with the initial hypothetical condition. Finally, we transfer the value belief for the outcome to become a proxy belief for the initial condition.

6

ENTERPRISE SITUATION-HANDLING

PREMISE: INDIVIDUAL SITUATION-HANDLING ACTIONS LEAD TO CONSOLIDATED ENTERPRISE BEHAVIOR

Whenever individuals or automated functions handle situations within the enterprise, their actions will affect enterprise behavior. In the aggregate, all individual actions within the enterprise result in the consolidated behavior that affects customer relations, product quality and features, cost effectiveness, employee morale, or any number of other behavioral characteristics.

THE ENTERPRISE SITUATION-HANDLING EXAMPLE

The Situation

Sales of Asterix Consolidated's large trucks, its major product line and the market leader, were declining. That happened in spite of recent innovations and new product features requested by customers. The decline seemed to continue, and unless sales picked up, drastic and undesirable steps would be required. Sales and Marketing did not have a clear picture of why sales were down — and that was a real problem. Recently, Asterix had also lost two large follow-up sales to long-time fleet customers. In both cases Asterix had been short-listed and had felt that it was both price and feature competitive to the point that it expected to win. The debriefing meetings had not provided concrete reasons for why Asterix lost. So, what was wrong? What did the company need to change?

Information Gathering

Ken Haas, Asterix chairman and CEO, frustrated that no one seemed to know, or had been willing to tell him why such a serious

155

situation had developed, created a taskforce to investigate in-depth. He chose four midlevel people known for their vigilance: an outside trucking industry expert and one expert each from Marketing, Manufacturing, and Research and Development (R&D). The team arranged to visit existing and potential customers to talk to both senior executives and rank-and-file representatives. After one week's intensive work and travel, the team had been surprised by what they were told, although other customers had earlier voiced similar opinions. The companies they visited were quite critical of Asterix, and all shared much the same opinions. That information had never been assembled into a single, coherent message, however. Over the weekend, the team organized their findings in a brief report that summarized the situation.

Sensemaking

The team pinpointed several issues:

Issue 1. Asterix customer support representatives (CSRs) did not give customers the impression of being motivated and competitively responsive. Many were late in returning calls and in responding to requests. Most CSRs were not proactive and would often wait to do something until problems became critical — even when they had known about them for some time.

Issue 2. The Marketing Department and the sales staff and their managers appeared to be convinced that Asterix was ahead of its competition. They also seemed to think that they knew most things better than their customers. They had become somewhat aloof and difficult to deal with.

Issue 3. Asterix clearly had worked hard to innovate, but mostly by focusing on perfecting existing features except when responding to customer requests. Many competitors, including the two that had won the large sales, had introduced radically new features that no customers had requested from Asterix.

Issue 4. Some new features were difficult to use and had quality problems. They appeared to be designed by sophisticated engineers who had their own ideas about how the features should be implemented instead of working closely with customer drivers.

Issue 5. Customers estimated the life-cycle costs of Asterix's trucks to be higher than those of most competitors, even though both acquisition costs and fuel consumption were lower.

When Ken Haas and his executive vice presidents were presented with the findings, they were dismayed. Initially, they did not believe that the situation could be that bad and that widespread. A heated discussion followed, but the evidence was compelling. There also had been earlier indications of similar problems, but they had been ignored. It was clear that Asterix had been complacent and had pursued a business-as-usual approach that now was resulting in problems.

Understanding the Situation

The executive team decided that Asterix needed to address all five issues and that they needed to work quickly. They decided that the situation was principally a result of senior management failure and that they themselves, including Ken Haas, were responsible. Now they needed to decide what to do. They agreed that they needed to be positively proactive instead of taking a negative reactive course.

Since time was of the essence and the problems were systemic, it was decided to pursue changes vigorously — as a major shakeup — and perhaps bring about a new corporate direction. They needed to determine what could be done quickly and at the same time start immediately to correct or improve what needed more time. However, they still needed to decide explicitly why and how they needed to change. They started by considering the five issues, but first they agreed that all signs pointed to four general problems:

1. Asterix's intended strategy, operational mode, and practices had not been understood by the rank-and-file and were therefore not being implemented effectively.
2. Both Asterix management and its rank-and-file had distanced themselves too far from their customers and did not understand customer thinking and attitudes sufficiently well.
3. Customers believed that the attitudes and mentalities of Asterix employees were not "good enough" to provide the service levels customers required — partly because of a lack of a common Asterix *esprit de corps* and partly because the employees lacked integrative understanding of Asterix's business and operations.
4. Whereas Asterix's executive management encouraged independence and distributed decision making, it was clear that the direction of work in many parts of the organization deviated

from the enterprise's intended strategy, operational mode, and practices. Moreover, much work was performed that did not contribute directly — or at all — to implement Asterix's strategy and intents.

There were other issues as well, but the executive team decided to narrow the focus and initiate actions as soon as possible by creating a very demanding program that would be given the highest priority, requiring the other issues to be postponed or canceled.

Decision-Making/Problem-Solving and Action-Selection

The executive team identified how to deal with each of the five original issues. It became a long list covering numerous areas and would require extensive resources. Nevertheless, the team decided that drastic measures were required and to proceed as follows (see the Chapter 6 Appendix for details on rationale, expected results, and the next steps of the action program):

Issue 1. Lack of motivation and responsiveness was caused by people's lack of understanding how their daily work was part of implementing Asterix's strategy.
Immediate Action 1-1: Help CSRs understand how their work implements Asterix's strategy.
Immediate Action 1-2: Create and implement positive incentives and control measures.
Immediate Action 1-3: Terminate individuals with incorrigible negative attitudes.
Longer-Term Action 1-1: Help all employees understand how to implement strategy.[1]
Longer-Term Action 1-2: Create and promulgate a service paradigm for everyone.[2]
Issue 2. The beliefs held by marketing and salespeople that Asterix was ahead of competitors were falsely based on inadequate competitor assessments and market intelligence.
Immediate Action 2-1: Undertake quickly a new, comprehensive marketing study.
Immediate Action 2-2: Request that Marketing, Sales, and others immediately share market intelligence.
Immediate Action 2-3: Create incentives to make it rewarding and natural to collaborate.

Longer-Term Action 2-1: Change the enterprise-wide personnel evaluation system.

Issue 3. Asterix needed to be more innovative in introducing competitive features.

Immediate Action 3-1: Review R&D projects to expedite those that support Asterix's strategy.

Longer-Term Action 3-1: Consider making available selected features at no cost on new trucks.

Longer-Term Action 3-2: Revise the R&D project plan for the next several years with new priorities.

Longer-Term Action 3-3: Create a framework for a flexible, forward-looking strategy.

Issue 4. Features needed to be created and tested in close collaboration with customers.

Immediate Action 4-1: Engage customers to review and test product features.

Longer-Term Action 4-1: Create strategic relationships with suppliers and customers.

Issue 5. Asterix sales staff had insufficient understanding of their truck's economic performance.

Immediate Action 5-1: Make life-cycle cost projections for several customer scenarios.

Longer-Term Action 5-1: Reevaluate pricing changes, cost reductions, and new product offerings.

Longer-Term Action 5-2: Reorganize spare parts logistics to maximize geographical availability.

As a result of this program, the nine immediate actions and nine longer-term actions were implemented with broad involvement of the whole Asterix enterprise.

General Aspects

Situation-Handling Aspects. Asterix's management discovered that the company faced a serious problem. Its chairman resolutely undertook high-competence information gathering and Sense-making activities to quickly make sense of the situation, which presented problems that centered around five issues. That provided the insight needed to understand the problem sufficiently well to identify remedial measures. Correcting the five problems required numerous actions (nine immediate and nine long term) that were implemented.

Knowledge Management Aspects. Asterix needed to manage knowledge much more decisively and systematically. Some KM efforts are short term, whereas others are significantly larger long-term efforts. The objectives of these KM efforts are to transfer insights and concepts to build knowledge in Asterix employees at all levels to understand its strategy, customers, and operations, and to build understanding of the markets.

Introduction to Enterprise Situation-Handling

Enterprise situation-handling is never simple. It is invariably a multi-objective exercise with conflicting issues and necessities to resolve dilemmas. Normally, important situations are evolving, and time is of the essence; slow situation-handling will cause lost opportunities or deteriorating situations. Compared to the personal case, within the enterprise environment it becomes important to recognize that completed situation-handling consists of three sequential "action" tasks where the last two rely on the results from the preceding ones. Thus, valuable time may be consumed from the instant a situation is recognized until its handling is completed. This means that situation-handling may often need to be expedited to be effective. However, that is not simple. As a rule, important situations, in addition to being multi-objective, also tend to be somewhat unfamiliar with new angles and lacking in full information. Hence, situation-handling also becomes an exercise in uncertainty.

Enterprises employ reference models in ways similar to the employment of mental reference models by people. Some reference models are culturally embedded as stories or as conventions of what people share, such as "this is the way work is done here." Others are embedded in the enterprise's structural IC in the form of practices, manual and automated systems and procedures, enterprise policies, and the manner in which the enterprise and its work processes are organized.

From a theoretical perspective, enterprises have situation-handling and organizational capabilities that are similar to those on the personal level. The primary tasks are also similar to those of personal situation-handling as indicated in Figure 6-1. However, their functional characteristics and underlying mechanisms are different. Although complicated, many are open to observation and analysis, and that permits insights which on the personal level may only be speculative.

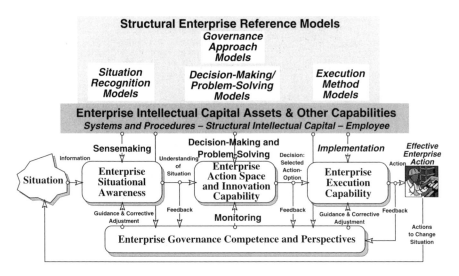

Figure 6-1
Organizational situation-handling depends on the enterprise's structural knowledge (IC) assets and capabilities. Copyright © 2001 Knowledge Research Institute, Inc. and Karl M. Wiig. Reproduced with permission.

To a large extent, the enterprise capabilities are determined by the personal proficiencies of the organization's employees. However, they also are shaped by structural resources such as systems, procedures, operational and managerial practices, organizational structure, availability of structural knowledge, and quality of information at the point-of-action. These resources are partly possessed by individuals but are also delivered through structural IC assets. Other factors such as managerial and enterprise attention and priorities influence the ability of the enterprise to act appropriately and effectively in many situations (Davenport & Beck 2001).

In the enterprise, routine situations — recurring day-to-day business operations such as many small steps in manufacturing, payroll, financial transactions, or basic order fulfillment — are handled automatically or by people who work with established systems and procedures within the organizational structure and according to the manner in which work is organized. All these mechanisms are designed to handle work effectively and efficiently to fulfill enterprise objectives. In reality, most of these mechanisms bear little resemblance to human mental mechanisms. However, from a more abstract systems perspective, they perform functions that are quite similar to the personal case. For decision making this is illustrated in Figure 6-2. Instead of knowledge and mental models, the enterprise draws

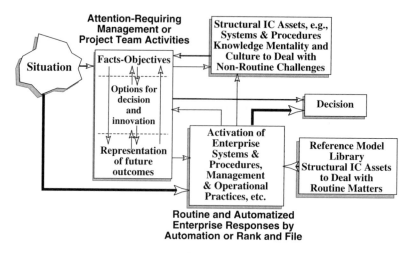

Figure 6-2

In the abstract, enterprise Decision-Making is similar to that of the personal domain. Simple work may be automated or tackled with routine procedures by rank-and-file. Unfamiliar or more complex work needs problem solving, often by project teams. Copyright © 1997 Knowledge Research Institute, Inc. and Karl M. Wiig. Reproduced with permission.

upon general capabilities such as employee competence and behaviors, structural IC, and the embedded capabilities in systems and procedures as discussed earlier.

There is a pronounced difference between information and knowledge within the enterprise. Situation information, we emphasize, is very different from reference models and other knowledge assets. Effective enterprise situation-handling requires good personal and structural knowledge (IC) assets and, separately, good information about situations. Hence, effective information management becomes an important aspect of the enterprise's ability to act effectively in both routine and complex situations. This attains particular importance when dealing with unexpected events where the need for comprehensive information may be required to understand the situation appropriately.[3]

THE FOUR ENTERPRISE SITUATION-HANDLING TASKS

The four primary tasks of situation-handling occur everywhere in the enterprise. In numerous, almost countless, occasions, situations must be identified, assessed, and handled. As they are handled, regardless of the degree of delegation, the activities must be monitored to some extent to ascertain that they are sufficiently well aligned to the enterprise intents and strategy and the particular needs of the context.

Tables 6-1, 6-2, and 6-3 provide three case examples of aggregated activities within the four primary situation-handling tasks. These

Table 6-1
Simplified example of situation-handing activities in fixing equipment failure.

	Situation-Handling Activities	Monitoring
Sensemaking	Diagnose reason for equipment failure	Ascertain that diagnosis is performed timely
Decision-Making & Problem-Solving	Decide how to repair the equipment or correct situation	Ascertain that specified corrections meet enterprise cost, time, and performance guidelines
Implementation	Correct situation (conduct the repair)	Ascertain that competent personnel is allocated to perform the repair
Metamonitoring		*Ascertain that Monitoring is performed in accordance with, and in support of enterprise strategy and intents*

Table 6-2
Simplified example of situation-handing activities in commercial loan application.

	Situation-Handling Activities	Monitoring
Sensemaking	Assess business situation of loan applicant	Ascertain that bank's risk criteria are applied
Decision-Making & Problem-Solving	Decide terms of loan given applicant's business situation	Ascertain that bank's framework is used to structure loan while observing budgets and available resources
Implementation	Negotiate terms and issue loan	Ascertain that bank's guidelines for negotiating terms are applied
Metamonitoring		*Ascertain that bank's Monitoring guidance is applied*

Table 6-3
*Simplified example of situation-handing in finding location, deciding type,
building, and opening a new store.*

	Situation-Handling Activities	Monitoring
Sensemaking	Identify geographic market to be served Assess cost-performance feasibility of potential locations	Ascertain that company goals for market size and profitability are observed
Decision-Making & Problem-Solving	Determine potential store designs for likely locations Select store location	Ascertain that company standards for store designs can be implemented
Implementation	Perform final store design Build, staff and open store	Ascertain that company criteria for contractor selection, contract terms, personnel policies, etc. are followed
Metamonitoring		*Ascertain that project is pursued and monitored according to company strategy and not as business-as-usual*

examples are highly simplified, and whereas many activities will normally be carried out in each task, these examples only highlight one or two. These cases include examples of "meta-monitoring", which refers to how the monitoring task for the particular situation-handling case is monitored from the enterprise's perspective.

The nature of enterprise situation-handling covers such a large range that it may be impractical to list representative categories of all variations. Therefore, in the following, we illustrate the primary tasks and their related competencies with case examples.

New Successful Services Strategy Made Possible by Costly Education

People throughout Financo, a financial services firm, were following developments in the marketplace closely. They were encouraged by the executives to identify customer and competitor behaviors and to assess trends and potential opportunities.

The executives were particularly interested in new strategic directions that would support CEO Paul McTierny's belief that they never should offer services that could be perceived to exploit customers. Instead, the firm should offer services that would provide as great a value to customers as possible. The basis for this philosophy was that success would be secure when their customers were served better by the firm than by competitors.

Based on inputs from everywhere, the Marketing Department and executive committee identified several market opportunities that could be created and exploited. They decided to provide a new service to give advice to customers that would build their understanding of how to make their own investment decisions. Such a service would be competitively novel and fall in line with the desired strategic intents as well as the CEO's philosophy of being of genuine help and value to customers. However, pursuing this strategy required delivering the new services to its customers with a great deal of expertise. The new services would require customer service representatives (CSRs) to possess additional knowledge, which they would have to acquire through additional costly education.

Nevertheless, the executive committee judged that the new strategic direction would be worth the risk. They therefore proceeded with implementation by creating a pilot program that would provide the new service to key customers using a small number of highly experienced and specially educated CSRs. This program was highly successful. The next step was taken to create an educational program for all service representatives, using the experienced CSRs as extra resources to share their approaches and deeper understanding of how to assist customers.

Comments: Without knowing it at the time, Financo divided its issue into the four distinct and separate situation-handling tasks as indicated in Figure 6-3. Financo's management handled the strategic situation by considering it from a knowledge perspective that resulted in comprehensive concept transfers and education.

The primary knowledge-related aspects of this case were the need for CSRs to build expertise in the form of a mental library of reference models that were required to deliver the new service with the proficiency Paul McTierny considered appropriate.

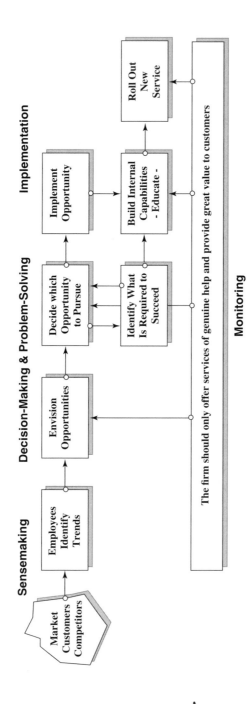

Figure 6-3

Financo's handling of its strategy opportunities involved all the tasks of Sensemaking, Decision-Making/Problem-Solving, Implementation, and Monitoring.

Sensemaking and Its *Situational Awareness*

Sensemaking is the initial — and perhaps the most important — area within situation-handling. However, it is often made difficult for several reasons.[4] Information may be insufficient or contradictory. The situation may be unfamiliar. Most situations are close-coupled and interwoven, with other aspects within or outside the enterprise. Hence, it may be difficult to delineate what to include or exclude in the target situation.

R&D and Marketing Leadership Find New Markets for New Products

The Marketing Department of the electronic equipment man-ufacturer Argis wanted to explore whether potential new communications products would be successful in the marketplace. The new products had capabilities far beyond the conventional products, which primarily served logistics operations. The sales staff and most of the marketing people argued that the new products were overengineered and that the new features would make them too expensive for the limited logistics market. Steve Hill, R&D head, and Paul Rhone, Marketing vice president, agreed that the "logistics only" perspective was too narrow and that Argis would be able to drive down costs if a larger market could be found to justify larger production runs.

The Market Research Department (MRD) had little market data outside the logistics industries and was reluctant to expand its product acceptance analyses. It felt that the new devices probably had little attraction for industries other than logistics and thought it would be a waste of effort. Steve and Paul decided that the MRD was too constrained in its views and that it needed assistance and insights by someone with a broader per-spective. Consequently, they created a taskforce composed of an outside group assisted by R&D and Marketing people who were convinced the new devices would be attractive to larger markets.

The taskforce returned with a wealth of information from focus groups and work meetings with operations people from several industries. They had found that no one else was offer-ing competing devices. Many potential users were enthusiastic about how the new devices would make their jobs easier and help their companies. The information included virtual user

scenarios — models — for how the devices would assist opera-
tions in practice. The taskforce also made up pro forma finan-
cial analyses to illustrate potential economic benefits. From
these models it appeared that the market for the new devices
easily could be double that of the logistics market. Steve and
Paul were able to summarize the findings in a succinct report
for the Argis management team which was to decide on whether
or not to pursue the new product line. They also explained the
deeper reasoning behind the concepts and findings in the report
in discussions with management, thereby transferring the
insights, and not just the results.

Comments: Argis was faced with an interesting situation and
needed to assess how it related to the potential marketplace. They
needed to understand if it made sense to pursue the situation.

The knowledge-related aspects of this case included the many
sales, marketing, and MRD people who appeared to have narrow
knowledge that prevented them from perceiving opportunities. The
taskforce learned to recognize potential new customers. Perhaps most
importantly, the taskforce was able to engage in deep knowledge
transfer to those who ultimately needed to use it, the management.

Sensemaking in the Enterprise

In unexpected, less known, and more complex situations, enterprise situation-handling becomes increasingly ad hoc. Under these
conditions, sensemaking is particularly important and requires thinking about the unexpected — "thinking outside the box." Sensemaking of what may appear to be a simple matter often requires
considerable effort as illustrated by the following example:

Production Line Investigation Finds Reasons for Cost and Delivery Problems

Morrison Company, an agricultural machine manufacturer,
experienced unacceptable rework and production delays in one
of their production lines. Joe Hanson, the plant industrial engi-
neer, investigated the problems to find out what was wrong and
pursued the task from different perspectives. He assembled
production statistics and information on production machine

downtime and repairs. He interviewed supervisors and line per-
sonnel. For hours, he observed activities on the production line,
paying particular attention to trouble spots. And he examined
parts that needed rework. Joe also followed information flows
and parts flows in his attempts to find discrepancies.

Joe uncovered evidence indicating that several things ap-
peared to be wrong. There were unaccounted interruptions of
the production line work flow. There were unacceptable quality
problems that the inspectors and testers identified at the end of
the production line. The quality problems were perplexing;
some appeared to be machining problems, whereas others might
be problematic materials. In addition, there were long down-
times when equipment failed. Most of these problems were new,
and it was uncertain what caused them. Morrison had recently
completed a cost containment program, and Joe suspected that
some problems might be related since they seemed to have
appeared after the program was implemented. That was hotly
denied by those who had promoted cost cutting. Nevertheless,
he explored the possibility of any connections. After thorough
analysis and collaboration with workers and supervisors, Joe
identified the following issues.

The cost containment had resulted in several separate moves
to reduce costs. Plant maintenance staff had been reduced,
production line overcapacity had been eliminated, and procure-
ment had changed to lower-cost suppliers for some materials.
Whereas these changes had resulted in somewhat lower costs,
they in turn had led to the observed operating problems in the
following manner.

- *The reduced maintenance staff led to maintenance scheduling*
  problems and long wait times — delays — to fix equipment.
  Also, since teams were measured by throughput, long main-
  tenance delays resulted in reduced productivity and a ten-
  dency to continue to operate with out-of-spec equipment,
  which resulted in out-of-tolerance quality problems at the
  end of the line. In Joe's mind, this could be avoided if the
  production line workers were allowed to perform selected
  maintenance on their equipment. However, that required
  additional education and new operating practices and super-
  visory functions.

- *Some new, low-cost suppliers delivered materials (such as*
  high-strength bolts) that failed during product tests and
  required repair and rework.

■ *The production line capacity reductions led to reduced flexibility. Morrison had always been proud to provide individualized customer service, including expediting orders from important customers. That had never caused problems since the overcapacity had absorbed the associated disturbances. Instead, the leaner production line could not absorb expediting and production delays, and other disruptions resulted.*

Comments: Joe Hanson was very experienced and did not always believe what he was told. In addition, he had been educated in systems dynamics and was personally interested in the higher order consequences of actions. In this situation, Joe received conflicting information and opinions. However, the symptoms indicated that there were underlying factors, and he was therefore motivated to uncover them.

The primary knowledge-related aspects of this case are related to the value of Joe Hanson's own expertise. A more permanent and strategic aspect related to the needs for greater and broader knowledge for production line workers and new management and supervisor understandings to support the new practices.

Enterprise Situational Awareness

Many enterprises are caught off guard as a result of misunderstanding situations and misinterpreting perceived consequences. Their Situational Awareness has been limited — the enterprise's reference models and the mental reference models of its employees have been limited — and therefore have become constraints in ways that lead to problems. Along the same lines, when enterprise management teams are faced with difficult situations that fall beyond their previous experiences — such as accidents or management failures — they may immediately execute self-preserving responses based on human reflex models instead of engaging in proactive Problem-Solving that examines implications from broader perspectives. Also, in many enterprises the information management function lacks the means, or have not been designed, to deal with issues beyond the expected. As a result, in these cases, the enterprise's intelligence assets lack the capabilities to deal with unanticipated challenges, hence leaving the enterprise vulnerable.

The extent of an organization's Situational Awareness often distinguishes a higher performing enterprise from one that only follows the industry leaders. Situational Awareness to a large extent is determined by the understanding and breadth of knowledge. When focus is narrow and understanding is limited, it may lead to significant business problems as illustrated by the following example.

Chief Engineer and Company Management Do Not Acknowledge Emerging Staffing Problems

Pierre Sonne, the human resource director for AeroCo, a medium-sized aerospace company, was quite concerned. He had discovered that more than half of the factory employees, including supervisors and plant engineers, were eligible for retirement within four years. Most of the remaining employees were quite new and, in general, not highly experienced. In addition, some specialty departments would be almost completely without workers when the eligible staff retired. However, there were no manufacturing department plans or budgets to hire replacements, transfer expertise to younger workers, or start building a new competent workforce by other means. Matters were made worse by the manufacturing management who reported to the chief engineer, who did not consider the situation to be worthy of attention.

Pierre was aware of the general shortage of a competent workforce in the general geographical area and the low supply of new engineers and people with associates degrees that could be expected from the regional colleges. He attempted to make the company management aware of the seriousness of the situation. The president and the vice presidents of operations and technology checked briefly with the chief engineer, Tom Jordan. Tom told them — and they believed him — that he was certain the situation would resolve itself. People would not all leave at the same time, he said, and there were more pressing issues that concerned the company.

The company's competitiveness was based largely on the factory's expertise involved in building sophisticated products. Hence, as personnel started to retire — 15 percent of the eligible group in the first year, 25 percent in the second year, 40 percent in the third year, and 20 percent in the fourth year — the problems that Pierre had foreseen quickly became apparent. Already in the first year it was difficult to find competent replacements, and during the next three years the expertise level within the workforce was drastically reduced. As a result, the company has experienced product quality problems and lost considerable business; a new management team has now been brought in to try to improve the situation.

Comments: AeroCo's management exhibited constrained Situational Awareness which limited its ability to act in time.

The primary knowledge-related aspects of this case included the chief engineer's lack of understanding of the dynamics of personnel retirements, replacements, and acquisition of expertise. Upper management also exhibited a lack of understanding of the same issues. Other aspects included the knowledge-building requirements to create a competent workforce, a process that required knowledge transfers from experts to novices, education, and learning on the job.

Decision-Making/Problem-Solving and *Action Space and Innovation Capability*

The quality of the enterprise Decision-Making/Problem-Solving capability is one of the most important functions for determining the enterprise's ability to survive and prosper. This capability may be risk seeking, daring, and creative to seek new and novel business opportunities. It may be risk-balanced, proactive, and innovative to support market leadership pursuit. It may be risk averse, reactionary, and conventional to support a business-as-usual direction. Clearly, within an enterprise of some size, Decision-Making/Problem-Solving capabilities will fall within all of these categories — within top management, operating divisions, departments, and among individuals.

How Shall We Utilize Our Retained Earnings for Best Long-Term Success?

Parity Corporation's president, Joe Hammack, struggled with the question of how to expand Parity's business. The last years had been successful, and the company had accumulated cash reserves from retained earnings beyond those needed to sustain operations during difficult times. They attributed much of their success to their advanced personnel policies and good salaries and bonuses, which provided a loyal and effective workforce.

In spite of present successes, market research indicated that Parity's existing medical diagnostic products would potentially be outdated within a few years. Within Parity, updated products were being prototyped, and new-generation products were under development. However, all were extensions of the present product line. Market forecasts for the health-care sector growth in general were quite favorable. Under these circumstances, it would be natural to pursue business-as-usual and use Parity's favorable situation to lower profit margins and prices to increase market share. Parity could then bank the cash reserves as insurance against future adverse conditions, or perhaps use reserves to increase dividends or otherwise reward owners and employees.

Nevertheless, Joe was not at ease. Joe, his Marketing vice president, and other members of the executive team believed that the present market trend would not continue for very long. Together they decided that Parity needed to consider new directions while they had the financial advantages to invest in new business. The issue was: Which directions should they pursue? There were many clear options, but they were still within the present market perspectives. Most would exploit Parity's R&D and manufacturing technology strengths, and they knew that direction could be managed with confidence. Then again, other firms would pursue the same options, and competition could be fierce, with no guarantee of successful outcomes.

Given this situation, Joe and his management team decided that, given their core strengths, they would try to create a new market niche that would provide them with durable opportunities for success in years to come. They set to work by first defining from a top-down and abstract perspective which core strengths they could use as foundation for new business directions. They focused on their R&D, engineering, manufacturing, marketing, and sales capabilities, assuming that they would have the management strength to deal with new markets. They decided to "think outside the box," and they created scenarios for wide-ranging customer and market futures. The initial scenarios still were based too much on conventional thinking. It was decided to step back and look at general principles and plausible scenarios for future health-care delivery and how technology would need to develop to support new thinking, new practices, new economics, and new health-care-related social values. In addition, they included the best thinking they could find on expected emerging technology and technological breakthroughs, both within and outside their present areas of expertise.

Several interesting scenarios emerged, some of which were isolated, others overlapped, but all required some technologies beyond Parity's present capabilities. The isolated scenarios were considered to be vulnerable and risky, whereas the overlapping ones were judged to provide both flexibility and greater likelihood of being realized. In addition, all the scenarios would require that someone — most likely Parity, if it proceeded — would need to build awareness and understanding in the marketplace of the improved quality of care and cost-effective opportunity associated with the new health-care delivery practices that would rely on its new products. The priority scenarios centered around diagnostic and treatment monitoring devices that ranged from simple and inexpensive applications of sophisticated technology with large market potentials throughout the world to high-cost machines with limited markets. All relied on new technologies, some of which might not be realizable and which therefore were risky.

Joe and his team agonized over the situation, which truly represented a dilemma with risks on all sides. However, it was generally agreed that continuing with any one of the business-as-usual alternatives would likely make Parity ultimately deplete its cash reserves to stay in business and become a mature corporation with few options for renewal. In the end, they elected to pursue a strategy that would work if several of the overlapping scenarios were realized. The strategy would be costly and risky but also quite rewarding if it could be brought about. The scenarios and the success of the strategy relied extensively on Parity's ability to develop radically new and affordable diagnostic and treatment monitoring devices that could revolutionalize selected areas of health-care delivery. Hence, they agreed that the responsibility for success was in the hands of Joe and his management team and, equally important, every employee at every level of the company.

To pursue the new strategy, Parity needed to more than double its R&D operations by bringing in senior researchers and their teams with expertise in four scientific areas. They were prepared to use considerable resources to acquire the necessary capabilities. They also needed to build greater medical expertise and develop additional strategic alliances with medical institutions, particularly with medical schools. In addition, the man-

agement team realized that it needed to rely on its rank-and-file employees to a greater degree than it had previously attempted to assist in implementing the new strategy. Given evidence that greater employee satisfaction increases productivity and innovation, the team decided to make Parity a more effective organization by providing employees at all levels with greater freedom to innovate and assume responsibilities. For that, management needed to create and engage in deep dialogues with each employee to make them understand how they could assist in implementing both existing and new strategies and how they would benefit personally from making Parity a success.

Comments: Parity's management confronted a challenging situation familiar to many management teams. Based on their best understanding of the situation, in spite of all its uncertainties and conflicting and partial information, they decided to pursue a proactive and comprehensive approach that required innovative Problem-Solving to determine what to do. Their goal was to re-create Parity to be successful in the long term. Their management philosophy was that they needed to rely on a loyal and effective workforce — to an even greater extent than previously. All these factors produced a complex situation.

There were several knowledge-related aspects of this case. Clearly, Parity's management team was very knowledgeable and had good understanding of its market, its capabilities, and how to make the organization operate effectively. However, to pursue its aggressive strategy, management needed to build additional knowledge capabilities. It needed to increase its R&D intellectual capital and also prepare its general workforce to understand how to participate in implementing the strategy in detail.

Enterprise Decision-Making

Much enterprise Decision-Making is immediate and often routine. Experienced managers respond to a myriad of varying situations, most of which are familiar — or nearly familiar to them. Work performed by rank-and-file employees is often immediate and routine and consists of well-established tasks and practices. Hence, to perform such work, proficient managers and other employees are often able to operationalize and execute personal mental reference models to perform their jobs. Within the enterprise one frequently finds that much work is performed by another class of Decision-Making cases that include predesigned responses embedded in automated functions such as payroll systems and in other types of systems and procedures.

Business Expansion Requires Hiring of Competent Staff

As a result of expanded business, Sally Struve, the human resources director of Holly Corporation, a public relations (PR) firm, was spearheading the hiring of 20 experienced PR specialists, advertising professionals, copy writers, and graphics designers. She assembled several hundred résumés for likely candidates. With her staff, Sally summarized the résumés and used a candidate evaluation software system to apply company criteria to screen and select about 60 candidates whom she and the department heads would interview in person.

To expedite the process, standard background checks were performed in parallel with inviting candidates for interviews, resulting in the disqualification of a few candidates. The remaining candidates were invited in for interviews by Sally and representatives of the departments involved. Eight were such obvious hires that they were given employment offers while still present.

Sally convened meetings with the department heads to staff the remaining 12 positions. They reviewed the interview results and ranked candidates according to Holly's proficiency, salary, and personality criteria. Based on these rankings, employment offers were extended to fill the remaining positions. However, since only 17 candidates accepted the employment offers, Sally, in followup efforts, was able to quickly extend offers to other candidates. In the end, all 20 positions were filled.

Comments: Holly had adopted a streamlined hiring procedure, with established criteria that allowed the company to make effective hiring decisions.

The primary knowledge-related aspects of this case included Holly's intellectual capital, which provided for an ordered hiring procedure with established criteria and pre-formatted employment offers and contracts. These structural IC assets constituted enterprise reference models for hiring. By following the hiring procedure, Sally and her coworkers were able to perform the hiring as a routine group decision.

Enterprise Problem-Solving

Enterprise Problem-Solving is performed by individuals, by teams, and, still very rarely, by automated means that contain embedded Problem-Solving methodologies.

Problem-Solving in the enterprise occurs in widely different cases, as indicated in Table 6-4. The approaches are in some cases determined by the urgency and other aspects of the nature of the situation. In other cases, the Problem-Solving approach may be determined by the capability or mentality of the decision makers.

Repairing Relations with Unhappy Clients

Parity Customer Solutions, a customer relations software provider that had grown rapidly, experienced problems with several major clients as a result of insufficient customer support made worse by a new software release that had disruptive reliability problems. Richard Posner, Parity's president and chief operating officer, led the effort to find ways to ameliorate the problems and, if possible, win back the confidence and loyalty that Parity had enjoyed in the past.

The problems were quite clear: they had caused not only clients' inconveniences but in several cases economic losses as well, although these were not large. Clients were unhappy, but none appeared to wish to break their contracts or take drastic measures. Nevertheless, Richard and his colleagues believed that it would be inadvisable to let time heal the situation and instead were intent on finding positive ways to fix the relationships. After all, Parity's expertise was customer relations, and that needed to be reflected by its actions.

Richard pulled together a team of six top people from Marketing, Sales, Strategy, Customer Support, and Software Development and Deployment. In the past, Parity had successfully repaired client relations by providing reductions in fees, but there was a consensus that the present situation required more drastic measures. What could they possibly do that would

Table 6-4
Characteristics of different Problem-Solving paradigms. Copyright © 1993 Schema Press & Karl M. Wiig. Reproduced with permission.

Paradigm	Characteristics	Approach
Leisurely & Unfocused Exploration	■ Goals are often fuzzy, unclear, & qualitative if explicit or may be tacit or implicit in general situations ■ Constraints are not explicit ■ Performance criteria are not explicit ■ Options, when generated & considered, are not made clear or remembered ■ Options may be internally inconsistent	■ Mostly performed alone ■ Unhurried & informal mental exploration ■ May disregard constraints & uncertainties, be internally inconsistent, with approaches that partially satisfy criteria & objectives. Uses idealistic, pragmatic, automatic knowledge ■ Relies extensively on associations & less on crisp or qualitative explicit reasoning
Crisis Problem-Solving	■ Sharp focus on what creates problem ■ Satisfactory solutions are sufficient ■ Situation may be constrained by Time, Resources, Information, & Knowledge ■ Goal is to alleviate crisis	■ Performed alone or in groups — often with considerable urgency ■ Approach is often "what comes naturally" rather than selected to match problem ■ Uses pragmatic & automatic knowledge
Routine Problem-Solving	■ Part of all regular knowledge work & needed to complete all normal tasks ■ Frequently overlooked due to its ubiquity ■ Well understood by participant(s)	■ Mostly performed alone ■ Often performed to analyze ■ Relies on pragmatic & automatic knowledge & on known routine cases, less on scripts

Systematic Problem-Solving	■ Goal is typically to develop approach to a challenge or produce a product ■ Group work may lead to disagreements due to diverse understanding ■ Situations are often only partially understood by problem solver(s)	■ Performed alone or in groups — often with considerable reflection & deliberation ■ Often performed to generate alternatives ■ Relies on idealistic, systematic, pragmatic & some automatic knowledge
Decision-Making	■ Goal is to produce a change or preserve status quo ■ Focus is on finding acceptable way to handle the *situation* & implementing it	■ Performed alone or in groups with varying degrees of reflection & deliberation ■ Often simplifies rather than vigilant ■ Uses systematic & pragmatic knowledge
Evolutionary Incremental Problem-Solving	■ Focus changes to present issues ■ Criteria for overall situation may be unknown & are not considered ■ Optimizes locally	■ Wait-and-see attitude to approach challenges as they present themselves ■ Uses whatever knowledge is required for local problem-solving
Exploratory Problem-Solving	■ Primary goal is to determine what the conditions of the situation are ■ Secondary goal is to determine if & how the situation warrants changes	■ Situation may be "perturbed" by changes to determine the nature of effects ■ Uses idealistic & systematic knowledge to explore & pragmatic knowledge to act
Innovating or Creative Exploration	■ Driven by "desire to make life easier" ■ May be highly practical & directly concerned with aspects of daily work ■ Criteria may be nonconscious ■ Constraints are considered explicitly ■ Sharply focused on desire to improve ■ Flexible, no particular solution sought	■ Mostly performed alone ■ Relies mostly on idealistic, pragmatic, & automatic knowledge ■ Uses idealistic knowledge to determine criteria & pragmatic & automatic knowledge to find solutions

have sufficient impact and value to their clients to correct the present state?

In spite of Parity itself employing customer relations experts, the team decided to explore the experiences and approaches that others had with repairing customer relations. They quickly contacted and interviewed anyone they thought could provide insights. Three members of the group sat down to examine how they would feel if they themselves had received Parity's treatment and how that would have affected them. They explored what they would require from Parity to set things right. In principle, the team engaged in divergent thinking to generate a spectrum of plausible approaches that might provide solutions to the dilemmas. They agreed that it would be important to go to some length, particularly if the measures were of great value to clients. However, Parity could not go too far in providing compensating measures.

After discussing and evaluating the potential approaches, the team decided that, for one aspect, special compensations should be provided to the affected clients. Quite another aspect — and perhaps a more important one, with greater market visibility and impact — would be to strengthen its customer support and software development, testing, and bug-fixing capabilities. They should also publicly acknowledge the problems and explain how they were being corrected to never occur again.

The team, and subsequently Parity, elected to immediately allocate additional customer service representatives to the affected clients and compensate those who had experienced losses. They also decided to expand both the customer service and software departments and to explain their actions openly and truthfully to the marketplace. In addition, there were indications that most customer support representatives (CSRs) needed to be better prepared — particularly by understanding Parity's products better and understanding how clients benefited from the products in their business. A comprehensive educational program — including knowledge sharing within the CSR community of practice — was therefore initiated. These actions were expensive but were judged to be both the best way to go and good investments with acceptable returns.

Comments: Parity's troubleshooting team collaborated to find the best solution to the customer situation by pursuing systematic Problem-Solving, as illustrated in Table 6-4.

The primary knowledge-related aspects of this case included the team's methodological Problem-Solving expertise, the knowledge sharing with the marketplace of Parity's intents and actions, and the educational program for CSRs.

Enterprise Action Spaces

Frequently, enterprise approaches become constrained by conventional thinking such as the "If it is not broken, don't fix it!" mentality. Action Spaces are often more constraining in the enterprise than in the personal situation and may be subject to "group-think" and committee behavior that reduces creativity to the "least common denominator." For these reasons, it is often helpful to bring in a different perspective, a different paradigm, or problem framing in which the group members have fewer constraints.

Restructuring Sales and Operations to Increase Profits Led to Action Space Expansion

LearnsSys, Inc. developed advanced computer-based educational materials for industry. Cecilia Cho, LearnsSys's president was dissatisfied with the effectiveness of their sales process. She also thought that their contract work led to excessive change orders and delays. This was in spite of LearnsSys's recent efforts to streamline its marketing-sales-proposal-contract execution-systems delivery value process, which was as good as advanced thinking in the industry could make it. Nevertheless, Cecilia was positive that a better approach could be devised to improve performance.

Cecilia argued with her team — who were quite proud of the present arrangements — to help find better solutions. They thought her wish was beyond reach. They agreed that the reason for what Cecilia considered to be a problem was that the market was limited. LearnsSys technology was too advanced and therefore amounted to a certain amount of hard-to-sell "technology-push" instead of "demand-pull" that customers would naturally ask for. They did not see any reason for a "rethink" or change.

All the same, Cecilia brought her team together to consider the marketing-to-delivery process from new perspectives. In the past, they had focused on information and work flows, but Bud Norman, the innovative R&D director, who also spearheaded LearnsSys's advanced technology, suggested that maybe they should look at what he called "understanding flow" instead. Bud felt that in executing the marketing-to-delivery process the salespeople and proposal writers did not properly represent LearnsSys's technological capabilities. Also, Sal Sanguese, head of software development, thought that many change orders could be avoided if better customer specifications were included in the contracts. And if change orders were reduced, that could lead to shorter execution times and lower execution costs.

As they argued and discussed, it became clear that most had opinions about the limitations of insights at several points in the process and that these might be caused by "understanding problems." Jane Quist, head of sales, suggested that, quite often, it was difficult for the sales team to explain how advanced features would benefit potential customers. She also indicated that at other times she learned later that valuable features that could be implemented quickly and inexpensively were not included in the proposed work due to lack of understanding. Others indicated additional limitations, all understanding or knowledge-related.

Initial suggestions for improving the situation (this was natural for an educational materials developer) were to provide an educational program for sales and proposal people to give them insights to represent LearnsSys capabilities better. That was quickly discarded for two reasons. First, conditions and technology changed too fast, and second, everyone already had enough to learn and keep up with. Hence, it was not possible to plan for more education.

After more discussion, a new model developed — that of placing people with relevant understandings and expertise in the various situations where they could make a difference. It was agreed that senior software and R&D people would join with the sales team to work with potential customers to conceptualize what LearnSys could do and how that would benefit the customer. The software and R&D people would only rotate in visiting roles. However, after conceptualizing a potential contract, they would next assist in writing the proposal, and if a contract was secured, the same people would participate in, or lead the contract work. In this way, there would be opportunities for a wide range of people to participate.

This model was built on the concepts that the presence of deep understanding of advanced technology and implementation in the customer situation would quickly help conceptualize the best possible customer solution. It would also build customer understanding and confidence. Next, the proposal would better reflect what was agreed with the customer and increase the probability of customer acceptance. Finally, the project work would benefit from automatic inclusion of customer understanding and agreements. This model was implemented, with the result that contract scopes increased on the average, the acceptance ratio increased, and execution costs and delivery time were reduced. There were other benefits. R&D and software people obtained a much better understanding of customer situations and issues, and they were better able to meet them in future work. By having people from different parts of the organization work together in different situations, new and valuable ideas and innovations emerged. In addition, improved customer relations increased followup work.

Comments: LearnsSys faced a typical business situation — that of needing to restructure work to improve profitability. Initially, the team's action space was constrained to business-as-usual as is often the case, particularly when a change for the better has already been implemented. For people who have been part of implementation, the psychological cost of discarding recent improvements is high. In LearnSys's case, by introducing a new paradigm — a new model and perspective — the team was able to expand its Action Space to create new ways of handling customers, proposals, project execution, and research and development.

The knowledge-related aspects in this case included the "understanding flow" within the marketing-to-delivery process as indicated in Figure 6-4. That paradigm provided the insights that allowed the LearnSys team to expand its Action Space, which in turn led to its innovative knowledge-bridging approach by assigning technology experts to follow each project through all its stages.

Enterprise Innovation Capabilities

Competitiveness appears to be a function of the degree to which an enterprise can innovate better and faster than its competitors. Its Innovation Capabilities provide the ability to innovate and are a result of many factors, such as enterprise culture and the mentalities of its employees, the degrees to which people are free to engage in

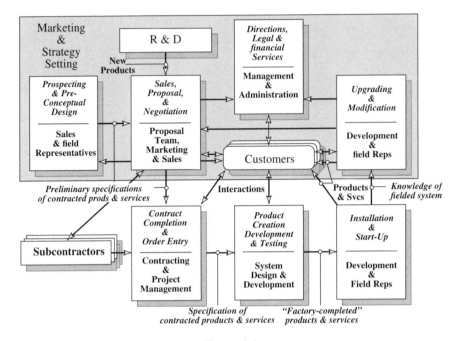

Figure 6-4

LearnSys, Inc.'s model of its "understanding flow" and value process.
Copyright © 1996 Knowledge Research Institute, Inc. and Karl M. Wiig.
Reproduced with permission.

creative and innovative activities, motivational factors and incentives, exchanges of viewpoints, perspectives and knowledge within the enterprise and with the outside, and the degree to which people within the enterprise understand customers, customers' customers, and the marketplace.

Innovation is a human activity, and there are many approaches to create an innovative environment within the enterprise. Among these approaches are those that expose people to new ideas. Equally important are approaches to expose people to novel needs and requirements. In addition, many organizations have discovered that creating opportunities for people from different parts of the organization to meet or work together often leads to innovative collaboration with great results. Perhaps the most valuable innovations are those that are associated with totally novel ideas and opportunities that are not yet perceived by the marketplace or by customers. At other times, opportunities are created by improving operations in ways that competitors have not understood as in the following illustration.

New In-House Technology Makes
Significant Cost Reductions Possible

Potter Industries was a leading commodity producer in a highly competitive industry. It had remained successful by developing and applying sophisticated technologies better than its competitors. However, other producers were catching up fast.

For its size, Potter had a comparatively small but very effective Research and Development Center that had been the nucleus for technology development. But R&D did not act alone. Plant process engineers and production teams experimented and assisted R&D in improving processes. R&D personnel visited the plants on regular rotation to work closely with plant employees for one or two weeks. As a result, the plant operators and engineers became conversant in technological matters, making it possible to implement equipment and practices that required extensive competence to operate. Plant engineers and union operators also rotated into the R&D Center but for longer periods of three to six months. This gave the R&D projects a practical direction that made it possible to implement many of them directly, without the need for R&D pilot plant operation.

However, most of the R&D effort had been focused on perfecting operations and making the present second-generation technology more efficient. Keith Esquivel, the company's thoughtful and broadminded R&D vice president, was not satisfied. Potter already operated the present technology close to its theoretical limit, and future improvements would be costly and not bring great improvements. Keith decided it was time to rethink the production process to introduce, if possible, new technology that either existed elsewhere or that Potter had to invent.

After considerable research at the R&D Center and in the plants, research that was both costly and risky, Potter was able to devise a new patentable third-generation process, which in pilot plant operation showed great promise for yield improvement and cost reductions. Thanks to the involvement of plant people in the initial research, pilot plant design, and operation, the scaling up to full production size occurred with only minimal problems. The anticipated economic gains were achieved.

Comments: By building an ongoing Innovation Capability, Potter was able to create a proprietary third-generation technology solution, which by its improved yield introduced significantly lower production costs, as indicated in Figure 6-5.

The knowledge-related aspects in this case included the valuable process that Potter created by rotating R&D and plant people. The continued interaction — both while working on projects and in leisure periods — formed an effective process for exchanging and creating ideas and innovation and transferring concepts between the R&D Center and the plants. In addition, the rotation created valuable networks and shared understandings and mentalities.

Implementation and Its *Execution Capability*

Problems with proper Implementation of good intents are perhaps the greatest difficulties in the world in general. Many excellent decisions and worthwhile projects and programs are derailed or even discarded because of inadequate Implementation. There are many examples of execution problems as indicated by Matta and Ashkenas (2003) and Bossidy and Charan (2002).

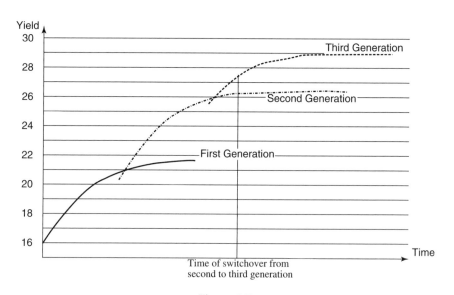

Figure 6-5
Potter's experienced yield of three technology generations and the time of switchover from second to third generation. Copyright © 1992 Knowledge Research Institute, Inc. and Karl M. Wiig. Reproduced with permission.

Often implementation becomes a problem because of ineffective communication of concepts and intents (bridging of purpose) from one person or functional entity to another. This is a particular area of concern in most enterprises. After a decision is made, the implementation team or department, at the same organizational level as the decision maker or at a lower level, often does not fully understand — or understand at all — the concepts or other underlying intents behind the decision. As a result, execution effectiveness suffers.

In the organizational domain, Implementation may involve large, complicated efforts that require extensive supports from specialized and competent personnel, systems, and other resources. However, most problems with implementation seem to originate with decision makers, who do not appreciate that the implementers cannot understand what is required (Mittelstaedt 2003).

The Strategy Is Not Implemented by Rank-and-File!

Stubb Corporation's president and CEO Paul Nary was appalled at how badly Stubb's strategy was implemented. Only four months ago, with the help of outside consultants, it was determined that Stubb's key strengths were centered around customer relations and quality leadership and their strategy should focus on attaining market leadership based on these strengths. Such a strategy was considered certain to succeed because the marketplace considered Stubb to have excellent relations and products. In anticipation of increased business, Stubb proactively increased its labor force by about 10 percent across all departments to ascertain that new workers were competent when they would be needed.

After a few months, however, the strategy was not being properly implemented by lower-level managers, supervisors, and rank-and-file. Instead of making tradeoffs in favor of quality and good customer service, they frequently focused on internal issues and minutiae such as maintaining low inventories, smoothing production line flows, minimizing scrap rates, and reducing the costs of supplies and consumables. Costly bickering and finger-pointing were also occurring between maintenance and production departments.

Paul called in a consultant, Pete Storm, who specialized in strategy implementation to find what was wrong. Pete found that several aspects worked against the strategy. First, whereas people throughout Stubb read and knew the strategy slogans, they did not really understand what the strategy entailed, and most did not see how their own work would help to implement the strategy. Second, people did not see how achieving good strategy implementation would be of value to themselves. They really were not interested in implementing the strategy. They were more interested in keeping their own work problem-free and maintaining good relations with coworkers and superiors. Pete identified internal Stubb initiatives that were counter-productive. Hence, operating cost containment efforts that dealt with inventories, scrap, consumables, and so on, ended up to be of greater concern than effective strategy implementation. In addition, current operating practice and culture did not support the rank-and-file's effort to make independent decisions to innovate and improvise on operational guidelines in order to achieve strategic benefits.

Pete recommended that a different approach be taken to communicating the strategy, its implementation, what it would mean for the company, how each job could participate in its implementation, and the value it would have for each employee to succeed. It would also be important to help people understand how they could resolve conflicts between strategy issues and other issues such as the cost containment efforts. These initia-tives would require considerable work on the part of manage-ment and the people throughout the organization. Pete also emphasized to Paul that, in order to achieve successful strategy implementation, it would be necessary to loosen management control and give people greater decision latitude — which in turn also required building additional expertise in the workforce.

Comments: Stubb's problems in implementing its strategy were created by a combination of lack of understanding, lack of interest in seeing the strategy succeed, and factors that were of greater immediate importance. In addition, many did not find it easy to establish priorities and to resolve conflicts between strategy issues and operating issues.

The knowledge-related aspects in this case included apprenticing and preparing new staff in advance of being needed for expanded business. An important knowledge problem became apparent when the actions of many employees indicated that they had not understood how to (or even that they were parties to) implement the strategy. The most important knowledge tasks were associated with communicating and transferring the insights of the strategy and enterprise intents with the associated implications to all employees. Also of importance were the knowledge flows required to build expertise sufficient for employees to assume responsibilities to handle distributed decision making.

Implementation in the Enterprise

A major implementation problem in the enterprise involves the handoff of the selected action-option from Decision-Making/ Problem-Solving individuals and teams to the Implementation team. The typical problem is particularly associated with the transfer of concepts and intents — the conceptual knowledge and insights — behind the action-option. These aspects of the action-option are rarely communicated deeply and appropriately and are crucial for understanding how to improvise when implementation requires adaptation to the reality and details of the implementation environment. When deep understanding is missing, the action-option implementation, therefore, typically suffers.

Implement Strategic Partnerships to Make the Enterprise Stronger

Paul Foh, Stihlo Corporation's vice president of marketing and strategy, had the executive committee's agreement to expand strategic partnerships with universities, several suppliers, and key customers. Stihlo provided financial analysis and backroom processing services to institutions and maintained its market position by being innovative, fast, and cost effective — all key factors within its market niche. Recently, Stihlo's competitors had been able to steal two of Stihlo's customers by demonstrating that they provided equal performance at lower costs.

Stihlo's management decided that they needed to improve on several fronts. They needed to become more efficient in internal operations to lower costs. That was necessary, but it would be still more important to innovate by improving, even redesigning, Stihlo's products and services to provide greater value to its

*customers. Hence, the concept was to expand strategic partner-
ships to obtain new ideas and potentially co-develop proprietary
solutions that would set them apart from competitors. Paul had
good ideas for new partnership candidates, which previously
had been limited to two suppliers and three customers.*

*Paul needed to delegate most of the strategic partnership
work to Helen Tracy, director of external relations, who was to
collaborate with Harry Thompson, the in-house analytical
genius. But Paul was concerned that the effort could fail unless
Harry, Helen, and their staff understood the underlying concepts showing why the partnerships were strategically crucial,
which ideas for technologies and solutions might be considered
in the short term and specifically, and the priorities of customer
services and benefits that Paul thought should be pursued. These
particulars needed to be central in the dialogues that Helen,
Harry, and others would have with prospective partners
when formulating and agreeing on the nature and content of the
partnerships.*

*In order to build the requisite understanding, Paul decided to
work closely with Helen and Harry and a few people from their
staff by meeting every day for two weeks in hour-long discussion and work meetings. They worked through the premises for
the strategic partnerships, the potentials for benefits for the partners and for Stihlo, and what might be obtained in terms of
insights, products, and other results. The motivation was for
Helen and the others to internalize the concepts and expectations and build strong mental models to the degree that the concepts and priorities would "be on the tip of their tongue" and
they could steer partner explorations extemporaneously and creatively. That was indeed achieved, and the partnerships that were
established produced both invaluable results and strong allies.*

Comments: Stihlo's management needed to ascertain that the
decisions and ideas to create strategic partnerships were to be
implemented creatively and to the fullest possible potential.

The knowledge-related aspects in this case centered on the transfer of ideas, concepts, priorities, and expectations behind the decision to create new partnerships. Another aspect, not made explicit in
the illustration, was the need to transfer enough understanding to the
partners to make them valuable and motivated supporters of Stihlo's
strategy.

Enterprise Execution Capability

Many enterprises excel by being able to execute successfully. They build internal capabilities, and practices that focus on developing a "can do" mentality. The mentality is backed up with broad individual and team expertise and systems, procedures, and practices to ascertain that all necessary resources are provided and that people are motivated and the enterprise is flexible and ready to assist when problems occur. Apart from providing the needed understanding as indicated in the previous illustration, successful Implementation depends upon the quality and sufficiency of the capabilities and resources that are made available to execute the decision — to implement the selected action-option. In many instances, execution failures are caused by budget limitations, miscalculations or misunderstanding, time pressures, and many other factors, as indicated by the following example.

The Project Is Late and Will Cost More Than Projected; Working Hard Instead of Working Smart Does Not Always Work!

Leon Pavarotti, project manager in Prego Systems' Information Services Division, was leading a new project to create the "Starburst" business system. Halfway into the project, Leon started to have problems. He was an accomplished project manager, but this project used a new and sophisticated technology with which both Prego and Leon lacked previous experience. The project was high priority and, when fully completed, would bring considerable benefits that were central to Prego's continued success. Hence, it was important to finish Starburst early and with all its planned features. However, now it appeared to Leon that the project would exceed both its schedule and budget. Worse, there were issues that Leon and his team did not seem to be able to overcome and Starburst might fail to meet some of its design criteria.

Frank Hayes, the chief information officer, had been warned that it might be risky to conduct the project with only in-house staff and that it might be wise to bring in outside expertise, which would at a minimum provide guidance. However, Frank had seen Leon lead difficult projects before and was confident that it would be quicker, less expensive, and a good learning experience for him to go it alone. When Leon reported problems, Frank decided to add several senior in-house people to the team to help out and asked that together they should work through the problems. Leon was not sure that it would work but agreed and told the project staff to work harder and start working overtime. He also asked professional friends outside Prego for insights into their problems but received little valuable help since the complexity of the project made it diffi-cult to get assistance without total immersion.

The project was not rescued. It was several months late and way over budget, it was missing several key features, and it was of limited value to Prego. Since Prego had relied on the new system for its success, the company suffered in the marketplace and needed to cut back its staff across the board. Leon was fired, but Frank — who was mainly to blame — was retained.

Comments: Prego made a typical mistake by initially allo-cating insufficient resources to the project. That problem was exacerbated by a management that neglected to support the execution team with sufficient competent resources after the project showed signs of failure.

The knowledge-related aspects in this case included insufficient expertise in the project team for the complexity of the tasks required for successful execution.

Monitoring and *Governance Competence and Perspectives*

Whereas delegated and distributed situation-handling proves very effective for an enterprise when employees are motivated and com-petent, there will always be a need to ascertain that work is per-formed according to the enterprise's intent and not in some other direction. Deviations from the intended direction may be caused by lack of competence, motivation, or understanding of what is required. Deviations may also be caused by people with self-serving agendas that are not aligned with the enterprise, and in some instances even by destructive or counterproductive actions. Hence, monitoring will always be important.

In other cases, such as when an enterprise pursues an exploratory direction with competent and motivated people, monitoring is impor-tant to redirect and improvise as new opportunities or constraints are encountered.

Company Works to Meet Societal Responsibilities

Atlee Chemical Corporation had been successful with its specialty chemicals, and the future looked promising. Over the years, Pete Reinecker, Atlee's president, had become convinced that Atlee needed to observe its responsibilities, not only to its owners and its employees, but also to the small town of Crossing in which they were located. Atlee was the town's largest taxpayer and also provided most of its payroll. Without Atlee, Pete was convinced, Crossing would cease to exist, and the livelihood of most of its employees would be destroyed. As a result, as business grew, Atlee's management decided to expand in Crossing instead of seeking more cost-effective locations elsewhere.

Not everyone agreed. Outside stockholders argued that the Crossing operations were too expensive and that they would like a more efficient plant that could yield greater profits. They also felt that Atlee's attempt to achieve total recycling with no emissions or effluents also was too expensive, although its profits were above average for the industry. A few of Atlee's employees complained that environmental concerns made it hard to operate the plant. Yet, Pete and his executive committee held on to their philosophy to pursue the company's broad responsibilities and decided to continue to honor the basic principles.

It was not easy to operate Atlee as a responsible and model corporate citizen. Throughout its operations there were constant needs to balance short-term, low effort, and cost actions against longer term and more societal-friendly actions. These dilemmas were particularly frequent in Atlee's physical operations which interacted with air and water quality and other aspects of the environment. Constant monitoring was required both by management to assist rank-and-file and by operators to ascertain that equipment functioned properly at all times and that proper maintenance was performed whenever needed.

Pete and his team believed that the present operating philosophy was both prudent and in the best interest for all concerned. First, they agreed that, whereas stockholders — owners — were an important group of stakeholders and their interests should be observed, they were not important to the exclusion of other stakeholders. Hence, other stakeholders included Atlee's employees who invested their working life in the company and relied on it for their own and their families' current and future livelihoods. The company also needed to be a responsible social citizen, which meant that it could not ignore its effects on local economics, social life, and the physical environment. Business analysts and many outside owners clearly disagreed, but Pete and his team decided that as long as they were profitable they would stay the course.

Second, Atlee was successful because of the effectiveness of its stable workforce. Worker morale was high, and turnover was low, both leading to unusually high competency among its workers. This was evident in operating statistics, which showed an unusually low frequency of operational mishaps and accidents, and low equipment repair costs since diagnosing and correcting malfunctions were considered everyone's responsibilities. There were other indications as well: product quality was reliably high, and everyone took pride in making the operations exemplary.

Comments: Atlee's approach to lasting and durable success was built around a management philosophy of acting as a model societal citizen and providing a highly attractive place to work. Their approach had many benefits that management found exceeded the costs of the efforts. The ability to maintain the high performance across several dimensions also required considerable monitoring effort, which was judged to be worthwhile.

The knowledge-related aspects in this case included creating a desirable work environment that made it possible to develop and retain highly expert employees. Another aspect was the high degree of competence required everywhere in the company to deliver the operating and management performance needed to meet the desired strategy.

Monitoring in the Enterprise

In today's business environment, single-factor situation-handling is a rarity except in highly routine cases. Most enterprise situations are fraught with dilemmas caused by conflicting objectives such as between quality and throughput, between satisfying a customer's special requirements and maintaining streamlined and efficient operations, between special treatment of fast-track employees and the general treatment and motivation of the workforce-at-large, and so on. In addition to being complex, many conflict situations also tend to be unfamiliar and are difficult to handle. Most need to be monitored — by superiors as well as by oneself — to ascertain that they are handled to the best of the abilities of the people involved.

Our People Do Not Make Balanced Decisions! They Focus on One Factor Only!

Bob Taylor, Bromley Corporation's operations manager, was appalled at the quality of decisions made by most people in his area. As he lamented: "Our people do not make balanced decisions! When they handle situations, they tend to focus on only one factor that will make it easy for them! And that results in erratic actions that go in whichever direction and do not support our corporate intents!" *He pointed to numerous examples where such sub-optimizing was carried to the extreme. Managers focused on controlling inventory turnover at the expense of acquisition costs, parts availability, and service levels. Service and sales representatives expedited customers' special orders in expensive ways without considering other customers, costs, or disruptions of operations. Plant operators wanted maintenance assistance to maximize their own production immediately without concern for others. Higher level managers and directors also tended to pursue single objectives: the logistics director on several occasions demanded that production be rescheduled to facilitate bulk shipping to reduce logistics costs without regard for production costs, customer commitments, and other factors.*

Bob felt that his people were not team players; they did not collaborate, cooperate with each other, or even coordinate their activities. They seemed to be interested solely in their own area of responsibility to the exclusion of all others and seemed to demand that everyone else would accommodate them. Bob was confused because these individuals were reasonable and flexible in other ways, and he could not understand their work behavior. When approached, they readily agreed with him on the need to deal intelligently with dilemmas and to balance the requirements of affected departments and operations. But when they needed to decide and act, the broader perspectives seemed to be forgotten, and that impacted the effectiveness of the whole operation. Bob could show that the unilateral behaviors cost Bromley money and affected its customer relations.

What then, was wrong? Since Bob was at a loss, he asked June Cousins, a Human Resources Department psychologist, if she could help. June took time to observe several people for hours and talked with them about what she had observed. It became clear that in most cases people engaged in operating decisions and situation-handling that had aspects of uncertainty in addition to multiple competing objectives. Information was often limited or inconsistent, and judgment was required to interpret the situation. Typically, situations presented dilemmas by requiring balancing tradeoffs between conflicting objectives. Common tradeoffs were needed for many kinds of situations such as between scheduling competent teams for night or weekend shifts while also accommodating personnel requests, between production expediency and product quality, or between minimizing short-term costs and building for the future.

Most found it difficult to make balanced, real-life decisions under such circumstances. Nearly all the decisions June observed also required quick resolutions. Hence, they were personal situation-handling cases that made it difficult to collaborate or use computer-based decision aids. Instead, they relied on the mental models held by experienced personnel. Furthermore, people handled most situations from concrete or, if they could, from routine points of view. That is, the decision makers attempted to frame situations from immediate and operational perspectives without considering decision implications related to other objectives, such as those associated with other departments or longer term effects. In effect, the decision makers tended to quickly focus on "first-order objectives" and to put "second-order objectives" aside, thereby creating single-objective situation-handling cases.

June discussed her findings with Bob, who became concerned. If this was how experienced people behaved, how could Bromley expect the balanced situation-handling needed for smooth and competitive performance? June suggested three reasons for people's tendency to simplify:

1. In general, most people tend to build practical mental reference models — expertise — that reflect immediate and concrete situations in which they are engaged and can observe. Unless otherwise assisted or engaged, they do not observe, or understand, implications or secondary effects outside their direct operations or those that appear at a later time.
2. Within Bob's operations, most had limited understanding of Bromley's intents and strategy. They did not appreciate how

their own actions were part of implementing the strategy or how they would benefit personally from achieving the strategy successfully. Hence, they were not motivated to observe or were not in a position to judge how past or present actions affected broader objectives. Their focus was mostly on the immediate operations.

3. *Although most people to some extent generalize and identify patterns when engaged operationally in complex situations, they do not appear to build broad and abstract mental models that can be referenced at later times. That is, they do not tend to build scripts, schemata, and procedural and declarative metaknowledge. Therefore, they become limited in their ability to make balanced judgments and decisions when similar complex situations occur.*

June suggested that things did not need to be this way. She referred to other organizations that assisted their employees to build mental approaches to generating and implementing balanced actions when handling complicated situations. That could also be done within Bromley. What was needed was to help employees understand the company's strategy and intents and how that related to their own work. To make that understandable, it would be necessary to engage in extensive discussions and furnish material that included example cases — stories — to facilitate quick mental model development. In this way the employees would be motivated and able to consider the higher order implications of actions and other changes.

In addition, people throughout Bromley needed to develop integrative perspectives and be encouraged to break down the existing silo mentality. They should be encouraged to learn more about operations adjacent to their own by networking and, if possible, by temporary personnel rotation. They needed to build understanding and appreciation for the wider workings of the corporate system. Only then would they be in a position to judge higher order effects. However, that would not be enough. People also needed assistance to build a methodological understanding of how to deal with uncertainties and conflicting objectives. That would best be done though approaches such as workshops and management simulation games. These did not need to be expensive but could be performed in many ways, like teams that competed during lunch hours with computer-based games. Other approaches would require costly offsite sessions.

Comments: By monitoring situation-handling effectiveness, Bob Taylor found that employees needed better approaches. Bromley undertook a thorough analysis to determine the underlying factors behind the lack of balanced decisions and found that corrective actions were needed to help employees use better methods. By observing their decisions, it was found that people needed educational support to develop better strategies to improve multiple objective situation-handling.

The knowledge-related aspects in this case included the need to help employees understand the enterprise strategy and direction. They also needed to build automatized methodological mental models to deal competently with situation-handling dilemmas.

Enterprise Governance Competence and Perspectives

The perspectives and competence of enterprise governance cover a very wide range, stretching from monitoring the ethical governance of the enterprise's societal responsibilities to monitoring its treatment of its employees and the effectiveness of its internal operations. In all cases, the effectiveness of governance is a reflection of management's philosophy, breadth of insights, and ability to determine practical ways of achieving the desired behaviors. One area that often is indicative of management's posture and perspectives becomes apparent when a situation requires damage control as in the following illustration.

Effective Damage Control after Product Failure in the Marketplace

Luis Galvis, president of Fancy Foods, received a late evening phone call from Stirling Way, his vice president of sales with bad news. Several people in Chicago had developed food poisoning apparently from eating Fancy Foods gourmet liver pâté. The potential link between the liver pâté and food poisoning had been determined by the Chicago Department of Public Health (CDPH), which was continuing to pursue the matter. The CDPH had not verified contamination in the pâté samples acquired from stores, but that did not exclude the fact that other batches could have problems. At the time, it was not clear which batches had been sold in Chicago or which batches might have caused the problems. Nor was it clear that Chicago was the only location of food poisoning.

Luis decided to spearhead the situation-handling to determine what Fancy Foods would do. Although it was not clearly established that the pâté was to blame, any doubt about the integrity of the company's food would affect its image in the marketplace. Hence, Luis wanted to be proactive, pull whatever products were at risk, and let the public know what was being done to assure that its products were safe.

The Georgia plant was the only source of liver pâté, and Luis immediately contacted the plant's manager, laboratory director, and logistics manager. Together, they began to check if any recent pâté batches had shown even marginal signs of contamination. They identified the batches that had been sent to Chicago and started the recall process. Just after midnight, Luis wrote a short press release that described the steps Fancy Foods was undertaking to prevent further illness and transmitted these to Chicago newspapers and as a general press release. The press release stated that although a firm link between the pâté and food poisoning had not been established, Fancy Food had taken immediate preventive steps. Fancy Foods also asked anyone who had experienced illness after eating its pâté to let them know about it and, if possible, submit the packaging and any remnants for examination.

Over the next days, Luis and his team collaborated with CDPH and reported to the press what steps were being taken. As for the source of the food poisoning, it was discovered that indeed it had been caused by Fancy Foods liver pâté. But the pâté in question was an old and outdated batch that a small food store had discovered in its warehouse and sold by mistake. No contamination was found in the regular product. Fancy Foods received positive press and market responses for its actions.

Comments: Fancy Foods executives decided to lose no time whatsoever to respond and to ascertain that its products were safe and that the marketplace was fully informed.

The knowledge-related aspects in this case rest on the president's and company's management philosophy and the shared understanding of how to follow up and take steps to implement philosophy intents in difficult situations.

ENTERPRISE SITUATION-HANDLING HAS MANY LEVELS

In any enterprise, situation-handling occurs on many levels. Top management needs to handle competitive, regulatory, and strategic situations, often resulting in quite aggregated decisions without opportunities to deal with implementation in detail. Most often, implementation (execution) of the desired actions will be delegated to lower organizational echelons. Typically, this is the way enterprise strategy is implemented. It is also the approach used in many other managerial decisions, such as promulgating new customer policies and new operational practices.

As always, the effectiveness of execution becomes a function of the knowledge available and other capabilities. In addition, it also becomes a function of how well the lower echelons understand the upper level decision. When execution is delegated to lower levels, it is important that the people who are asked to implement it understand both the details and background of the decision. They need that understanding to fashion and carry out the practical steps and improvisations that are required to achieve the decision objectives under circumstances that normally will have been unknown to the decision makers on higher organizational levels and therefore could not be part of the plan.

A schematic illustration of the four-level delegation of enterprise strategy implementation is depicted in Figure 6-6. From this perspective, delegation of decision execution at one level results in a whole new situation on the next level that must be interpreted, and implementation details must be decided upon and executed. At each lower level the situation-handling is monitored throughout, both from the perspectives and goals of the present and higher levels. There is a constant need to know that the planned actions are implemented in accordance with the top level's wishes.

THE IMPORTANCE OF THE SITUATION-HANDLING MODEL

Initially, we may ask: "Why is the situation-handling model important? What valuable insights does it provide? Why should we be concerned with such level of detail?" There are many answers to these questions, all having to do with improving the effectiveness of people and whole organizations. Whereas this book is cast from the perspectives of KM, the situation-handling model pertains to most people-focused, organizational, and technology-based action-oriented

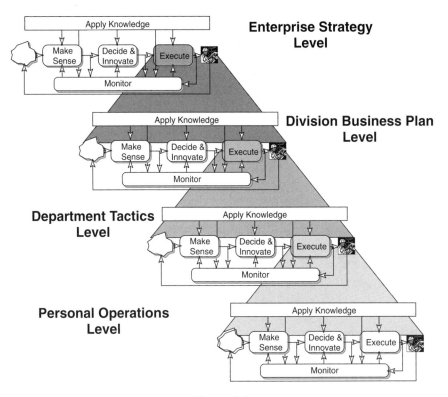

Figure 6-6

Enterprise situation-handling takes place on many levels. Copyright © 2001 Knowledge Research Institute, Inc. and Karl M. Wiig. Reproduced with permission.

systems, be they simple and small or complex and large. The model — as all models — is a simplification, and from a systems perspective it is a variant of a regulatory feedback system. It does not depict specialized processes, many feedback loops, and other functional pathways associated with learning, innovation, dealing with uncertainty, or evolving situations, although some aspects of these are mentioned.

The model depicts the situation-handling process from Sensemaking to Implementation of action-options to the best of our current understanding. It treats the process from a particular perspective in a simplified and aggregated fashion that also leaves room for other interpretations. Many premises included in this model are still under investigation by the scientific community and may well cause us to revise our understanding and thinking as time goes by.

The model outlines the structure of the situation-handling process from beginning to final action. It incorporates understanding from recent research and practical experiences, as well as the role of stories for equipping people and organizations to become proficient and it ties the integrative effects of stories to the building of knowledge in the form of mental models and structural IC assets. In addition, the model provides a framework for analyzing and synthesizing personal and organizational action-oriented processes.

Many of today's business problems are knowledge-related, as are many of today's business opportunities. Unfortunately, people in general have limited insights into the knowledge-related processes and mechanisms that affect business performance. Hence, many problems are not recognized, and many opportunities are missed. The situation-handling model provides an easily explainable framework for understanding knowledge-based action-oriented activities that are of direct importance to business.

Enterprise Situation-Handling Model Insights

The model relies extensively on the role of previous experiences such as reference models (for example, patterns and paradigms) in personal and organizational situation-handling. The model explains action-oriented functional operations and partitions the process into separate tasks. That allows us to describe the general resource requirements, operations, and limitations of these tasks from the knowledge perspective. In its focus on knowledge, it identifies in the aggregate the nature and roles of personal mental models and organizational reference models for performing the primary tasks.

The situation-handling model becomes a vehicle for providing everyone within the organization with general insight into the roles of personal and structural IC assets for delivering competent work. Such widely distributed insights are key in organizations that pursue knowledge vigilance and build a knowledge-aware intangible assets management mentality among its employees. Such a mentality creates a knowledge-friendly culture and fosters collaboration, and IC assets focus on planning and daily operations. The model integrates understanding from several fields into a single structure. It borrows from cognitive sciences, management theory and science, information technology, and management and social sciences.

The situation-handling model provides several important insights. Whereas the model is knowledge-centric, other enterprise contexts also facilitate — or hinder — effective situation-handling. They include:

- Widespread rank-and-file understanding of enterprise strategy and intent.
- Personal understanding by everybody of "What's in it for me?" by participating in implementing enterprise strategy.
- Individual motivation fostered by providing independence, recognition, and permission in order to shape work products to serve individual contexts and enterprise intents and to be permitted to engage in fulfilling work.
- Role models provided by the consistent behavior of enterprise, business unit, and department managers and leaders.
- Natural work processes and practices that represent preferred ways of working.
- General knowledge-leveraging mentality built on understanding the power of maintaining and applying competitive knowledge and other intellectual capital (IC) assets.

In most of these cases, deliberate and systematic management of knowledge-related processes and activities (knowledge management) becomes a cornerstone for success.

A competent person will understand the context and fundamental nature of new and slightly different situations and readily initiate and pursue options and innovate within her Action Space and Innovation Capability. However, she may at times be uncomfortable and unwilling to consider actions outside this domain that prevent effective behavior. Hence, an assembly worker experiencing quality problems with parts supplied by another department may not wish to diagnose the situation. Instead, she may only feel comfortable by following accepted procedures for reporting the issues to the supervisor who then will handle the problems "by the book." With better contextual knowledge and with increased motivation, authority, and independence, she will develop a broader Action Space and Innovation Capability and might feel comfortable about contacting the supplying department directly to fix the problem quickly and productively without added supervisory overhead. Unfortunately, personal and organizational constraints often cause better and more effective actions to fall outside workers' Situational Awareness, Action Space, and Innovation Capability. That hinders effective Sensemaking and Decision-Making/Problem-Solving. Similar constraints exist in Situational Awareness, Action Space and Innovation,

Execution Capability, and Governance Competence and can often limit the effectiveness of the situation-handling tasks and thereby contribute to impaired enterprise performance.

A new generation of KM systematically and deliberately provides precisely such understanding, knowledge, and empowerment of individuals and enterprise departments alike. Understanding the mechanisms that underlie situation-handling models provides significant insights. By analyzing activities within the enterprise, its work functions, personnel capabilities, and competence from these perspectives, KM may be used to improve the enterprise's effectiveness appreciably. It is possible to improve knowledge diagnostics, practical knowledge transfer by, for example, learning on the job and focusing on stories in addition to memorizing facts and principles. It is also very important to secure the availability of pertinent knowledge at the point-of-action and just-in-time, provide synthesis of effective knowledge-related efforts, and foster new practices, to name a few.

The four functional proficiencies (Situational Awareness, Action Space and Innovation Capability, Execution Capability, and Governance Competence and Perspectives) constitute important practical issues in any organization. Fortunately, many limiting factors in personal situation-handling can be alleviated by increasing employees' task and general knowledge. Of particular importance are their understanding of enterprise goals and how they, as individuals, benefit from working effectively. Organizational situation-handling can also be enhanced by building structural intellectual capital in many different forms within the enterprise. Experiences indicate that action-oriented enterprise policies and practices increase both personal and enterprise Action Space and Innovations and Execution Capabilities, resulting in improved business performance. When guidelines and policies are flexible and people understand the desired enterprise direction, they pursue enterprise intents to a greater degree by innovating and adjusting actions to fit the circumstances. With such an understanding, employees truly participate in implementing enterprise strategy.

Why Should We Be Concerned with Details?

The view of organizational situation-handling in this model framework provides an important tool for knowledge diagnostics, one of the least understood aspects of knowledge management. By identifying the major tasks in handling specific situations and challenges, one can quickly understand the strengths and weaknesses of the different functions of the enterprise Situational Awareness, Enterprise Action Space and Innovation Capability, Enterprise Execution Capability, and enterprise Governance Competence and Perspectives. Such insights also provide a vehicle for understanding knowledge- and resource-related problems and opportunities. The situation-handling model provides important support for organizational knowledge diagnostics by providing functional structure, definition of elements, and identification of tasks and variables.

When analyzing the causal effects behind operating and other business problems, the understanding of the underlying factors and how to deal with them is directly dependent on the depth of insights into situation-handling mechanisms. We believe that competent knowledge diagnostics requires considerable expertise about the details of knowledge-related processes. The situation-handling model gives important support for organizational knowledge diagnostics by providing functional structure, definition, and identification of the main process tasks and variables. As indicated in Figure 6-7, the model

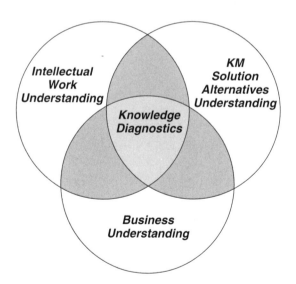

Figure 6-7
Knowledge diagnostics requires combined insights into intellectual work mechanisms, knowledge-related solution alternatives, and business processes. Copyright © 2002 Knowledge Research Institute, Inc. and Karl M. Wiig. Reproduced with permission.

supports knowledge diagnostics by providing specific comprehension of intellectual work understanding with additional insights into KM solutions.

Appendix
Action Program Details of the Enterprise Situation-Handling Example

The executive team stated that they needed to deal with each of the five original issues as follows:

Issue 1. It was judged that lack of motivation and responsiveness was caused by each person's lack of understanding about how his or her daily work supported and was part of implementing Asterix's strategy and intents — and how the employee benefited from making the strategy succeed.

Immediate Action 1-1: Work quickly with selected CSRs to identify their understanding of Asterix's strategy and how in their work they could implement the strategy and intents and, in return, how the CSRs themselves would benefit. Immediately follow up with senior management representatives to work with every CRS in small groups to create understanding of the strategy and make them appreciate how important they are.

Rationale: Employee emotion, loyalty, mentality, and resulting motivation were impaired by not understanding and appreciating the key roles they played and how their behavior affected Asterix's market standing and success and therefore their own future.

Expected Result: CSRs would understand and be motivated to participate in implementing Asterix's strategy.

Next Step: A task force was named, led by the vice president of Planning (a major force behind Asterix's strategy), an innovative Human Resource manager, the director of Customer Service, and most of the CSRs, a few at the time. They were to complete their task over the next two weeks.

Immediate Action 1-2: Create and implement positive incentives and control measures to promote better responsiveness by CSRs.

Rationale: CSRs needed both quick positive reinforcement and monitoring to ascertain that their actions were appropriate.

Expected Result: CSRs would have strengthened motivation and would quickly change behavior.

Next Step: The director of Customer Service working with his senior CSRs would create an interim incentive and control program for presentation to the executive team within one week. (Coordinate with Immediate Action 2-3.)

Immediate Action 1-3: Identify any individuals with incorrigible negative attitudes for reassignment or termination for cause.

Rationale: Some individuals might be beyond redemption and should not remain.

Expected Results: Reducing bad influences makes it easier to strengthen group behavior.

Next Step: The vice president of Human Resources working with her senior staff and Legal would identify individuals and prepare for termination after personal consultation with Ken Haas — starting immediately.

Longer-Term Action 1-1: Repeat the work to identify how the strategy should be understood and implemented with all other units.

Later, it would be possible to communicate the strategy by conducting "knowledge-café" discussions or similar sessions after determining implementation details for new strategies.

Rationale: People everywhere in the enterprise should understand how their work supports strategy implementation.

Expected Result: Much better strategy implementation everywhere.

Next Step: The original team led by the vice president of Planning would continue work throughout the enterprise. The team should consider whether Asterix should acquire knowledge management expertise to assist in the effort.

Longer-Term Action 1-2: Create and promulgate a "Service Paradigm" for all rank-and-file, supervisors, and managers.

Rationale: People need clear guidelines, frameworks, and role models to behave effectively in all facets of their work life.

Expected Result: A supported mentality and culture resulting in more effective employee behavior.

Next Step: The executive team with assistance of Human Resources should lead to the creation of the service paradigm.

Issue 2. The belief held by Marketing and Sales people that Asterix was ahead of competitors was falsely based on inadequate competitor assessments and market intelligence.

Immediate Action 2-1: Undertake a new marketing study — vigilantly, quickly, and with new methods and sources. Employ outside parties if necessary.

Rationale: Present market intelligence monitoring was inadequate and needed to be replaced, immediately by a quick study and in the longer term by a new system.

Expected Result: Better and more realistic understanding of markets, competitors, and Asterix's achieved position relative to other parties.

Next Step: Marketing to sequester two senior employees to perform the study with the help of Sales and others as required. Report back weekly with findings.

Immediate Action 2-2: Marketing, Sales, and all others with outside contacts to immediately share market intelligence results by posting on new bulletin board and engaging in personal interactions.

Rationale: Marketing and Sales people and others needed to be given incentives to collaborate on customer and competitive intelligence.

Expected Result: Improved market understanding would build better insights into Asterix's strengths and weaknesses, with the result that Marketing and Sales efforts would be better targeted and lead to greater sales.

Next Step: Marketing, Human Resources, and Information Management collaborate to create the intranet bulletin board to be operational within one week. Marketing and Human Resources to facilitate discussion groups and other people interactions to be started within a week.

Immediate Action 2-3: Create incentives to make it rewarding and natural for Marketing and Sales people to collaborate and provide disincentives to pursue interdepartmental rivalries.

Rationale: Current reward systems reinforced individualism instead of collective group success and ability to build consolidated understanding of the market.

Expected Result: Collaboration to obtain better understanding of competitive and market forces, threats, and opportunities.

Next Step: One director from Marketing and one from Sales would create an interim incentive and control program for presentation to the executive team within one week. (Coordinate with Immediate Action 1-2.)

Longer-Term Action 2-1: Change the enterprisewide personnel evaluation system to reinforce integrative behavior and enterprisewide success through collaboration.

Rationale: The present personnel evaluation system promoted behavior counter to desired management philosophy.

Expected Result: Increased collaboration and cooperation would over time lead to better networking, faster and more effective actions, fewer wasted efforts, lower costs, quicker time-to-market, greater customer satisfaction, and so on — all leading to greater success.

Next Step: Create taskforce led by personal involvement of CEO with head of Human Resources and five others from throughout the enterprise. Legal counsel in advisory capability. The new evaluation system should be operational within three months.

Issue 3. Asterix needed to be more innovative in introducing competitive features. They needed to live up to the adage that "No longer is it enough to learn faster than our competitors — we must also innovate faster and better than they do!"

Immediate Action 3-1: Review all existing R&D projects (as well as some that have been discontinued) to expedite those that best supported Asterix's strategy and competitive position. (Coordinate with Immediate Action 4-1.)

Rationale: Several members of the executive team doubted that every R&D project provided the best possible benefits. Some R&D, Marketing, and Engineering personnel also had voiced similar opinions.

Expected Result: Fast-track implementation of features that would be of value to customers and make competitive differences.

Next Step: Marketing, Engineering, and R&D vice presidents to review all projects while consulting with others as required. Report back to executive team in 14 days.

Longer-Term Action 3-1: Consider the notion of making available five selected soon-to-be-manufactured new features as no cost enhancements (standard equipment) on new trucks and perhaps also as no-cost retrofits on trucks sold within the last year.

Rationale: These features, some similar to features offered as standard by competitors, were both visible and valuable and would be noticed by customers.

Expected Result: New trucks would be more competitive. Customers with recent purchases would be pleased. Market image would be improved. Expectations for future performance would increase.

Next Step: Marketing, Sales, Engineering, and Manufacturing would create a taskforce to decide how to handle the situation. The taskforce would report back in one month.

Longer-Term Action 3-2: Create a revised R&D project plan for the next few years with new priorities, new funding requirements, new schedules. The plan would make explicit how each project would support Asterix's strategy and intents. The plan would include scenarios for how trucks, trucking, and movement of goods might change over the next five to ten years.

Rationale: Prior R&D plans were inadequate and based on business-as-usual.

Expected Result: A product development program that would be competitive for years.

Next Step: Vice presidents of Planning, Marketing, Sales, Engineering, and Manufacturing would participate and act as a taskforce.

Longer-Term Action 3-3: Create a framework for maintaining a flexible forward-looking strategy for Asterix to pursue as the transportation world changes.

Rationale: It is likely that the nature of goods transport and trucking at some time will deviate from present business-as-usual, and at that time it will be important for survival that Asterix is prepared to participate in the changes (but not necessarily lead them).

Expected Result: A strategic posture that can adopt new directions before it will be too late, making it possible for Asterix to remain viable and vibrant for a long time.

Next Step: Form a taskforce consisting of an executive team and the vice presidents of Planning and Marketing.

Issue 4. Features and innovations needed to be created and tested in close collaboration with customers and with better ergonomics.

Immediate Action 4-1: Engage customer managements and operating personnel to review and test recent or forthcoming product features. Consider potential redesign and new priorities for features. Report back within one month. (Coordinate with Immediate Action 3-1.)

Rationale: Some recent features had problems, and it was quite possible that new features would also have problems unless vetted by customers.

Expected Result: More reliable and acceptable features.

Next Step: Create a temporary taskforce with a total of four representatives from R&D, Marketing (Customer Service), Engineering, and Manufacturing.

Longer-Term Action 4-1: Create strategic relationships with suppliers and both large and small customers to propose, evaluate, review, and test new truck features. Consider obtaining ergonomics capabilities by hiring, consulting, or developing university relationships.

Rationale: People who manage and use trucks and truck fleets often have ideas about valuable changes and new features. Suppliers have new solutions. New truck features need to be considered desirable, valuable, and practical.

Expected Result: Advanced, practical, reliable, desirable, and highly competitive product and service features introduced in a timely fashion.

Next Step: R&D and Marketing vice presidents set up permanent taskforce to create and manage strategic product relationships.

Issue 5. Asterix sales staff had insufficient understanding of their truck's economic performance.

Immediate Action 5-1: Make life-cycle cost projections for several scenarios to understand reasons for customer concerns and estimates. Contact selected customers to identify the life-cycle cost assumptions and procedures that they use. Also, attempt to create life-cycle cost scenarios for main competitors' trucks for comparison.

Rationale: Since life-cycle costs were part of customer decisions, it was imperative to understand how Asterix's trucks performed under different scenarios.

Expected Result: Understanding of the strengths and weaknesses of the life-cycle cost elements for each of Asterix's trucks under different customer scenarios.

Next Step: Marketing and Accounting create taskforce with the assistance of Customer Service and Sales to perform the analyses and to report back in three weeks.

Longer-Term Action 5-1: Evaluate which pricing changes, production cost reductions, new product and service offerings, etc., should be considered to improve the economics for different truck models for different customer scenarios.

Rationale: Insufficient attention had been given to optimize the economics of Asterix's trucks as seen from different customers' perspectives.

Expected Result: Greater competitive economics.

Next Step: Marketing to create a two-month taskforce to propose changes.

Longer-Term Action 5-2: Reorganize spare parts logistics to maximize spare parts geographical availability and reduce waiting time to minimize customer truck downtime.

Rationale: The present philosophy had been to minimize spare parts inventories at the expense of availabilities and Customer Service.

Expected Result: Increased customer satisfaction and economics.

Next Step: Logistics director with the assistance of CSRs and Accounting were to form taskforce to address inventory and customer service issues.

As a result of this program, nine immediate actions and nine long-term actions were implemented, with broad involvement of the whole Asterix enterprise.

Notes

1. The problem of having the rank-and-file understand the enterprise strategy is recognized as very serious for many, perhaps most, enterprises and has led to both dissatisfying performance and business failures.
2. See Chapter 7 for a discussion of service paradigms.
3. Experts often require little but selective information to handle situations, whereas people dealing with unfamiliar situations, such as novices, require a much larger complement of information to handle them.
4. Sensemaking within the organization has been treated extensively by Weick (1995) who emphasizes how disorderly — complex and ambiguous — the organizational environment is. Weick provides insights into how organizational sensemaking is created retrospectively and retroactively, hence providing building blocks for both personal mental reference models and institutional reference models such as organizational systems, procedures, and practices. Such sensemaking provides understanding of the World-That-Was and may not be valid for dealing proactively with the World-That-Comes.

7

PEOPLE-FOCUSED KNOWLEDGE MANAGEMENT IN DAILY OPERATIONS

PREMISE 7-1: KNOWLEDGE DRIVES ENTERPRISE PERFORMANCE

Knowledge is the primary driver of enterprise performance. Knowledge affects performance by making it possible for people to perform good and effective actions. Application of better knowledge provides opportunities for better performance.

PREMISE 7-2: KNOWLEDGE MUST BE MANAGED

The mechanism by which knowledge affects performance is through people; hence, we must facilitate and strengthen the knowledge-related processes, activities, and practices that make it possible for people and organizational entities to make effective actions. The efforts to facilitate and organize knowledge production and utilization is knowledge management.

PREMISE 7-3: EFFECTIVE KNOWLEDGE MANAGEMENT MUST BE PEOPLE-FOCUSED

Enterprise performance is determined by knowledge-based people-actions, and the effectiveness of actions results from knowledge utilized to handle situations. It is clear that KM must be people-focused.

PREMISE 7-4: SIX FACTORS DETERMINE PERSONAL KNOWLEDGE-RELATED EFFECTIVENESS

The effectiveness of personal knowledge-related actions is directly affected by (1) management philosophy and practices; (2) deliberate

213

and systematic knowledge management; (3) knowledge and other resources; (4) motivation and personal energy; (5) opportunities; and (6) permission (as discussed in Chapter 2).

THE VIGILANT KNOWLEDGE COMPANY EXAMPLE

Paul Horner, chairman, president, and CEO of Palmera Corporation, was delighted with the performance of his company. Palmera was the world's leading manufacturer and supplier of high-technology consumer goods and had been able to increase its competitive lead through intelligence and dedication. The company was known for its innovative research and development that often were made into market-ready products faster than any of its competitors could match. Yet, Palmera employees did not seem to work harder than anyone else. Instead, they seemed to enjoy themselves and achieved a balance between their work lives and private lives that others could only dream about. How did they do it?

Palmera is a company with a century-long history of adapting to new markets and challenges by proactive thinking and an internal culture that has favored expertise, innovation and daring, flexibility, fairness, and a strong sense of family. When Paul became CEO a decade ago, he supported these values implicitly but decided to make them explicit and provide business reasons to back them. On top of his agenda he placed the goal for Palmera to be a combined global market and product leader, which was ambitious since Palmera was breaking into new products.

Paul, supported and assisted by his management team and Board of Directors, stated Palmera's intentions by outlining principles for management beliefs and company and personal competence objectives that can be summarized as follows.

Management Belief-Related Principles
- The individual — whether an employee, business partner, or customer — should be respected, which entails open communication, fairness, mutual trust, and learning from human differences.
- A balance is to be achieved between work content and personal interests and needs; that balance has an impact on employee well-being in order to maintain work-life balance according to employees' changing needs and life situations.

- Palmera will pursue approaches to treat people with dignity and opportunities based on the strong evidence that organizations experience a 30 to 40 percent productivity advantage when they treat their people "right."
- The four fundamentals of the management philosophy are: Palmera values, achievement-based recognition, professional and personal growth, and work-life balance.
- Stakeholders are: Palmera as an operational entity, employees and their families, customers, shareholders, suppliers and other contractors, nongovernmental organizations, governments and authorities, and citizens in areas where Palmera operates.
- Palmera's impact on society comes with responsibilities that go beyond providing useful, safe, and quality products. By conducting business in a responsible way, Palmera can make a significant contribution to sustainable development and provide a strong foundation for economic growth.

Company and Personal Competence-Related Objectives
- Employees are persuaded to develop an understanding of what is expected from them, how their individual achievements support Palmera's overall strategy, and how they benefit and are rewarded as a result. Employees are motivated to be responsible for their own development and to take advantage of the available development opportunities that Palmera provides.
- Continuous learning encourages employees to develop themselves and to find ways to improve their own and Palmera's performance. Employees continuously look for ways to stay at the forefront of technological development, share experiences, take risks, and learn together.
- Continuous learning is not just studying and training; it also means that people support each other's growth, develop and improve their relationships through common exchanges, and develop ideas in open discussion and debate. On-the-job learning is also heavily encouraged.
- Coaching is regarded as a vital part of continuous learning and provides role models and opportunities to build mental reference models.
- Participating in different teams fuels employees' development and provides them opportunities to share ideas and goals with innovators and industry leaders.

- Employees are encouraged to improve their competencies through changing their positions. The aim is to give Palmera people the opportunity to manage their own careers.
- Personal growth is to be fostered in a challenging environment, with clear visions, goals, and shared management and operational principles.
- R&D's five rules for competitive innovation are to spread people around to maximize interaction opportunities; keep teams small to allow all voices to be heard (listen!); use flat hierarchies to minimize bureaucracy; encourage unusual ("crazy") ideas beyond normal boundaries — celebrate tinkering and side projects; welcome mistakes, for if there are no mistakes, we don't push the envelope hard enough!

The company and personal competence-related objectives in effect rely extensively on active pursuit of new generation knowledge management (NGKM), which is practiced widely, deliberately, and systematically throughout Palmera. However, the term *knowledge management* is not used, at least not officially. Instead, the active management of knowledge — development of personal and structural knowledge and intellectual capital (IC) and associated innovation and competitive quality of work — is considered to be a natural and integrated part of Palmera work styles and culture.

NEW GENERATION KNOWLEDGE MANAGEMENT

What is Deliberate and Systematic Knowledge Management?

Knowledge Management is the Major Enabler of Enterprise Performance. People's behaviors are guided and shaped by what they know, understand, and believe, consciously or tacitly. Knowledge, therefore, is the fundamental factor — the major enabler — of enterprise performance. Consequently, a major task for any enterprise is deliberately and systematically to ascertain that personal and structural knowledge — intellectual capital assets of all kinds — are created, captured, shared, and leveraged to improve performance, and are also recycled to continually be improved. The initiatives and activities undertaken and the practices pursued to achieve this goal are what we mean by knowledge management.

Hence, knowledge management is the systematic and deliberate creation, building, renewal, application, and leveraging of knowledge and other intellectual capital (IC) assets to maximize the individual's and the enterprise's knowledge-related effectiveness and returns.

Our primary interest in operating any enterprise is to make it perform well. Through its actions, we want the enterprise to succeed and prosper to the best possible extent by fulfilling its objectives. To achieve that purpose, we focus on the individual since the enterprise's overall behavior is the aggregation of individual actions by people and entities throughout the organization.

In daily operations, knowledge enables effective enterprise performance by making it possible for people to handle situations in ways that are in the enterprise's best interest. Other factors also influence people's actions, but knowledge — understanding, competence, expertise, skills, etc. — becomes the central factor in as much as it directly influences motivation and other subordinate factors. However, it is knowledge that provides insights into what happens in a given situation, why and what to do with it — how to handle it, and how to do what is needed — how to act to change the situation to the best advantage.

Consequently, the issue of assisting the workforce to act effectively by being knowledgeable becomes a major concern. We need to strengthen the knowledge-related processes, activities, and practices by conducting active knowledge management. And if we agree that KM is that important, we need to make it part of our daily operations and pursue it deliberately and systematically. Given these premises, we must consider how we facilitate the processes that make people better actors. Since enterprise performance is determined by people's actions and people's effectiveness results from the knowledge they utilize to handle situations, it is clear that KM must be people-focused.

The focus of KM changed from artificial intelligence in the early 1980s to information technology (IT) during the 1990s, a focus that for many is still dominant. However, with experiences within many advanced and proactive organizations, the focus has started to shift toward KM as a major enabler of the performance of individuals. The focus becomes centered on how we assist people in performing their daily jobs better and how we motivate them to align their work closer to the enterprise's intended direction. The need for a new generation KM (NGKM) has emerged, a direction to govern knowledge-related investments, activities, and support systems that are people-focused and people-friendly and frequently supported significantly by IT. Those who now practice NGKM find it important to practice it systematically to obtain the desired benefits and to make it part of their employees' daily work-life.

NGKM relies on practices that make it a natural part of people's daily work-life. In part, NGKM focuses on "natural knowledge management," which makes it second nature and provides emotionally preferred approaches to work. Our emerging understanding of how people and organizational entities function, make decisions, and handle situations with mental models and other reference models has also changed our approaches to the "management" of knowledge. Although knowledge itself cannot be managed, knowledge-related processes, activities, and practices can be managed, as can conditions related to knowledge creation, innovation, and use. Our understanding of the deeper workings of these processes is emerging, notably our understanding of the role of stories for education and the transfer of concepts, paradigms, and methodologies. Stories also provide important foundations for developing the mental reference models that we use tacitly and naturally to handle situations — by "covert activation of biases related to previous emotional experiences of comparable situations," as stated by Bechara *et al.* (1997, p. 1294). NGKM becomes strategically and operationally important by the explicit recognition of the human as a central knowledge-creator, keeper of knowledge and knowledge-driven performer of work, and in the aggregate the source of enterprise actions and behavior.

New Generation Knowledge Management Is Different

Compared to earlier KM generations, NGKM is more highly integrated with the enterprise's philosophy, strategy, goals, practices, systems, and procedures and how it becomes part of each employee's daily work-life and motivation. NGKM is different because its concern is for the overall enterprise performance as well as each individual within it. Its emphasis is on utilizing all available scientific and professional insights to provide the best possible KM support for the enterprise. These differences lead NGKM practitioners to pursue KM approaches that are systemically combined with all other practices and activities, both within the enterprise and in interactions with all outside parties. The characteristics of NGKM include the following.

- *Broad and Proactive Business Philosophy and Management Beliefs — Not Static and Mechanistic Control*
  NGKM pursues anti-Tayloristic and anti-Command-and-Control management models. Its model rests on the need to provide clear leadership and the belief that employees perform better and support the enterprise more effectively when they are competently knowledgeable, given appropriate action freedom and authority, work in a supportive culture, and still are held accountable for their actions. The NGKM model, as practiced by many organizations, relies extensively on management and leadership examples, proactive mentality, and agile and adaptive behaviors to take advantage of opportunities and adapt to changes. The model is supportive of employees' welfare and motivations. Furthermore, it minimizes the technology-based view of KM. Instead, it adopts people-focused views of the enterprise's work, its ability to innovate and learn, and the role of human intellectual capital (IC) in the enterprise's capital accounting. For discussion of intellectual capital, see Amidon (2003), Edvinsson (2002), Roos *et al.* (1998), Stewart (1997, 2002), and Sveiby (1997).
  The philosophy and beliefs behind the management model embrace perspectives that are much broader than those found in many businesses. It adopts what many studies have verified that organizations experience a 30 to 40 percent productivity advantage when they treat their people "right." In particular, in addition to considering short-term operational and survival needs (to meet financial obligations, for example), there is a focus on the long-term viability of the enterprise. Furthermore, beyond concerns for first-order impacts of actions, there are concerns for second- and higher-order implications of actions as they affect stakeholders of all kinds, including employees, the society, and the environment. These considerations are not new. They have been observed by enterprises for centuries and are common traits within enterprises that have been in

existence for over 100 years in many organizations (de Geus 1997).

■ *Knowledge-Focused Business Strategies and Practices*

Enterprises that pursue NGKM exploit knowledge-related opportunities and strengths in their strategies. Some enterprises target new markets with specially developed knowledge capabilities, such as when customer service representatives in the financial industry develop expert ability to deliver new areas of advice to clients. Others collaborate extensively with clients and suppliers to develop new products and services that are based on specifically developed knowledge assets. These approaches differ from regular research and development (R&D) activities by their specific focus on creating and leveraging knowledge flows in new ways.

■ *Knowledge and Intellectual Capital Stewardship Mentality*

As discussed further in the next section, NGKM practitioners develop widely shared mindsets across their organizations. Since people's mindsets are major drivers of the organization's culture, the culture becomes knowledge-focused, even knowledge-vigilant.

■ *Systemic, Self-Sustaining, and Self-Renewing KM Practices*

NGKM practices are systemic. The practices have become part of the culture; they are distributed, understood, and generally pursued by employees everywhere within the enterprise. The wide distribution and utilization have led them to be adopted by people across the enterprises. They have become self-sustained. In addition, people at all levels innovate to make the KM practices better and more effective, with the result that the practices are steadily improved and renewed.

■ *Systems Perspective of Enterprise and Environment*

In the proactive enterprise, managers and people at any level tend to adopt systems perspectives of knowledge-related processes.[1] They perceive the enterprise as consisting of many closely coupled dynamic systems or processes that influence each other and change as a result of external influences or internal dynamics. They also perceive the enterprise to be part of a larger system — the society, the environment, the economy, with customers, competitors, suppliers, governments, and so on.

When working with systems perspectives, people see their work and actions as part of a much larger whole. In the extreme, it could make them helpless to deal with an impossibly complex world. However, healthy systems perspectives set priorities and focus on expediency and target processes while considering wider implications.

- *Vigilant Application of State-of-the-Art KM Practices and Infrastructure Capabilities*

    KM methods and practices are under constant development. New and more effective state-of-the-art options are steadily becoming available. Increasingly, these approaches build on improved understanding of IC-related processes and mechanisms, which may be cognitive, psychological, social, organizational, economic, or technical. As new KM methods are developed, some replace other practices, but overall, current, well-established KM practices are effective and continue to deliver good business value. NGKM practitioners pursue knowledge-vigilant practices. Whenever possible, they adopt KM approaches that will provide the most favorable cost effectiveness as seen from enterprise objectives.

In addition to adopting concrete operational practices, NGKM practitioners also subscribe to abstract models of how to manage knowledge. They develop advanced visions and plans for shaping and taking advantage of KM for improving strategies and operations. Practitioners develop management philosophies that build partly on insights from state-of-the-art KM concepts and experiences in other organizations. When conducting benchmarking, NGKM practitioners focus not only on what was done successfully, but also on the associated costs and results. They are as concerned with the conceptual considerations of "What is the context?" "Why was it done?" "Why was it done in the particular way?" "What did it require in terms of added expertise and management and operating practices?" "Which cultural changes needed to be introduced?" "How did personal motivations need to be influenced?" and "Which problems were encountered, and how were they overcome?" These factors are different from traditional benchmarking methods but are important for obtaining the required insights.

NGKM relies on natural and commonly pursued practices such as storytelling, knowledge sharing, apprentice nurturing, collaboration, and other behaviors that are instinctive and effortless for people. The reliance on such practices is particularly apparent when such behaviors are supported by the reigning cultures. Some of these behaviors are innately natural, whereas others become the most natural choices when fostered through management examples and incentives.

New Opportunities Require New Efforts and Directions

Enterprises that pursue NGKM operate differently from other organizations in several ways. Most importantly, they plan strategic moves based on existing and developing knowledge and IC assets to pursue new directions. They create increased competitive value through innovation, expertise, and other results from their knowledge and from IC assets, which are continually improved by NGKM. They foster and maintain open and supportive, yet goal-oriented and accountable, environments by pursuing widespread IC stewardship mentality. This mentality is promoted by senior management participation, particularly when they are positive role models. The focus is on maximizing enterprise effectiveness and performance and on adopting long-term perspectives and performance objectives subject to short-term health and survival. They pursue interdisciplinary approaches for NGKM and for integrative management, seeking to provide the most conducive conditions for effective work, motivation, and employee dedication (Buckman 2004).

Perspectives on New Generation Knowledge Management

Practical KM work requires effective communication and sharing and understanding across all levels within the enterprise. For that purpose, it is helpful to understand the concerns and perspectives held by people in different positions. Knowledge management and the broader responsibility, intellectual capital governance, can be viewed from different perspectives ranging from national-societal levels, enterprise-business levels, to operational-implementation levels. For an overview of five main perspectives, see Figure 7-1.

Societal/Global Perspectives focus on building knowledge-related capabilities to improve regional and societal competitiveness and capabilities. Examples include a systematized educational process for the current and future workforce and the development of quality industrial and business expertise.

Strategic Perspectives focus on creating and expanding relationships with customers, suppliers, and other stakeholders to create strategic products and services. Examples include developing new strategies based on knowledge capabilities, outsourcing innovation to suppliers, and bartering IC.

Tactical Perspectives focus on exploiting knowledge processes to achieve more effective enterprise operations. Examples include

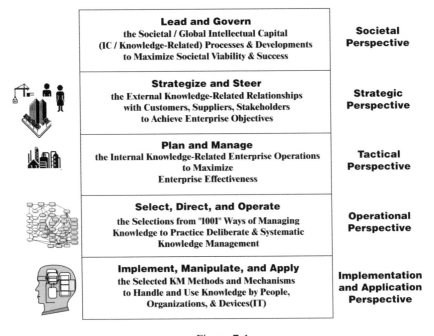

Figure 7-1
*Five levels of role perspectives on IC governance-KM. Copyright © 2000
Knowledge Research Institute, Inc. Reproduced with permission.*

KM-supported innovation to reduce operating costs, reduce time
to market, reduce employee turnover, and to improve quality.

Operational Perspectives focus on creating and fostering general
KM practice and initiating and managing individual knowledge
processes. Examples include implementing KM practices such
as lessons learned programs, expert networks, and knowledge
landscape mapping.

**Knowledge Implementation, Manipulation, and Application
Perspective** focus on manipulating and applying knowledge to
reflect how people, organizations, and inanimate devices deal
with knowledge. Examples include matching knowledge to
thinking style and work requirements and transferring expertise
to other workers.

Selected aspects of the five IC governance and KM perspective levels are presented in Table 7-1. As the perspectives of people
change with different roles, their perceptions of work scopes also
change from broad and long-term considerations and policies to

Table 7-1

Focus, scope, and examples for the five IC governance-KM perspective levels.

Perspective	Focus	Scope	Example Activities	Theoretical Field Examples
Global/Societal Perspective	■ Intellectual capital governance	■ Build knowledge-related capabilities to improve societal competitiveness and capabilities\	■ Systematize education for future workforce ■ Rely on best expertise anywhere in the world	■ Socioeconomic science ■ Political science
Strategic Perspective	■ Intellectual capital governance	■ Create products and services ■ Create and expand relationships with customers, suppliers, other stakeholders	■ Outsource innovation to suppliers ■ Learn what makes customers successful ■ Barter IC	■ Market theory ■ Management theory ■ Economics
Tactical Perspective	■ Knowledge Management	■ Exploit knowledge ■ Operating costs processes to achieve more effective enterprise operation	Innovate to reduce: ■ Time to market ■ Employee turnover ■ Low quality	■ Theory of the Firm ■ Management science/Operations research
Operational Perspective	■ Knowledge Management	■ Create and foster general KM practice ■ Select, initiate, and manage individual knowledge processes	■ Lessons learned programs ■ Expert networks ■ Knowledge landscape mapping	■ Management science/Operations research ■ Social science
Implementation & Application Perspective	■ Knowledge Management ■ Knowledge engineering	■ Manipulate and apply knowledge to reflect how people, organizations, and inanimate agents deal with knowledge	■ Match provided knowledge to thinking style and work requirement ■ Transfer expertise to other workers	■ Cognitive science ■ Systems science ■ Information science

task-specific (narrow) and short-term focus on matters that support concrete work, be it teaching a class, reviewing a loan application, or repairing a diesel engine.

In any population, shared understanding is important — even required — for effective leveraging of IC assets in situations such as the knowledge-intensive work delivered by rank-and-file to implement enterprise strategy. A majority of people appear to be interested primarily in the aspects of practical work — implementation and application — while a smaller group is interested in aspects of supervisory and managerial work. Higher-level (broader perspective) work seems to interest even smaller groups. This means, at least initially, that obtaining shared understandings of the wide range of perspectives associated with IC governance and KM work may require smart approaches and focused effort.

Deliberate and Systematic Knowledge Management

Enterprises that pursue broad and systematic knowledge management — comprehensive KM — find that they pursue several practices, which in total contribute to the overall success. They are vigilant in making knowledge work effectively as the chief enabler of enterprise success. These subpractices include efforts to

Foster Knowledge-Supportive Culture — Characteristics of the general culture include a safe environment, ethical and mutually respectful behavior, minimal politicking, collaboration, and a common focus on delivering quality work without delay — that is, "getting the right thing done as soon and with as little fuss as possible!"

Provide Shared Understanding — The idea is to develop a broadly shared understanding of the enterprise's mission, current direction, and the role of the individual in support of the enterprise and the individual's own interest.

Focus the Knowledge Management Practice to Align with Enterprise Direction — Practitioners of comprehensive KM identify the intended business direction of the enterprise to ascertain that the associated knowledge-related factors receive appropriate attention and are well maintained.

Practice Accelerated Learning — A broad range of knowledge transfer activities are pursued to ascertain that valuable knowledge is captured, organized and structured, deployed widely, and used and leveraged. The impetus is to make important knowledge flow rapidly, in proper quantities, in well-represented and effective ways, and to all valuable destinations.

Pursue the Six Success Factors — These factors focus on providing managers and all employees with:

1. **Management Philosophy and Practice** — General beliefs that people will act effectively and responsibly when satisfied with their conditions, given the chance to contribute and when they understand that it is in their interest. However, it must also be realized that a few employees may have adverse personal agendas.

2. **Deliberate and Systematic Knowledge Management** — Personal knowledge and structural IC assets are the most important factors behind enterprise success, and these assets must be managed diligently. They must be created, renewed, and exploited for the greatest benefit to all concerned by deliberate and systematic KM. That includes creating a widespread intellectual asset management mentality and culture.

3. **Knowledge and Resources** — Professional, craft, and navigational knowledge and metaknowledge, information, and other necessary resources must be made available for employees to deliver quality work products that satisfy the requirements of the situation and the general service paradigm. Employees must also possess requisite skills and attitudes (that is, personality traits). They must be supported by their ability to think critically and creatively by being provided with relevant metaknowledge.

4. **Opportunities** — Employees must be placed in situations where they have the opportunity to use their capabilities. Work flows must be organized to take advantage of people's capabilities and to exploit the potentials for innovation and application of diversity.

5. **Permission** — Employees must be provided safe environments. They must therefore be given permission to innovate, improvise, and "stretch" enterprise policies and practices beyond predetermined scopes to serve the enterprise's, and the stakeholders', best interest.

6. **Motivation** — Employees must be motivated to act intelligently, "to do the right thing," by being shown that their actions will be of value to stakeholders, the enterprise, and, most importantly, to themselves. This factor is most important but difficult to effectuate. It requires adopting new approaches to effective and active communication.

Provide Effective Governance for the Knowledge Management Practice — Management must monitor, evaluate, and guide the KM activities and their plans, results, and opportunities.

Create Supportive Infrastructure Capabilities — Management must implement new or adapt existing capabilities to provide needed and effective supports for KM.

Deliberate and systematic KM does not mean top-down autocratic determination of which knowledge must be utilized to perform desired work competently. Instead, it means the creation of a knowledge-vigilant culture guided from the top with a stewardship mentality, where each individual and each department, as part of their daily work, continually look out for the knowledge perspective to ensure that appropriate expertise and understanding are used to deliver the desired work. Such practices lead to the creation of synergistic knowledge-focused mentalities and cultures. The comprehensive KM culture recognizes a particular aspect of personal behavior. This aspect deals with the realization that many individuals deliver outstanding work in unusual situations without having extensive topic knowledge. Instead, as discussed in Chapter 2, they have strong metaknowledge that enables them to make sense of novel situations and create effective approaches to handle them.

New Generation Knowledge Management Foci

In some ways NGKM provides a whole new direction for corporate leadership and practices as has been demonstrated by several organizations. It requires new efforts from both suppliers and user organizations. By being better engineered cognitively, socially, and technically, NGKM practices are easier and more natural to use and become the preferred modes of operations by managers and the workforce alike.

NGKM leads to higher levels of effectiveness and performance in personal, enterprise, and regional or national innovation, and success in securing competitiveness and viability.

People Focus

- Cognitive sciences research, which provides practical insights into how people learn, possess knowledge, use knowledge in different kinds of work, innovate, and become motivated. These developments provide the foundation needed to create KM approaches that will effectively support work environments and gain broad acceptance.

- Research on the nature, role, and use of stories and other KM-related knowledge-sharing processes that fit naturally and easily into people's work styles and enterprise business functions. This research includes new methods for transfer cognitive skills between people.
- Approaches to build and teach metaknowledge such as critical thinking to make people competent to tackle unfamiliar challenges and opportunities.
- Methods to provide educational and other means for people to build libraries of mental reference models relevant to the work complexities they face.
- Increased understanding of how to prepare and furnish IC assets to individuals and organizations to improve knowledge work. This includes business and work functions simulators and "games" for fast, effective training and creation of work-related operational mental model libraries for routine work and for development of critical thinking and abstract mental models for the more general and infrequent challenges.
- Knowledge-related situation-handling and other analysis and action-oriented behavioral models that explain and provide frameworks for analysis and development of KM capabilities. As was indicated in Figure 5.2, from a situation-handling perspective, decision making is an integral part of a chain of tasks starting with observation and receiving situation information and resulting in action.

Enterprise Focus

- Understanding that competitiveness requires innovating and learning faster than competitors and that deliberate and systematic KM is the key to achieve objectives.
- Understanding that strategies are implemented by the rank-and-file and that the workforce needs in-depth understanding of enterprise goals and of how they, as individuals, contribute and benefit from delivering effective work.
- New approaches to make personnel at all levels know and understand enterprise strategy and appreciate how they, as

individuals, can participate in implementing enterprise strategy and intents.

- Powerful new methods for transfer of personal knowledge into structural IC, including targeted ontologies.
- Knowledge diagnostics and related analysis approaches to identify, describe, and find the means to address critical knowledge functions and opportunities. Most of these approaches require expertise and insights into several disciplines and are based on an understanding of underlying knowledge-related mechanisms that affect work and performance.

A new awareness is emerging among KM practitioners and theoreticians that KM in the global economy must become more effective. Several issues have emerged.

- The KM scope must be broadened not only to include operational considerations, but also to be colinear with the enterprise (company, city, country) strategy, direction, and purpose. (Buckman 2004)
- The KM scope must be broadened to focus on long-term viability, constrained by the needs to secure short-term survival (to avoid bankruptcy, for example).
- Enterprise KM must be practiced according to "benevolent IC governance," that is, utilizing gentle and flexible top-down visioning and planning while avoiding regimentation and bureaucratization.
- KM efforts must be self-sustaining and self-renewing, requiring that KM (i.e., IC leveraging mentality) become an automatic and integral part of everybody "living the job."
- KM must be people-focused, not technology-centric, and must rely on people-related mechanisms such as storytelling, communities of practice (CoP), and social networking.
- KM must be in harmony with culture and with the joint values of the enterprise, employees, and external stakeholders.
- Modern IT is vital, at this time primarily for simple automation and the KM-infrastructure, but at a later time also for intelligent applications (in part to offload reasoning and other mental tasks from knowledge workers).
- There is a need to conceptualize an integrated perspective of all the "pieces" of KM into a greater, systematic, and coordinated whole. The effectiveness of KM is reduced when many efforts, such as knowledge sharing, storytelling, communities of prac-

tice, knowledge harvesting, and IT-based KM systems, are found to work in isolation and at cross purposes.

Technology Focus

- Broad artificial intelligence (AI) technologies for automation of reasoning in operations, diagnostics and trouble-shooting, research and creative exploration, and information management.
- Natural language understanding (NLU) and reasoning for information management tasks such as abstracting, prioritizing, and routing, and for automated situation-handling of cases with varying complexity.
- Automated performance support systems (PSS) to complement knowledge workers with reasoning and other capabilities for complex tasks.
- Mathematical modeling of business and social processes to support "soft computing" and other exploratory and computational synthesis methods.
- Greater reasoning sophistication of computer-based systems to reduce operating costs, improve reliability of routine tasks, and free employees to perform higher value work.
- State-of-the-art information technology-based infrastructure functions to support communication, collaboration, and many other processes.

The Bar Has Been Raised — NGKM Implications

NGKM provides new opportunities and many challenges for researchers and KM capability suppliers, whether consultants, technology suppliers, or other parties. Researchers in areas such as the cognitive sciences, epistemology, the social sciences, organizational sciences, management theory, economics, and AI and informatics will need to tackle a range of new issues. A number of topics require investigations of how people and organizations create and utilize knowledge and how one might enhance and deal effectively with these processes with operational methods and technologies.

KM products are becoming increasingly more sophisticated, and suppliers need to include new capabilities to build their wares on firm and fundamental understandings of underlying processes and mechanisms, as explained by scientific findings and practical experience. We expect a clearer distinction between supplier types such as:

- Providers of services to create KM capabilities and associated management systems.
- Providers of tools for knowledge audits and analysis such as knowledge mapping, knowledge diagnostics, knowledge inventory management, and IC navigators.
- Providers of KM capability development tools, such as automatic reasoning tools, knowledge discovery in databases (KDD), tools to build structural knowledge from personal knowledge, and tools to create ontologies.
- Providers of support facilities for KM capabilities such as collaboration environments.
- Providers of KM capabilities such as expertise knowledge bases and educational systems.

Starting the Knowledge Management Practice

Enterprises pursue deliberate and systematic knowledge management for clearcut reasons: they wish to make people — and the whole enterprise — act intelligently, operate more effectively, and satisfy their stakeholders better. However, the practical issues of how to expand the knowledge management practice are more complex.

When knowledge management practices are implemented in an enterprise, they become part of a continued process that will be ongoing for years. Initially, "bite-sized" targeted efforts with clear bottom-line business goals should be pursued. These efforts should later be complemented with other efforts that together will create increasingly valuable capabilities for the enterprise. The nature of the process to implement capabilities in evolving situations is the foundation of a successful KM implementation process. A well-planned introduction of KM practice normally requires that nine agenda items are pursued up-front. In order of importance, these items are as follows.

- Create an **environment** of trust, ethical behavior, mutual respect, support, and open communication about individual employees' functions, roles, and importance of contribution — in part based on individual responsibility and accountability.

- Develop a **broad vision** of the knowledge management practice and obtain **buy-in** from management. Champions must have a flexible mental outline of how knowledge management might be conducted and organized to support the enterprise. This vision provides the guide for creating the needed capabilities and infrastructure and for setting priorities. It should be documented in brief discussion papers.

- Pursue a **targeted knowledge management focus** determined from knowledge landscape mapping and other insights and based on priorities that align with enterprise objectives. Undertake small and sharply focused initiatives with clear benefit expectations. These initiatives should build cumulatively to implement the broader knowledge management vision over time.

- Build a small **professional team** and allow it to **focus full time** on knowledge management. Designate one or a few highly competent employees to work almost exclusively with implementation. Avoid the common mistake of giving them additional responsibilities. This is difficult to do since these individuals tend to be some of the most valuable in the organization. The practitioners must have good understanding of "knowledge" (in contrast to "information"), its role in conducting knowledge-intensive work in target situations, methods for diagnosing, eliciting, acquiring, transferring, and organizing knowledge, and so on. These are often new professional areas for the enterprise.

- Install and agree on knowledge management **impact and benefit evaluation methods** and other instruments for providing feedback on KM progress and effects.

- Implement **incentives** to motivate individual employees to manage knowledge on personal and enterprise levels, collaborate broadly, and act intelligently — to innovate, capture, build, share, and use knowledge. The enterprise must express its support clearly. Employees on all levels must be helped to understand personal benefits resulting from active knowledge management. **Disincentives** must be removed.

- Teach **metaknowledge** to everyone. When allowed to develop metaknowledge for creative and critical thinking, knowledge workers at all levels demonstrate significant increases in their effectiveness and ability to develop and take advantage of improved subject knowledge. Metaknowledge is important for areas as disparate as situation-handling (including problem solving and decision making), systems theory, interpersonal situations, and technical work topics and may include techniques such as topic-, methodology-, and structure-related conceptual maps.

■ Select knowledge management activities that will support the six critical success factors by providing **opportunities, capabilities, motivations,** and **permissions** for individuals and the enterprise to act intelligently. Realize the full value of personal knowledge and structured knowledge assets by utilizing these assets to deliver products and services effectively. Effective intelligent behavior can only be achieved when the conditions of opportunity, capability, motivation, and permission are satisfied.

■ Create supporting **infrastructure.** Build upon existing capabilities and gradually add new ones as required to facilitate effective knowledge management, particularly in the chosen target areas. Supporting infrastructure capabilities range widely, from information and communication systems to virtual corporate universities.

Teams that have not been able to acquire a sufficient working understanding of knowledge management theory and practical approaches often yield disappointing results. Practical work requires expertise at several levels. The team must have access to expertise to deal with central issues such as:

■ Providing insights to set knowledge management priorities and strategic direction.

■ Understanding broad, enterprisewide requirements to determine needs for incentives, infrastructure, and other supports.

■ Working with knowledge-intensive functions (that is, how people — and organizations — obtain, create, hold, share, use, and apply knowledge) to determine needs and opportunities.

■ Diagnosing knowledge-related problems and opportunities by understanding how knowledge affects the ability to perform and enhance capabilities to deliver.

■ Dealing with and manipulating knowledge itself — elicit, organize, encode, deploy personal and structural knowledge for direct use, or build it into intellectual capital such as products, services, technology, or knowledge-based systems (KBS) applications.

Problems with Conventional Knowledge Management

The forays of Informatics (Information Management/Information Technology — IM/IT) into KM during the 1990s were largely ad hoc and were not solidly founded on a deeper understanding of such fundamentals as cognitive processes of people-at-work, business functions, or management philosophies and practices. The lack of customer sophistication and understanding may partly be to blame for unsophisticated market offerings and supplier focus on relatively simple solutions. When acquiring a KM/ERP system, many organizations are still surprised to find that they have installed not only a broad-ranging IM/IT capability but also a rigorous system of management and operations practices that are at odds with their management philosophies and business practices. Yet other problems have surfaced:

- Idealistic KM system implementers working in isolation from senior management create capabilities that match their personal beliefs and understandings of best operating practices but not those that the enterprise prefers. It is thereby provided with a capability that may not be used fully — or will force operating practices that may not be in its best interest.
- KM systems have been promoted to have unrealistic capabilities, with resulting frustrations, disappointments and, frequently, cancellations.
- Instead of focusing on business needs and opportunities, the focus has been on introducing KM as a generic capability of unquestioned but unspecified value. Many such KM efforts have been found to be of limited business value.
- Many KM efforts have failed after having been introduced without allocating sufficient effort — capable personnel and other resources.
- KM problems caused by lack of understanding of the long duration before the initial KM efforts translate into enterprise bottom-line results.

Most KM practitioners are aware of such problems and are working to heighten the level of understanding of what KM requires and to improve KM and related practices. As a result of these efforts, NGKM has emerged, providing KM practitioners with increasingly effective capabilities.

Fahey and Prusak (1998) highlighted another perspective on the problems often associated with conventional KM as "The Eleven Deadliest Sins of KM":

1. Not developing a working definition of knowledge
2. Emphasizing knowledge stock, not knowledge flow
3. Viewing knowledge as existing mainly outside people
4. Not understanding that a fundamental KM purpose is to create shared contexts
5. Paying little heed to the role and importance of tacit knowledge
6. Separating knowledge from its uses
7. Downplaying thinking and reasoning
8. Focusing on the past and present and not on the future
9. Failing to recognize the importance of experimentation
10. Substituting technological contact for human interface
11. Seeking to develop direct measures of knowledge

New Generation Knowledge Management Challenges

KM touches on human behavior, attitudes and capabilities, business philosophies, models, operations and practices, and complicated technologies. Creating and operating KM capabilities cover many disciplines and introduce new perspectives as illustrated in Figure 7-2. They often require integration to provide functions that are of appropriate strategic and operational support and use within the target operations.

The world around us changes constantly. Businesses invent and pursue new strategies, develop new products and services, and devise better ways of running their operations — all in the interest of remaining successful and viable. Scientists make discoveries and extend our understanding in many fields. Technologists create new devices and methods. All these developments bring new opportunities for development and, when implemented, progress. Two broad KM development areas are advancing in tandem and are influencing the value and acceptance of KM. The areas represent demand pull and supply push.

1. Management and operating philosophies and practices developments create *demand pull* to pursue IC-related capabilities in order to make enterprises perform better and more effectively.

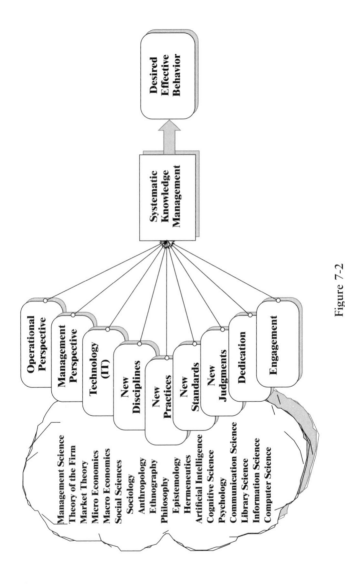

Figure 7-2

New disciplines are required to provide deliberate and systematic knowledge management and adoption of new business practices. Many diverse practices and disciplines are introduced and may be novel in the business world. Copyright © 2001 Knowledge Research Institute, Inc. Reproduced with permission.

The resulting culture reflects positive practical experiences with KM, and with marketplace and societal pressures to increase the focus on IC assets for competitive reasons and the greater understanding and capabilities of KM approaches and technologies.

2. Science and technology developments make it possible to provide *supply push* to create new solutions built on solid, relevant, and practical understandings of underlying mechanisms.

Globalization has placed businesses everywhere in new and different competitive situations where knowledgeable, effective behavior provides the competitive edge. Enterprises are turning to explicit and systematic KM to develop the intellectual capital needed to succeed. Further developments provide benefits resulting from changes in the workplace and in management and operational practices. Changes will come partly from information technology and artificial intelligence developments. However, more important changes are expected in people-focused practices to build, apply, and deploy knowledge and understanding for the support of innovative and effective knowledge-intensive work.

Much remains to be done. Our understanding of knowledge and how people use it to work has a long way to go. We need a theory of knowledge and perhaps a new theory of the firm to create a solid foundation for future KM. Still, users can expect significant benefits from KM as it develops over the next decades.

Knowledge-Focused Mentality and Corporate Culture

What's required is new accounting, a new measurement system which should be instituted internally within organizations. And we need a change in mentality.
Baruch Lev in *Business Week*, June 18, 2001, p. 30 D

No matter how intelligent a leader's strategy for change, it will fail without the dedicated support of the rank and file. Winning that support often requires more effort than devising the strategy itself.
Carol Hymowitz, "In the Lead," *Wall Street Journal*, April 24, 2002

NGKM practitioners develop widely shared mindsets across their organizations. The typical mindset focuses on three aspects:

1. The psychological, social, organizational, economic, and technical mechanisms that make knowledge and other IC assets strengthen operational and strategic situation-handling and the effectiveness of resulting actions.
2. The management of knowledge and IC assets from operational performance and investment points of view to support the enterprise and its stakeholders (including the employees themselves).
3. The equitable balance between dilemmas, such as long-term versus short-term goals, work-life versus personal well-being, "use what we have" versus invest to improve, and so on.

The mindset embraces proactive, exploratory, and innovative perspectives with the notions of the careful and responsible management of knowledge and IC assets. The mindset amounts to a benevolent knowledge and intellectual capital stewardship mentality (NGKM), which brings constructive and actionable knowledge perspectives to everyday situations, automatically and naturally. Building the mentality is achieved by helping people develop in several ways. They need to develop an understanding of options for developing, obtaining, and leveraging knowledge assets for everyday work; they need to be provided with role models; they need to be motivated; they need to understand the advantages for themselves, their customers and stakeholders, and the enterprise.

In organizations that pursue NGKM, the new mentality becomes a natural part of the daily "living the job," resulting in automatized operational considerations for how to acquire and apply the best possible expertise by collaborating, discussing with experts and peers, hiring, accessing knowledge bases, using computer models, and in numerous other ways. From strategic perspectives, NGKM makes people consider options and tradeoffs for how to invest time, effort, and resources to build knowledge and IC assets for future needs.

A new awareness for NGKM is emerging among KM practitioners and theoreticians.

- Benevolent knowledge and IC stewardship involve gentle and flexible top-down monitoring, visioning, and coordination, while avoiding regimentation and bureaucratization.
- The NGKM scope is broadened beyond operational considerations. It is colinear with enterprise (company, city, region, country) objectives, strategy, direction, and purpose.
- NGKM is in harmony with the culture and joint values of the enterprise and stakeholders.

- NGKM focuses on long-term viability, constrained by the need to secure short-term survival.
- NGKM builds knowledge and IC capabilities and assets for the future while utilizing existing ones for present effectiveness.
- NGKM efforts are self-sustaining and self-renewing. The IC leveraging mentality becomes an automatic and integral part of "living the job."
- NGKM is people-focused (not technology-centric), recognizing fundamental knowledge mechanisms.
- Modern IT is vital, designed primarily for simple automation and KM infrastructure, but later for intelligent applications to offload mental tasks from knowledge workers.
- The many isolated variations of KM thrusts such as knowledge sharing, storytelling, communities of practice, knowledge harvesting, and IT-based KM "systems," need to be conceptualized into a systematic whole for NGKM.

The Enterprise Culture

The culture within an organization is driven by many factors ranging from tradition to the behavior and philosophy of its leaders. In general, we may think of the culture as driven by and reflecting the mentality of people in the organization.

When an enterprise builds and orchestrates an internal practice to deal systematically and deliberately with knowledge by having people share insights and seek assistance from one another, a new and open culture begins to emerge. In such a culture, people find it easy to discuss difficult issues, emerging ideas, and tentative opportunities with one another. They are willing to take "mental" risks that would be unthinkable in more conventional environments. They seek collaboration to achieve better results quicker, and they are not afraid to build upon the ideas of others, or to let others build on their own ideas. In this way they, in effect, expand their action space.[2]

As people expand their action spaces, and as they become stronger through stronger collaboration, the whole enterprise improves. Complex tasks are addressed better and more quickly, but more importantly in the longer run, innovations abound and make the enterprise more capable and able to engage in activities that previously were infeasible.

Behaviors and beliefs that we find in the knowledge-vigilant cultures include:

- Belief that applied knowledge is a dominant factor in personal and enterprise effectiveness and growth.
- Actions to ascertain that the best available knowledge is applied.
- Practices to assess knowledge needs, availabilities, and potentials to build or source knowledge.
- Tendencies to build knowledge-related assets by investing wisely.
- Knowledge-cognizant organization of work, knowledge location, and organizational structure.
- Widespread exploration to improve work products.
- Threats, Opportunities, Weaknesses, Strengths (TOWS) assessments are made of knowledge needs, availabilities, and potentials to build or source.

Four Key Knowledge Management Thrusts

Experience shows that the introduction and sustained practice of coherent knowledge management which supports the success of the enterprise require the continued pursuit of four objectives:

- To develop and pursue a shared vision for the knowledge management practice that is explicit and systematic — that is, connects to and integrates with the enterprise strategy and direction and is embedded in each person's daily work.
- To understand the enterprise's overall strategy and direction and each function's service paradigm and the associated knowledge required — that is, for each point in the organization, understand the expertise and facilitators required to deliver the service paradigm.
- To create and conduct effective knowledge transfer methods — that is, deliver to the workplace the desired balance between deep and conceptual knowledge versus concrete "surface" knowledge.
- To provide incentives, infrastructure, and other supporting capabilities, including reorganization of work — that is, facilitate intelligent behavior in both individuals and the enterprise resulting from sound and effective knowledge management activities with positive support by all personnel.

The Power of Role Models, Examples, and Practices

As discussed in Chapter 4, mental reference models have a significant and dominant influence on people's instinctive and natural situation-handling. This carries over into the effects that mental models have on a person's daily behavior at work, at home, and in society generally. Mental models that govern our behavior are to a large extent based on the behavior of influential people around us whom we consider important or interesting in one way or another — our role models.

Our role models teach us and influence our behavior in many different ways. From the enterprise and societal view, good role models can show us how to be effective and work with the enterprise's intents and society's interests at heart. Bad role models can teach us to be selfish and deceptive and to handle situations that are only in our own self-interest.

Within the enterprise, the observed behavior — the individual actions — of managers serve as examples for accepted ways to deal with many aspects of the organization's affairs and operations. Managers set examples as to how to deal with ethics and truth and legal issues; customers; suppliers; fellow employees; finances and budgets; innovatation and acceptance of risk; situation-handling; short-term versus long-term issues; and a host of other aspects.

Within the enterprise, people's tendency to imitate their role models becomes a very significant issue. Leaders, whether managers or from the rank-and-file, permanently affect the behavior of others by their example. From a NGKM point of view, behavior-related mental models are taught through processes that can be shaped and monitored. Hence, we can be teamed with individuals whose actions and behaviors we might copy and imitate.

Making Everybody Understand

A major function of managing knowledge is to facilitate processes that will give people throughout an operation a common understanding. Shared understanding promotes shared goals and increases the ability to coordinate and collaborate to deliver joint work results. NGKM carries this objective further by proven approaches to build shared understanding across the enterprise (also see Dixon 2000).

Understanding the Enterprise Direction and Context

In the example at the beginning of this chapter, the business motivation for understanding enterprise direction and context is stated clearly in two of Palmera's objectives:

- Employees are persuaded to develop an understanding of what is expected from them, how their individual achievements support Palmera's overall strategy, and how they benefit and are rewarded as a result. Employees are motivated to be responsible for their own development and to take advantage of the available development opportunities that Palmera provides.
- Continuous learning encourages employees to develop themselves and to find ways to improve their own and Palmera's performance. Employees continuously look for ways to develop so that they can stay at the forefront of technological development, share experiences, take risks, and learn together.

The Service Paradigm

Proactive enterprise managements look beyond daily work; in addition, they pursue durable performance over the long term by maintaining broad awareness. They emphasize that they themselves and their employees not only deliver work products directly associated with their functional job descriptions and immediate work but also act productively and responsibly in other respects as well. In particular, proactive enterprises expect that all employees, departments, and organizational entities, as part of their daily activities, will support a wider scope of work and participate in the implementation of enterprise strategy and the principles of governance.

Within an enterprise, each operating entity — department, unit, team, and individual employees — is expected to deliver business services in the form of work products in support of the enterprise's purpose. The desired business services can be defined explicitly within narrow scopes and in considerable detail as explicit job descriptions, or they can be quite general and broad. Many organizations utilize *service paradigms* to outline the broader nature of the desired services, at times as a complement to the job description. Service paradigms define expectations for employee and entity behaviors from the perspectives of external and internal customers, the enterprise, and other stakeholders. In general terms, the service paradigm describes how products and services are delivered and how employees are expected to act and perform. The purpose of service paradigms is not to specifically outline which deliverables should be produced and how they should be created and delivered; other vehicles do that.

Service paradigms serve several purposes. On a higher level, their main purpose is to delineate what each operating entity is expected to deliver from strategic and tactical perspectives. The service paradigm for a unit is an expression of how the unit and its personnel envision and practice the enterprise philosophy, direction, and strategy.

A second purpose is to define a set of expectations against which the general performance of the unit can be judged qualitatively. A service paradigm cannot be used as the yardstick against which the specific performance can be measured quantitatively; that requires different mechanisms.

A third purpose is of direct interest for KM and is perhaps the most important one: it outlines requirements for knowledge and other resources and conditions needed to fulfill the assigned responsibilities. It guides identification of the resources and capabilities needed to deliver the service paradigm productively and competently.

Service paradigms describe what the enterprise, and individual units and people within it, ideally should do for the enterprise, customers, and stakeholders and how they should appear to observers through their work products and behavior. Hence, the service paradigm scope may cover several areas and in particular the enterprise's expectations for how the employees and operating units — including departments — will behave.

Following is one example of the basic service paradigm for employees in a large service organization. This service paradigm covers four basic areas:

1. **Produce and Deliver Products and Services Reliably and Competently** (expectations for delivery of the basic work products of the unit).
   — Conduct and deliver work according to high professional and craft standards and in the enterprise's overall interest.
   — Ascertain that deliverables are consistently of high quality.
   — Ascertain that deliverables are consistently on time.
   — Take responsibility for "completed staff work."[3]
   — Always use best available knowledge.
   — Always apply critical thinking

2. **Secure and Improve Customer Relationships and Internal Contexts** (expectations for maintaining or improving contexts — within the work environment, between different departments and enterprise entities, between the enterprise and its customers, and between the enterprise and other stakeholders).
   — Understand and satisfy customer needs and requirements while meeting enterprise strategic intents.

   — Maintain and improve customer-enterprise relationships and contexts.

   — Collaborate, help coworkers, build positive relationships, and network.

   — Help implement corporate governance and curb and control improper behavior.

3. **Conserve Enterprise Resources** (expectations for dealing efficiently with enterprise resources, including time).

   — Work productively — on target, efficiently, and be engaged.

   — Use slack-time to improve the work environment, capture knowledge, establish valuable internal and external contacts, and so on.

   — Use every opportunity to learn, share, and embed knowledge — that is, build intellectual capital.

4. **Renew Enterprise Capabilities** (expectations for aiding in the renewal of the enterprise).

   — Innovate to improve enterprise capabilities in work processes, the work environment, and all other areas.

   — Envision opportunities for, and pursue improvements of, new products and services.

Some service paradigms can also include factors that pertain to the function's major responsibility areas. Such general responsibilities include:

- Producing regular work deliverables
- Dealing with difficult or unexpected challenges
- Dealing with customers and markets
- Dealing with learning, innovation, and growth
- Conducting management, operational, and work practices
- Dealing with enterprise and strategy
- Dealing with the external world
- Exhibiting appropriate appearance and general behavior
- Other responsibilities

The second and fourth areas listed for the basic service paradigm represent investments, whereas the first and third areas represent activities of value realization. Models for what performance is required and expected within an enterprise vary widely. Management philosophies can differ greatly, and consequently, the authority given an operating function or individual may be quite broad or, conversely, very narrow.

(1) pragmatic focus on effective delivery of "Today's Work"; (2) operational focus on improving work methods and environment; (3) tactical focus on improving products and services; (4) strategic focus on improving the business for long-term viability; and (5) visionary and societal focus on enterprise role in the world-at-large. It is possible to migrate people to a broader focus in parts of their domain through education, peer influences, and cultural conventions.

2. Action space: the domain that lies within the boundaries (constraints) that circumscribe the outer limits of the actions within which the person (or enterprise) is comfortable to operate.

3. Completed staff work is the study of a problem and presentation of a solution by a staff member in such form that all that remains to be done on the part of the recipient is to indicate approval or disapproval of the recommended action. The words "recommended action" are emphasized because the more difficult the problem is, the more the tendency is to present the problem to the recipient in a piecemeal fashion.

8

PEOPLE-FOCUSED KNOWLEDGE MANAGEMENT EXPECTATIONS

PREMISE: PEOPLE-FOCUSED KNOWLEDGE MANAGEMENT SUPPORTS GLOBAL EXCELLENCE

The global economy's reliance on personal knowledge and structural IC has flattened the global playing field. In the aggregate, new generation KM — including national educational systems and efforts — will potentially provide worldwide exchange of intellectual capital and the ability to operate enterprises anywhere at globally competitive levels. Workers everywhere will accordingly be able to achieve livelihoods that in the past only workers in industrialized and developed nations could realize. It will also be possible to reduce the gaps between rich and poor nations and individuals within nations.

THE GLOBAL LEADER EXAMPLE

Solitus Inc. is a medium-sized company that develops and produces high-technology nonmilitary devices, with associated software capabilities for industry and governments. Solitus has technical and manufacturing operations in North America, Latin America, Europe, Asia, Africa, and Australia. Apart from its focus on remaining a market leader in its field, Solitus considers it strategically appropriate and beneficial to support and improve the societies and environments in which it operates.

In an annual "town meeting" with more than 1,000 worldwide employees and with video connections to all major facilities, Hans Schelling, Solitus's chairman and CEO, described the company's direction in the following manner:

During the last year, many of you have joined our ranks and I would like to talk to you about how we operate and perceive ourselves since

248

we find it to be imperative for our success that all of us understand, agree, and believe in what Solitus is all about.

To begin, let me state some basic beliefs on which the Board of Directors, the senior management team, and many throughout the company agree. We believe that corporate excellence and success in the global competitive environment is secured by a knowledgeable, collaborating, motivated, energized, and ethical workforce that is compensated well, has growth opportunities, and is proud of its accomplishments. We believe that a workforce can be effective only when treated equitably and with respect, allowed to exercise its capabilities, and when its members enjoy good personal lives. We believe that for long-term survival, we must not only learn faster than our competitors — we must innovate faster than they do. We believe that misalignment between corporate direction and personal goals leads to ineffectiveness. We believe that greed, politicking, bureaucracy, and dishonesty are counterproductive at any level of the company.

Our intent is to continue to make Solitus a very different company. Therefore, as during prior years, our main objective has four separate thrusts, and they are:

- To encourage and support world-wide employee mentalities and cultures that make you, the employees, proud to work with (not for) Solitus in ways that you find to be challenging, interesting, fulfilling, and promising — and that energizes you to engage to make your work effective in all respects and closely aligned with Solitus's purpose. You are our brains and you implement each and every action and we rely upon your expertise, motivation, and conviction that ours is the right approach.
- To make our customers select us as their preferred supplier as a result of the quality and cost/performance of our goods and services and the manner in which we treat them. Our customers must trust us and realize that they can work with us to receive the best available goods and services.
- To build broad capabilities and good quality of life in the communities in which we operate. That means that we will work actively to assist the building of educational capabilities and societal facilities of many kinds. Particularly in developing nations, we will provide better salaries than our competitors to attract the best talents and we believe that world-wide we need to compensate people equally according to their contributions although adjusted to local conditions.

- To sustain our performance so that it is consistently durable — profitable in the short-term and successful in the long-term with secure reserves to buffer unexpected setbacks. We will achieve this by being diligent and effective and willing to take risks to advance our leadership. We will always be ready to tackle unwelcome surprises. We cannot afford to be vulnerable since we are serious about our responsibilities to you, our employees, or our other stakeholders, particularly our customers.

This philosophy brings many conflicts, because we also believe in the basic right of each human to live a worthy life. However, there are many ways to achieve these objectives. On the personal level, we need to make it possible for you to achieve an attractive balance between your work life and your professional life. At work, we need for you to understand the goals, intents, and strategy of our company down to the level where you specifically and instinctively know how you can participate in achieving these purposes. And, very importantly, we need for you to agree with these purposes and feel that they are right and that you will be proud to pursue them.

On the company level, we must be honest and operate with highly ethical principles and provide a safe environment where we can deal openly with opinions, criticism, and ideas. We must be equitable in our dealings with you, the employees, with customers, with suppliers, with owners, with all other stakeholders whoever they are. We must participate actively in supporting this society and communities and the environment in which we all live. We must provide products and services of which we can be proud. We must be profitable and provide financial results that satisfy our investors, make it possible to compensate you appropriately, and satisfy all other stakeholders.

There is more. We must make it easy for each other to conduct work. That means that each of us must find ways to build personal knowledge and increase our structural intellectual capital since these are basic pillars that make us able to be effective and excel. We must develop concrete personal knowledge to deal with routine work and highly abstract knowledge to handle novel challenges and difficult assignments. We will help you!

We must transfer all possible personal knowledge to structural knowledge so it can be available for general use to everybody's advantage. The ever-increasing personal knowledge base must be complemented with intelligent work aids, excellent and relevant information, and availability of advanced and easy-to-access structural intellectual capital assets. All of this will make it possible for us to work effectively and to innovate in ways that will make our company the very best. It will also make it possible for all of us to work smart, and not to work unduly hard. By being knowledgeable and by understanding what we need and want to do, by cooperating and collaborating to achieve shared goals, by working with systems and procedures designed to help, as well as by providing prudent but not restrictive controls, we will be able to do our work by exerting little effort and feel that much of what we do is both natural and second nature.

We must be critical of inappropriate and unethical behaviors by our coworkers, superiors, and subordinates. We shall have zero tolerance for unacceptable behavior and actions and must observe the laws of the countries in which we operate. There will be no room within Solitus for those who want to pursue different agendas. However, while observing strict principles, we must remember that situations are not always what they appear to be at first glance. We need to be flexible and allow pursuits of approaches and opinions other than our own.

We must accept risky ventures and actions as long as they hold beneficial promises. At the same time, we must accept that risky ventures can fail without faults of the people involved. In other words: "We must push the envelope and think outside the box!" We must be prepared to enter areas where no one has been — even areas where others have failed.

One more thing. Our company should not be a command-and-control or top-down company. Nor should it be a bureaucratic silo organization where communications are restricted to "channels." We must be open to suggestions, disagreements, and supportive comments from everyone to anyone. Personally, I will be glad to receive inputs — just make them short and to the point! The management committee and I need swiftly and regularly to learn about what works, what does not work, what could work, and relevant ideas for improvements and new directions. All of us need to work together to innovate faster than our competitors! And, the people who often know best are those who are close to the action.

These are our goals but it will not happen automatically. Nor can we expect all of this to happen flawlessly. But by working together, let us continue on the path that we already have chosen — and let us excel, both as a company and in our professional and personal lives! Thank you!

As a result of its management's efforts to build employee capabilities, understanding, and agreements, Solitus has built a highly capable and motivated workforce. It continues to be the leader within its market niche, constantly providing new or improved products and services. It is profitable in the short term and has built considerable reserves to ensure long-term survival.

Solitus is a leader in engaging in social and cultural activities in all locations where it operates. The company supports community initiatives and, for example, has policies to support its employees to participate in activities such as tutoring in public schools on company time. It provides company-based health services and daycare, and it provides flextime work arrangements. Every year, Solitus employees consistently work fewer overtime hours compared to its competitors and other high-technology companies. Solitus is considered to be the preferred employer and has low personnel turnover, with the result that workforce expertise has grown to become high and well distributed.

Hans Schelling and his management team are convinced that the company's performance and success are a result of its management philosophy, principles, and objectives. Accordingly, they plan to continue to build Solitus strategy on this foundation.

What Future Knowledge Management Business Users May Expect

Globalization has placed businesses everywhere in new and different competitive situations where knowledgeable, effective behavior has come to provide the competitive edge. Enterprises have turned to explicit and systematic knowledge management to develop the intellectual capital needed to succeed. Further developments are expected to provide considerable benefits resulting from changes in the workplace and in management and operational practices. Changes will come partly from information technology and artificial intelligence developments. However, more important changes are expected in people-focused practices to build, apply, and deploy knowledge and understanding for support of innovative and effective knowledge-intensive work.

Next generation KM methods will still be crude. We need new theories of the firm and of knowledge to establish new perspectives of enterprise operation and performance. In the meantime, users can expect significant benefits from KM as it develops over the next decades.

Explicit and systematic KM methods are now recognized as important approaches to improve enterprise performance, either through knowledgeable people delivering work more effectively or through other ways of leveraging intellectual capital (IC). KM has been treated by many authors.[1] Significant advances have been made during the last decade, and we can expect further changes, creating entirely new directions or refining present methods. KM in part deals with human understanding and mental models and with how these are used in work. Consequently, we may see advances for a long time to come — however, we may not associate all these changes with KM; many will integrate systematic KM into daily work and no longer consider it knowledge management.

We could focus on how KM methods and the KM market can be expected to develop. Instead, let us explore how future KM may affect organizations, people, and society where the real value of KM is realized. From that perspective, we are particularly interested in what explicit and systematic KM may come to mean from the perspectives of users and adopters.

Our interest is in KM from the perspective of how it is conducted within the enterprise, but other views exist. One such view is that commercial KM also incorporates the marketplace of KM-related software, information and content services, professional information technology and KM-related services, and business process management.

During the last several decades, KM has become a central management topic throughout most of the world. With globalization opportunities and pressures, coupled with worldwide communication, emphasis on personal and structural intellectual capital assets has become a necessary cornerstone for competitive behavior in the knowledge economy. Although KM is still in its infancy, it has already become very valuable for those enterprises that practice it. During the last 15 years, KM has changed from one generation to the next through constant improvements and new perspectives. A new generation knowledge management (NGKM) is emerging with fresh objectives, methods, and results. Enterprises that practice NGKM pursue broader concepts and in other ways depart from earlier KM approaches by exploiting underlying mechanisms, whether economical, social, psychological, organizational, or technical. Organizations that have adopted NGKM (without calling it KM!) include the SAS

Institute, Nokia, Chaparral Steel, Buckman Laboratories, W. L. Gore & Associates, and Malden Mills.

The Business Environment Is Under Pressure

Already, we see increased requirements for better knowledge in the workplace to deliver competitive knowledge-intensive work. Demands for customized and more sophisticated products and services have increased. Globalization pressures have changed business — and correspondingly work — worldwide. Nations that earlier supplied manual labor have started to compete with Europe, Japan, and North America by offering competent intellectually based work. Thanks to the Internet, knowledge workers everywhere can access the latest information on advanced concepts, methodologies, and business issues. However, technology access is still far from uniform, and most people in Africa, Asia, and South America may have to wait a long time before they are fully competing in the workplace. Even so, to maintain their viability, institutions and nations that have long been the intellectual leaders will need to build and apply intellectual capital much better. They increasingly must manage knowledge systematically.

Other developments that are causing changes in business and work are the new cognitive science understandings of how people make decisions and work with their minds (Cannon-Bowers & Salas 1998; Klein 1998, 2002; Wiig & Wiig 1999); new management and operational practices; improvements in information technology (IT); and powerful and practical artificial intelligence (AI) techniques. We are learning what motivates individuals and how to integrate individual goals with those of the enterprise. We are discovering the value of new ways to organize work and interpersonal networking to maximize opportunities for people to deliver their best. In addition, we are obtaining practical experiences about how to manage knowledge in different KM arenas.[2]

With all these forces pressuring business, we have learned to prepare our workforce better, automate many routine functions, and organize work in ways that allow us to deliver higher quality products and services more effectively. The nature of work is shifting toward more complex work (see Chapter 1), with identifiable targets for intelligent automation in routine areas and potentials for application of greater understanding and expertise in more demanding work.

Handling all work tasks competently and with outcomes that fulfill quality requirements requires that the organization and systematization of work and individuals apply all required resources effectively. Hence, among proactive enterprises, increased efforts have been made to make individuals, and therefore the enterprise itself, act as effectively as possible.

Management teams are unwilling and unable to allocate resources to new directions unless they promise to deliver clear and important benefits. Hence, they continue to ask specific questions such as: "Will active KM allow us to deliver a more competitive service paradigm?" "Will active KM make it possible to create more competitive products?" "Will active KM improve the effectiveness of work and thereby reduce operating costs, allow us to be more responsive, improve our market image, and otherwise become more successful?"

Success Relies on Knowledgeable Behavior

Effective behavior is vital. Sustained success and viability require the effective execution of internal functions and interactions with environment — that is, effective behavior. When individuals act effectively within an effective framework, the enterprise can act effectively — operationally, tactically, strategically, and in support of markets. In practice, effective behavior means that both people and the organization adjust actions to the context by improvising with a given strategy, tactics, and policies. It also means acting creatively and responsibly in order to achieve the best results possible.

Often effective behavior requires collaboration in a collegial culture in which politics and bureaucracy are bypassed. A major operational objective is to make the customer successful by customizing products and services to satisfy individual needs while at the same time implementing the enterprise goals.

The success of an enterprise depends on the interplay of many factors, some beyond the enterprise's control and others associated with the leaders' strategic moves. Still others (and these we consider here) are associated with how the enterprise arranges its internal affairs. Among these factors we find:

- The ability to deliver desired service paradigms by individuals, departments, and business units, and by the overall enterprise.[3]
  — The ability to act in a timely fashion.

— The capability of employees to deliver the products for which they are responsible.
- The effectiveness of interpersonal work (teaming and networking) through coordination, cooperation, and collaboration.
- The ability of work at all levels to support implementation of enterprise strategy and direction.
- The ability to create, produce, and deliver superior products and services that match present and future market demands.
- The effectiveness of outcome feedback on how well products perform in the marketplace as well as within the enterprise.
- The degree to which innovations occur, are captured, communicated, and applied.
- The ability of individuals, teams, units, and the enterprise itself to deal with unexpected events, opportunities, and threats.
- The effectiveness of enterprise systems, procedures, and policies.
- The degree to which undesirable and dysfunctional personal or systems behaviors are controlled and corrected.

All of these factors depend to significant degrees on the effective availability and application of good knowledge. Consequently, broad and systematic management of knowledge and intellectual assets becomes a key support activity to ensure enterprise success and viability.

Enterprises pursue different KM strategies aligned to their business strategies. Hansen *et al.* (1999) report two separate approaches, which they call *codification strategy* and *personalization strategy*. These strategies focus on the automation and application of IT and on the learning organization, respectively. Others discuss a third strategy — *strategic management of intellectual capital* to build, manage, and exploit "structural" knowledge-related assets (Cannon-Bowers & Salas 1998; Wellman 1999; Winograd 1988). A fourth focus is also pursued — the *enterprise effectiveness strategy*, where the emphasis is on applying any and all available knowledge and intellectual assets in the best interests of the enterprise. These isolated, but complementary, strategies suggest that they in fact are separate tactical approaches within a comprehensive KM strategy, as indicated in Figure 8-1. As organizations develop their KM practice further, during the next decade most enterprises will likely pursue all four thrusts as part of their overall KM strategy.

To be competitive over the next decade, proactive enterprises will increasingly manage knowledge systematically — although many KM activities and functions may be implicit in each employee's and

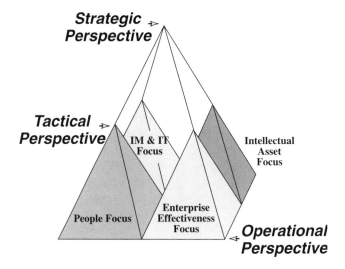

Figure 8-1
*Four tactical perspectives of knowledge management focus areas. Copyright ©
1995 Knowledge Research Institute, Inc. Reproduced with permission.*

department's daily work and practice. As of now, the enterprises will
continue to be motivated by several end-goals, the main ones being
securing short-term success and long-term viability. A particular KM
objective in support of whichever strategy the enterprise pursues is
to leverage the best available knowledge and other ICs to make
people, and therefore the enterprise itself, effective in implementing
the enterprise strategy (Buckman 2004).

Expected Knowledge Management Developments

KM promotes the development and application of tacit, explicit,
and embedded intellectual capital — that is, leveraging understanding, action capabilities, and other intellectual assets to attain the
enterprise's ultimate goals of profitability, long-term viability, or
quality services. This perspective of KM suggests a number of developments in the coming years.

- A developing area of increasing insight is the role that understanding — or meaning-connected knowledge — and abstract
  mental models play in intellectual work. The 1990s notion that
  "knowledge is actionable information" and similar early per-

spectives will be displaced. Insights from emerging cognitive research and business experiences with the importance of deep knowledge will make it plain what, and how, people need to understand in order to handle complex challenges competently.

- Future KM practices and methods will be systematic, explicit, and relatively dependent upon advanced technology in several areas. However, overall we expect KM to become more people-focused as the recognition spreads that the networking of competent and collaborating people forms the basis for any organization's success (Cannon-Bowers & Salas 1999; Dawson 2002; Wellman 1999; Winograd 1988).

- By building on extensive experiences from many organizations, the manner in which KM is organized, supported, and facilitated will change. The more obvious changes will be associated with placement and organization of the KM effort itself, be it with a high-level chief knowledge officer (CKO) or with a distributed effort. Changes that deal with reorganization of work and the abolishing of whole departments that are integrated into other operations will be less apparent but prevalent.

- Management and operating practices will change to facilitate KM in many different ways. Incentives will be introduced and disincentives eliminated to promote innovation, effective knowledge exchange ("sharing"), learning, and application of best knowledge in all work situations. Cultural drivers such as management emphasis and personal behaviors will be changed to create environments of trust and concerns for finding the root causes of problems without assigning blame.

- Efforts will be made to embed KM perspectives and considerations in regular activities throughout the enterprise. An example of how broadly KM may affect an organization is indicated in Figure 8-2. It highlights some sole and shared-responsibility KM-related activities within Research and Development (R&D), Human Resources (HR), Information Management and Technology (IM & IT), and a KM supervisory function.

- New practices will focus on desired combinations of understanding, knowledge, skills, and attitudes (KSAs) when assembling work teams or analyzing requirements for performing work (Cannon-Bowers & Salas 1999). The emphasis on complementary work teams will coincide with the movement toward virtual organizations where many participants in in-house teamwork will be external workers who are brought in for limited periods to complement in-house competencies for

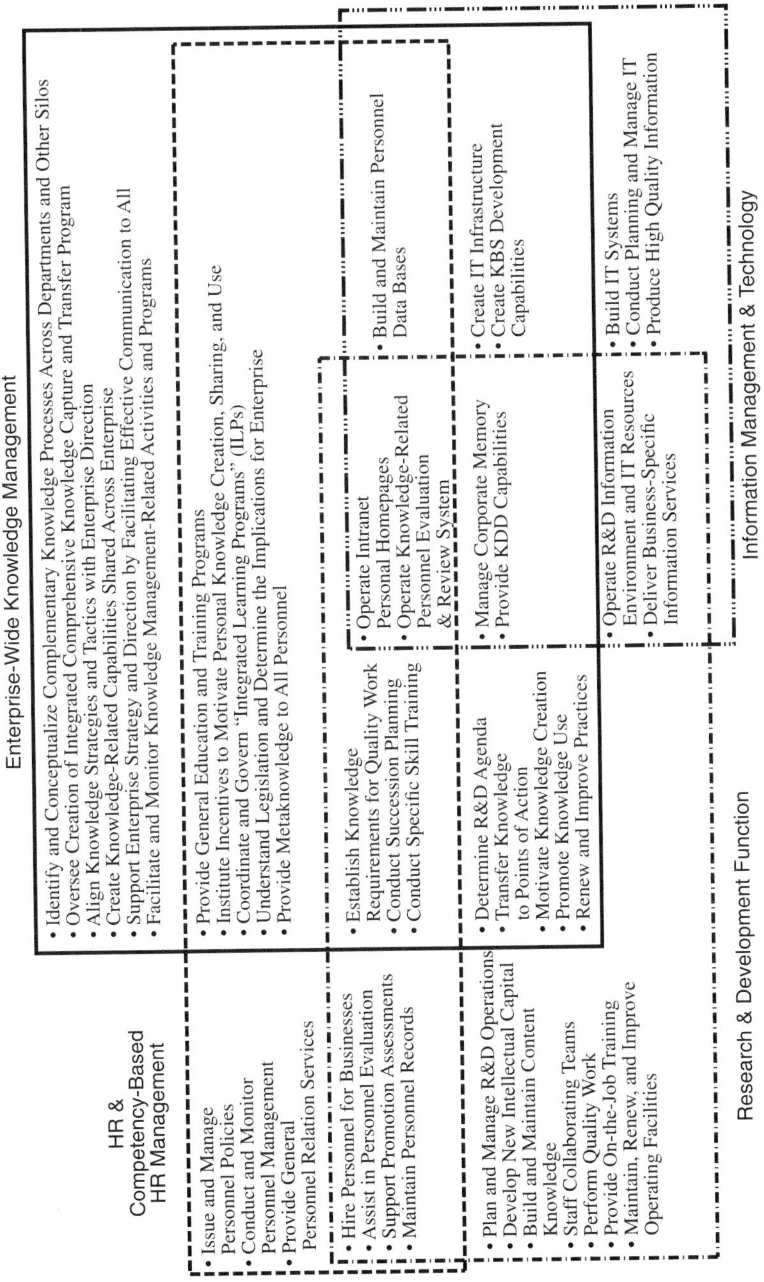

Enterprise-Wide Knowledge Management

- Identify and Conceptualize Complementary Knowledge Processes Across Departments and Other Silos
- Oversee Creation of Integrated Comprehensive Knowledge Capture and Transfer Program
- Align Knowledge Strategies and Tactics with Enterprise Direction
- Create Knowledge-Related Capabilities Shared Across Enterprise
- Support Enterprise Strategy and Direction by Facilitating Effective Communication to All
- Facilitate and Monitor Knowledge Management-Related Activities and Programs

- Provide General Education and Training Programs
- Institute Incentives to Motivate Personal Knowledge Creation, Sharing, and Use
- Coordinate and Govern "Integrated Learning Programs" (ILPs)
- Understand Legislation and Determine the Implications for Enterprise
- Provide Metaknowledge to All Personnel

- Establish Knowledge Requirements for Quality Work
- Conduct Succession Planning
- Conduct Specific Skill Training

- Determine R&D Agenda
- Transfer Knowledge to Points of Action
- Motivate Knowledge Creation
- Promote Knowledge Use
- Renew and Improve Practices

- Build and Maintain Personnel Data Bases

- Operate Intranet Personal Homepages
- Operate Knowledge-Related Personnel Evaluation & Review System

- Manage Corporate Memory
- Provide KDD Capabilities

- Create IT Infrastructure
- Create KBS Development Capabilities

- Operate R&D Information Environment and IT Resources
- Deliver Business-Specific Information Services

- Build IT Systems
- Conduct Planning and Manage IT
- Produce High Quality Information

Information Management & Technology

HR & Competency-Based HR Management

- Issue and Manage Personnel Policies
- Conduct and Monitor Personnel Management
- Provide General Personnel Relation Services

- Hire Personnel for Businesses
- Assist in Personnel Evaluation
- Support Promotion Assessments
- Maintain Personnel Records

- Plan and Manage R&D Operations
- Develop New Intellectual Capital
- Build and Maintain Content Knowledge
- Staff Collaborating Teams
- Perform Quality Work
- Provide On-the-Job Training
- Maintain, Renew, and Improve Operating Facilities

Research & Development Function

Figure 8-2

Examples of individual and shared responsibility for knowledge-related activities within an enterprise. Copyright © 1997 Knowledge Research Institute, Inc. Reproduced with permission.

specific tasks. The present use of consultants from large consulting houses is one manifestation but is expected to increasingly involve self-employed external knowledge workers.

- Most organizations will create effective approaches to transfer personal knowledge to structural intellectual capital (SIC). Increased transfer will allow better utilization and leveraging of the SICs. It will also have a positive side effect for external subject matter experts who may be able to provide, that is, sell their expertise to many enterprises for continued use. We already have seen this in isolated instances; for example, with refinery operations experts (Dixon 2000).

- Comprehensive approaches to create and conduct broad KM practices will become the norm. For example, designing and implementing comprehensive multimode knowledge transfer programs will be common (Wiig 1995, p. 358). Such programs take systematic approaches to integrating all primary knowledge-related functions, including major internal and external knowledge sources; major knowledge transformation functions and repositories, such as capture and codification functions and computer-based knowledge bases; major knowledge deployment functions, such as training and educational programs, expert networks, and knowledge-based systems (KBSs); and the different knowledge application or value-realization functions where work is performed or knowledge assets are sold, leased, or licensed.

- Education and knowledge support capabilities such as expert networks or performance support systems (PSSs) will be matched to cognitive and learning styles and to dominant intelligences. That will facilitate workers, particularly full-time employees, in all areas to perform more effectively. In addition, new, powerful, and highly effective approaches to elicitation and transfer of deep knowledge will be introduced. Such capabilities allow experts to communicate understandings and concepts and facilitate building corresponding concepts, associations, and mental models by other practitioners.[4]

- One area of considerable value will be the development of comprehensive and integrated processes for knowledge development, capture, transformation, transfer, and application.

- KM will be supported by many artificial intelligence (AI) developments, including intelligent agents; natural language understanding and processing (NLU and NLP); reasoning strategies; and knowledge representations and ontologies that will continue to develop and, by providing greater capabilities, will be relied on to organize knowledge and to facilitate knowledge application to important situations.[5]

- Information technology will continue to progress and will bring considerable change to many KM areas. They will include "portable offices" that roam anywhere with their owners; communication handling systems that organize, abstract, prioritize, make sense of, and in many instances, answer incoming communications; and intelligent agents that not only will acquire desired and relevant information and knowledge, but will reason with it relative to the situation at hand.

To create broad and integrated capabilities, most of the changes that are introduced by these developments will not be stand-alone, but will be combined with other changes, many of which have foci different from KM.

There are specific expectations for business benefits in terms of strategic, tactical, and operational improvements when pursuing KM actively. Practical experiences with systematic and explicit KM reported by advanced and early adopting organizations indicate that benefits can be substantial. Most direct benefits tend to be operational, while tactical and strategic benefits often are indirect and take longer to realize. Nevertheless, strategic advantages tend to move enterprises to pursue KM actively. There has been an increasing trend toward pursuing strategically oriented revenue enhancement instead of the early search for the "low-hanging fruits" of operational improvements. During the coming years, enterprise management teams will expect to obtain specific benefits resulting from KM advances, some of which are in the early stages of use. Illustrative examples are as follows.

Examples of Strategic Benefit Expectations

The enterprise will build an increasing competence to provide improved enterprise service paradigms and the ability to produce and deliver products and services with higher knowledge content than previously possible. This may be achieved by having knowledge workers who possess and have access to better applicable knowledge, and organizing work to facilitate the application of best knowledge.

The organization will develop a broadened capability to create and deliver new products and services and a greater capacity to deliver products and services to new markets. It can also be expected to enjoy greater market penetration and competitiveness.

Examples of Tactical Benefit Expectations

The enterprise should experience faster organizational and personal learning by better capture, retention, and use of innovations, new knowledge, and knowledge from others and from external sources achieved by:

- More effective knowledge transfer methods between knowledge workers.
- More effective discovery of knowledge through KDD and other systematic methods.
- Easier access to intellectual capital assets.
- More effective approaches to ascend Nonaka's knowledge spiral by transforming tacit personal knowledge into shared knowledge (Nonaka & Takeuchi 1995).

Better transfer of tacit to personal knowledge can be expected to lead to availability of more highly competitive knowledge.

Less loss of knowledge through attrition or personnel reassignments should be achieved by:

- Effective capture of routine and operational knowledge from departing personnel.
- Assembly of harvested knowledge in corporate memories that are easy to access and navigate can be expected to lead to greater ability to build on prior expertise and deep understanding.

More knowledge workers will have effective possession of, and access to, relevant expertise in the form of operational knowledge, scripts, and schemata. In addition, employees will obtain greater understanding of how their personal goals coincide with the enterprise's goals.

Examples of Operational Benefit Expectations

Employees will have access to and be able to apply better knowledge at points-of-action achieved by, for example,

- Educating employees in the principles of their work (scripts, schemata, and abstract mental models).
- Providing knowledge workers with aids to complement their own knowledge.
- Training knowledge workers to operationalize abstract knowledge to match the requirements of the practical situations they handle.

These changes can be expected to lead to lower operating costs caused by fewer mistakes, faster work, less need for handoffs, ability to compensate for unexpected variations in the work task, improved innovation, among a few of the operational benefits that are often reported.

- Operational areas will experience less rework and fewer operational errors.
- The enterprise will achieve greater reuse of knowledge.

As a further illustration of how KM changes may affect enterprise, we may consider the dynamic progression of effects from the initial KM activity until it has been translated into bottom-line benefits. Figure 8-3 shows the effects and benefits that can be expected from creating and deploying knowledge-based systems (KBSs) to support production workers in a plant that manufactures high-technology products.

Realization of most of these examples will require noticeable changes within the enterprise. These development will influence the culture, which may change to promote greater initiatives and greater job satisfaction among employees. With increasing virtual organization operations, it will also tend to change the roles of permanent employees when outside expertise is imported with temporary employees (Buckman 2004).

The Changing Workplace

Not only do we expect the enterprise to change, but advances in KM practices will also change the workplace — in many places drastically. Visible changes will be evident by the increased application of, and reliance on, technology compared to the KM information technology focus of the 1990s. However, less visible changes will be more important since they will tend to improve the way people work

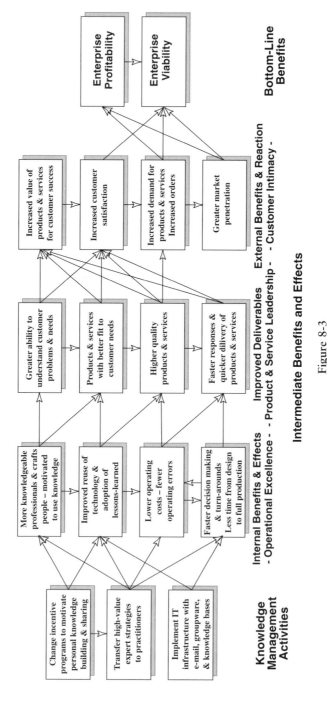

Figure 8-3

Example of how results from knowledge management activities propagate through event chains to deliver bottom-line benefits.
Copyright © 1989 Karl M. Wiig. Reproduced with permission.

with their minds. The changes that people will experience in the workplace include:

- Greater emphasis on performing work using interdisciplinary teams, with focus on ascertaining that the best mix of competencies and understanding will be applied to the work at hand.
- A major change in the workplace resulting from the increasingly common temporary nature of many employment situations. As greater emphasis is placed on assembling short-lived teams with requisite knowledge profiles to address specific tasks, people will have reduced allegiances to the temporary employer and make increased efforts to improve their expertise to maintain their personal competitiveness.
- Good understanding of the need to rely on strong associations and conceptual knowledge to guide the direction of work.
- Better understanding by knowledge workers of how to influence the implementation of enterprise strategy by each small decision or act that is part of their daily work.
- Greater degree of collaboration and willingness to coordinate and cooperate with associates and other activities.
- Increased personal understanding by employees of how they personally benefit from delivering effective work.
- Greater job security and less hesitation and procrastination to undertake complex tasks after they build increased metaknowledge and professional or craft knowledge about the work for which they are responsible.
- Increased reliance on automated intelligent reasoning to support work. As an example, when confronted with a complex situation, automation may assist knowledge workers by identifying and making available relevant support information and knowledge, making preliminary sense of the situation, and locating and presenting suggestions for how to handle it.
- Deployment of intelligent agents internally and externally who will offload "data detective work" that is now required to locate and evaluate information required in many knowledge worker situations ranging from plant operators to ad hoc strategic task forces.
- New organization of the physical work environment which will change the way people work together and will allow richer interaction. The new work environments will be designed to foster knowledge transfer and exchange through networking and collaboration and will facilitate serendipitous innovations.

In the aggregate, KM can be expected to lead to less effort to deliver present-day service paradigms. However, as was indicated earlier in Figure 8-1, work will change to satisfy the ever-increasing requirements for new features and increased capabilities of products and services. Hence, personal job-related understanding will be increased through better script and schema knowledge, and work will expand to take advantage of the new capabilities. Even so, knowledge workers will feel more confident and have better understanding of jobs to be done. In addition, better knowledge support will allow more jobs to be done correctly the first time, adding to confidence and job satisfaction.

Knowledge Will Be Bought and Sold

New approaches to trading knowledge in various forms have already emerged as a viable business for many parties. Among many interesting examples is Lotus, the English car maker, which reportedly receives greater revenues from advising other car makers on building engines than it receives from selling its own products. Individuals are able to advertise and sell marketable knowledge products worldwide over the Internet to recipients, either directly or through knowledge exchanges.

"Packaged knowledge" has traditionally been passive and has been provided in the form of books or similar media that must be "read" by recipients. The marketplace will increasingly provide active forms of packaged knowledge that (e.g., through reasoning) will address frequently encountered problems of importance to business and the general public. Much of this knowledge will use powerful, perhaps semistandardized representations and ontologies and will apply reasoning capabilities that increasingly will be based on natural language. We already see emerging sources of prepackaged knowledge of this kind. In the distant future, natural language processing, supported by powerful information technology, may be so advanced that knowledge can be communicated in free-form language. All these developments will allow users to incorporate knowledge quickly and reliably into their deliberations — as long as these are explicit. For tacit evaluations and decisions, which most are, the obtained knowledge must be internalized in advance of being required. When the situation arises, it must already be resident in the person's mind in the form of tacit associations and mental models. In other words, knowledge workers must have learned and internalized the requisite knowledge.

Electronic advisory or consulting services are already emerging. Knowledge-based performance support systems (PSSs) can be bought in areas ranging from legal and tax advice for individuals to operating advice and water treatment guidance for thermal power plants. Knowledge acquisition will become more reliable, and the marketplace will become more organized. At the same time, we will create capabilities and functions to validate explicated knowledge. We can expect that individuals with every kind of expertise will capture what can be made explicit and present it for sale in the marketplace. Individuals will trade their knowledge in ways that we now can only glimpse by acting as free agents to virtual corporations. Now, we normally see free agents as consultants that are asked to assist clients with particular problems. A likely next step is for experts, for a fee, to let clients harvest part of their knowledge to incorporate it into structural IC that fits their operations.

Societal Side-Effects

From a societal perspective, there will be numerous effects of systematic and deliberate management of knowledge. Most will have positive societal values as people become better educated and more knowledgeable. Also, elaborate knowledge discovery processes will provide powerful insights into the preferences and behaviors of the general public by institutions that aim to serve public needs and demands. To make this knowledge more valuable for use, particularly when communicated to end-users whose behavior it is expected to improve, knowledge building will be combined with advanced speech-act theory and other communication techniques. That will allow the message to be communicated more effectively. However, there are potentials for disuse by parties that are not always honest.

The effects of better KM will not always be positive and desirable. Our KM expertise will not always work to society's or individual's advantage. Biased and self-serving uses will abound. Companies, political parties, and others will wish to gain greater understanding of how to influence their customers through advertising, sales tactics, and even through misinformation and propaganda. Part of this misuse has already been experienced in simple formats on the World Wide Web and is likely to become parts of political campaigns.

On the other hand, we will see emerging availabilities of reliable expertise — knowledge, insights, information, and explanations — for direct access by consumers and packaged to provide understanding and mental model development, giving them understanding and insights to counter undue influences. This trend is expected to be important, allowing the average person to defend against the avalanche of "influence information." Consequently, we can expect to see a broad, worldwide, "yin-yang battleground" of subjective influencing countered by objective and vetted knowledge, where both sides draw upon extensive KM expertise to sharpen their weapons.

We Are Far From Finished!

As noted throughout this book, we really do not understand much yet about knowledge. Our understanding of the cognitive aspects of human functioning (as related to work) is marginal, and we have no accepted economic "theory of knowledge." Nor do we have a general understanding of how to undertake comprehensive and systematic knowledge management within an organization. We may need an entirely new theory of the firm for us to manage knowledge effectively — and to tie it properly to enterprise strategizing, tactics, and daily operations while recognizing that people and their behaviors contribute much more to enterprise success than conventional assets.

- Advanced management teams are already aware that they need to manage knowledge-related activities systematically and explicitly. They have numerous options, and we see many different approaches to applied KM. As the world gains further experience, we expect to see strong patterns of what works well and what may be questionable or what only applies in specialized situations.
- A new competitive battleground is emerging in which knowledge and ICs are the ammunition. We can foresee difficulties for "old guard" management teams who rely on tangible and visible aspects of work and on conventional wisdom. There will be greater differences between those who act proactively and those who follow.
- New advances in KM and the adoption of broad KM practices will bring about great possibilities for creating new economically important products and services.
- From a KM perspective, we need to develop and capture more successful working methods and approaches, including computer-based tools.

We hope that KM will become a great equalizer between the haves and have-nots, both within different nations and between nations.

Clearly, the knowledge possessed by a person is a separator ("knowledge is power"), and good education provides a considerable edge. However, when working in the developing world, we have often found that people's mental machinery — their intelligence and attitude — is a greater resource than what they know and understand. Given that finding, as well as the increasing levels of education in many developing nations, we have the potential that people everywhere can participate in the knowledge economy more equitably than before.

One key lesson is that we need to adopt greater people-focused perspectives of knowledge. To be viable, we need constant learning, led by constant innovation. Technology only goes so far; it can only provide us with rudimentary reasoning devoid of innovation and with rather concrete analyses of the past through approaches such as knowledge discovery in databases. People are the real intelligent agents, those that see and act on new opportunities that really are creations of the mind. It is those opportunities that will bring the world forward.

In spite of all present limitations, KM is already very useful, even when its scope is narrow. The saving grace is that the playing field is quite level. For the next decade, most everyone is a beginner!

New Enterprises and Integrative Management

The modern enterprise must adopt integrating practices to ascertain that internal operations everywhere are developed and conducted in harmony. Mutually dependent functions need to support each other during operations and to change in coordination with others when adapting to new business situations. Integrative management and analysis formalize collaborative practices that combine modern human resource practices such as cognitive science-observant people management with systems perspectives, management science methodologies, and considerations for interactions between operational entities' and stakeholders' short-term and long-term objectives, marketplace performance, and conducive management philosophies. Needs for integrative management are driven by increasingly complex business environments and workplaces. Implementation of integrative management in most organizations leads to considerable changes, particularly in terms of new incentives, policies, practices, and infrastructure.

The enterprise's ability to adopt and practice integrative management rests on its intangible capital. It also rests on people's knowledge, understanding, and motivation and on pertinent infrastructure, including information management, the knowledge distribution system, and automated methodologies such as comprehensive dynamic simulation models. The success of integrative management is a function of the enterprise's ability to act — the value of its intangible capital and its distribution throughout the organization.

The integration of activities within the enterprise is not new. However, explicit and systematic integration of management and operational plans and actions with broad perspectives is new. Durable success and viability have always required coordination of activities in different parts of the enterprise. However, integrative management, as it is now seen, goes further. By considering enterprise strategy and short-term and long-term objectives held by relevant stakeholders, it involves the integration of current activities and future plans while exploring potentials for joint, synergistic approaches. It also considers impacts such as important peripheral and long-term implications and side-effects that affect operational departments and the creation of products and services. Integrative management recognizes the interconnectedness of mutually dependent functions and pursues systems perspectives that incorporate dynamics and interactions between all affected subsystems.

Objectives of Integrative Management

Integrative management provides capabilities and practices, with resulting decisions and actions that implement enterprise strategy and directions effectively to ensure durable success. By introducing long-term viewpoints and broad-based collaboration, systems perspectives, and methods, it expands decision making to include considerations such as the business value of intangible benefits, hidden costs, and overall life-cycle costs and benefits. Integrative management surfaces shared needs and opportunities that may be neglected in other environments. It also provides a stronger basis for innovation and agility — for smart behavior. In short, integrative management provides the foundation for a strong competitive enterprise. As indicated schematically in Figure 8-4, integrative management coordinates creative interactions between most internal and external entities, which in some way affect the behavior and effective performance of the enterprise.

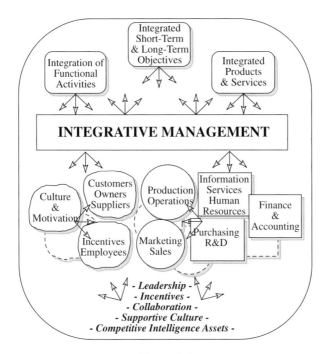

Figure 8-4
Integrative management leads to coordination of many entities.
Copyright © 2002 Knowledge Research Institute, Inc. Reproduced
with permission.

It has always been obvious that integration is required between codependent entities such as operating functions and scheduling activities of different areas of production. Information services also are typically well integrated with departmental activities. What is not so obvious — as evidenced by problematic practices in many organizations — is the need to integrate and coordinate daily activities and future plans with marketing, R&D, culture, strategy, incentives, corporate direction and intentions, the management of intellectual and information capital, and the objectives of relevant stakeholders. In the past, narrow foci have often led to problems. Two problem areas come to mind: business process redesign (BPR) and enterprise-wide information systems such as those provided by SAP, Oracle, and others. The performance and success of many efforts have fallen short of expectations, mostly because of pursuing narrow scopes. Dimensions such as culture, people's tacit work approaches and mental styles, established networking and collaborating behaviors, and the knowledge and expertise needed for competent delivery of intellectual work products were often neglected.

In Complex Businesses, Better Practices Are Required

Many people question why integrative management has surfaced at this time as an important issue. There are several reasons. Globalization has forced the need for greater enterprise effectiveness. Increased sophistication and customer demands place new requirements on customizing products and services. Work is becoming more complex, and that requires greater integration among entities and more expertise at the point-of-action to make the enterprise operate smoothly and to deliver quality work with desired competence. New complex work environments require hands-on knowledge management by innovation, knowledge gathering, organizing, deployment, and so on. On a larger scale, constructive coordination of operations, departments, and business units is also required.

One major requirement for integrative management is the need to identify, design, and implement shared capabilities, facilities, and systems and procedures that individual entities either cannot identify the need for or justify by themselves. Examples include shared IT capabilities and a shared incentive system that foster and influence the desired integrative management mentality, culture, and behavior.

Previously, organizations pursued practices that increasingly were considered outdated by proactive organizations. Bureaucratic operational and management practices led to suboptimizing and "silo operations," often indirectly through continued use of inappropriate incentives and performance measurements. These practices need to be changed to prevent enterprises from falling behind (Quinn *et al.* 1996). Many business schools have traditionally prepared managers to make quick, narrow, and simple-minded "dominant factor" decisions based on the rote-learning of archetype concrete case examples that isolate the decision space to operational areas such as marketing, manufacturing, or finance. Future managers are not taught to "think strategically," according to Professor Martin of the University of Toronto's Rotman School of Management (Anonymous 2000). To prepare students better, the school teaches "integrative thinking" rather than focusing narrowly on specific methods and operational actions. Other business schools now offer courses in integrative management as well. Students develop a general understanding of underlying mechanisms and their interactions in the business world. In the process, they also develop mental strategic action models of governing principles and general approaches to guide their handling of business issues, although that is not discussed by Professor Martin. Cognitive science researchers have recently pointed out that such models are the foundation for our decision behavior, and their proper development by necessity is becoming required for survival in today's business environment. The implications of how we train and educate our workers are significant.

Intellectual Work Is Indeed Complex

Preparing people to work effectively in complex environments relies on recent cognitive science findings on how people build knowledge, make decisions, and implement actions. In the past we may have had an improper understanding of how to prepare and support people as decision makers and implementers. That is changing as research and practical experiences provide new insights. We also increase our knowledge of how to manage intellectual capital, particularly through adoption of people-focused knowledge management.

Obviously, integrative management and integrative analysis that attempt to take into account all issues can lead to "analysis paralysis." That clearly must be avoided since timely and proactive decisions must always be the goal. Time is always of the essence. How then, with the need to coordinate and consider wider implications of decisions, can managers pursue integrative management effectively — and what is required?

Good managers must make quick decisions based on established judgments, while considering broad implications and the novelty of the situation at hand. Such behavioral models must remain our ideal. For integrative management to be effective, several conditions must be present. Managers — and every employee with any level of responsibility, including factory floor workers — must be provided with the awareness to consider the broad consequences of their decisions — upstream, downstream, adjacent operations, over the longer term, and while taking into account how relevant stakeholders are affected. As achieved by Chaparral Steel, workers must be provided with an understanding of what is expected of them (Wiig 1999). They must have clear communication of their role in implementing enterprise strategy, objectives, and direction, and they must be able to explore what it will mean for them, personally, in order to build operational mental models and understanding. They must also understand service paradigms that spell out the nature of the services they are asked to provide. These communications and discussions can be conducted through "knowledge cafés" and similar processes.

How Do We Implement Integrative Management?

Integrative management cannot take place unless the enterprise leadership and the pervasive culture recognize and reward the desired behavior and resulting performance. Peer recognition and all other implicit aspects of culture must be supportive. Individual supervisors and managers will need to take responsibility for looking at their operations in detail. They need to collaborate constructively and innovatively with upstream, downstream, and adjacent functions to decide how tasks and detailed work may be shared or changed. That requires taking others into their confidence, thinking broader about the business function beyond amassing personal power, staff, and responsibilities, and realizing that their personal success is closely tied to enterprise success, both in general and as a result of the new incentives and environment (Buckman 2004).

Integrative management is not automatically achieved overnight. Incentives, operations and management practices, and education with extensive communication must be practiced. That will foster an environment — an integrative management culture — of collaboration and cooperation based on the clear understanding that personal and enterprise success are intertwined and follow from working together toward common goals. More than anything else, integrative management relies on quality intangible capital — the knowledge and understanding of people backed up by facilities such as expert networks, knowledge-based systems, knowledge bases, and information services.

Informed and competent decision making is of crucial importance for integrative management. Without knowledge management (i.e., systematic and deliberate development, maintenance, renewal, and maintenance of knowledge and understanding) integrative management cannot take place. Decision-Making/Problem-Solving followed by implemented action consists of matching knowledge assets with corresponding information assets to make it possible for individuals, and the enterprise as a whole, to collaborate, understand interactions, and implement broad, effective actions required for integrative management. As indicated in Figure 8-5 in a simplified financial industry example, both appropriately matched knowledge and information are required. Excellent information about situations is required to describe conditions appropriately, and excellent knowledge is applied

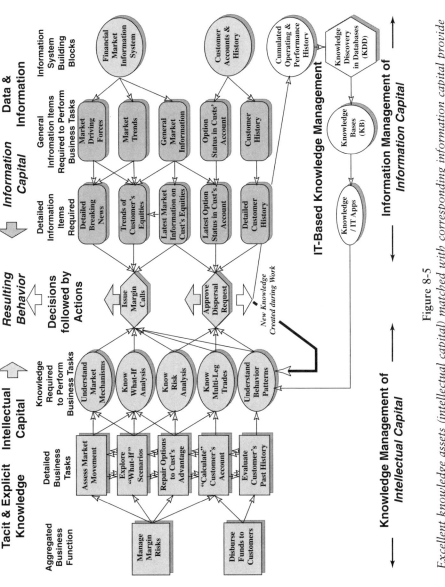

Figure 8-5

Excellent knowledge assets (intellectual capital) matched with corresponding information capital provide the capability to act effectively — a financial industry example. Copyright © 1999 Knowledge Research Institute, Inc. Reproduced with permission.

to interpret what situations mean and decide how to handle them effectively.

Integrative management provides the capability to "run" the enterprise in ways that make it more effective and viable. That is achieved by making decisions followed by actions that avoid undesirable side-effects. A central premise is that "decisions-in-the-large" (i.e., senior management, strategic, and many tactical decisions) may not lead directly to final actions and implementation. Instead, most produce initiatives that outline desired enterprise directions and are implemented through numerous "decisions-in-the-small" (minute tacit decisions) by people (or in some instances, automated agents) who work on the operational level of the enterprise, "on the line." It is one of knowledge management's roles to see that these people and agents are adequately prepared and supported. Similarly, effective information management is required to provide the descriptions of the world that are required to fuel decisions. Hence, integrative management relies extensively and separately on knowledge management and information management.

Integrative management cannot flourish and provide value without general participation throughout the enterprise. Not only must managers practice integrative management, but it must become a practiced aspect of the general culture. Employees everywhere must be aware of the conditions and requirements of neighboring functions, their future directions, and how those might affect their operation. Such awareness requires knowledge and understanding that must be developed through widespread knowledge management and adoption of asset management mentalities for dealing with intangible capital. The awareness also requires effective information management to provide high-quality information to those with a need to know. Hence, to be effective, integrative management requires many changes and improvements throughout the enterprise. These changes will also serve other initiatives that, when implemented, will together provide additional intangible capital that further supports the enterprise's potential for viable success.

FINAL THOUGHTS

Our Present Direction

The story is far from finished. During the last 20 years, considerable research has been conducted to learn more about how people and organizations handle situations and make and implement decisions, and about how knowledge and other factors influence the effectiveness of such processes. Researchers in areas such as cognitive science, organizational theory, management sciences, economics, and other fields have provided important understanding of these areas (Bechara *et al.* 1997; Damasio 1994, 1999; Davenport & Beck 2001; Dixon 2000; Fauconnier *et al.* 2002; Glimcher 2003; Klein 1998, 2002; Kuhn 2000; Simon 1976, 1977a; Sowell 1980; Weick 2001). And the research continues with greater depth and more sophisticated methods.

Extensive progress is being achieved in other areas as well. We have an increased understanding of the modes and values of effective networking (Dawson 2003), collaboration (Bartulovitch-Richards 2000; Bennis & Biederman 1997; Schrage 1995), and independent work (Loehr & Schwartz 2003). We also are obtaining better insights into the efficacy of different kinds of leadership (Badaracco 2002; Bennis 1994; Bennis & Thomas 2002), the benefits of treating people right (Lawler 2003; Mintzberg 2002; Pfeffer 1994), the advantages of energizing people and making them become engaged in work (Loehr & Schwartz 2003), and many other aspects that make organizations sustain durability and continued success.

Whereas enterprise performance and competitiveness to some extent rely on the application of modern and advanced technology, the results of these investigations and our increasing understanding of what is important become quite clear (Brown & Duguid 2000). The differentiating factor for performance is the effective behavior of people — people who are knowledgeable, motivated, energized, flexible, and ethical; people who are managed according to principles and philosophies that understand how people react, behave, and engage themselves in work, and who are managed by leaders who are just, principled, and effective role models and who can be imitated to create behaviors that are beneficial to the enterprise and its objectives (Ackoff 1994; Buckman 2004; Collins 2001; de Geus 1997; Drucker 1999; Handy 1997, 1999; Mintzberg 2002; Pinchot & Pellman 2000). These are keys to success.

We find broad ranges of opinions as to what effective leadership entails. Many models and perspectives exist, ranging from the autocratic dictator to the soft do-gooder. As in all other aspects of life, the extremes are not effective and tend to be counterproductive. Leaders must understand to strike balances and deal with dilemmas. For example, balance has to be achieved between the dilemma of delegating and empowering on the one hand, and leadership, guidance, and control on the other. It appears that "leading quietly" with decisive, proactive, and long-term goals is a worthy contender for success (Badaracco 2002; Bennis 1994; Bennis & Thomas 2002).

The Societal Conundrum — What Shall We Do?

Increased reliance on and influence of knowledge as a significant ingredient in business will lead to many changes and shifts in economic and trade balances between nations. For example, as the global playing field is flattened, opportunities for industrialized developed nations (North America, Europe, Japan, etc.) to obtain low-cost goods and services from developing nations (e.g., India, Pacific Rim, Latin America, and Africa) will be diminished.

Developed nations have been able to create and sell prized goods and services in part as a result of high educational levels in both their professional and rank-and-file workforces. Historically, developing nations have provided goods with less knowledge-intensiveness at relatively low costs. These goods are produced by workforces with lower educational levels who receive much lower salaries and possess reduced qualities of life. Consequently, developed nations have bought a wide range of goods (and to a smaller extent, services) from developing nations at lower costs than they themselves could deliver — to a large extent through the sacrifices of people with less economic and political clout.

Presently, the educational gap is in the process of being reduced. For example, at the time of this writing, India has more people with doctorates in engineering and science than any other nation, although it still has significant illiteracy. Educational levels in the United States and parts of Europe seem to be stagnant or even deteriorating both in absolute terms and compared with those in many up-and-coming nations. At the same time, increasingly more knowledge-intensive and sophisticated work is being outsourced to developing nations. Immediately, the issues surface: "Which advanced and knowledge-intensive products will the developed world be able to create and deliver to maintain its current living standards if it falls behind in educating its workforce?" and "What will the world look like if we all become equally knowledgeable and empowered?"

From a societal perspective, applying deliberate and systematic people-focused knowledge management that emphasizes enterprise performance is both desirable and appropriate — for now. More effective personal and enterprise behaviors will certainly provide societal value according to current objectives. However, it is not clear that current objectives are appropriate for long-term societal stability and balance (Malone & Yohe 2000; Mintzberg 2002).

As we consider the progress of our ability to manage knowledge and to make enterprises more effective, the question arises: "What is the purpose of these endeavors?" The objectives for the directly affected enterprises for the next year and the next decade are quite clear. Narrowly, they have to do with enterprise survival and success and quality of life for employees and their families and those directly affected by the enterprise's operations and functions. The broader, longer-term objectives are not so clear. From myopic and self-serving societal perspectives, the long-term objectives may be for selected nations to prosper. From global perspectives, issues such as equality among nations and "the gap in wealth and health that separates rich and poor" (Landes 1998) start to emerge. Malone and Yohe (2000 p. 368) state it clearly: "Continued exponential and asymmetrical growth in both population and individual economic productivity would propel world society along a path that is environmentally unsustainable, economically inequitable, and hence socially unstable." Potentially, we may use the building and application of knowledge and understanding worldwide as the tool with which we can level the global playing field. This, we believe, is the real challenge for deliberate and systematic *societal* knowledge management.

Unless the enterprise centers its attention and focus on people, on their knowledge and ability to work effectively, it will be at a competitive disadvantage. That will be the case whether the enterprise is a company, a nongovernmental organization (NGO), a government department, or a nation.

The required people-focus must address several aspects, which must be balanced. They cover the knowledge empowerment of employees, their decision autonomy, their need to understand enterprise policies, direction, strategy, and obligations to stakeholders and society, and lastly their accountability. Many organizations have gone overboard in one direction or another by emphasizing a single aspect and only that one. However, that does not work. As elsewhere in life, a balanced approach is required here as well.

NOTES

1. The special issue on knowledge and the firm in the *California Management Review* (Spring 1998, Vol. 40, No 3) may be of particular interest.

2. Typical KM arenas are KM activities associated with ascertaining that effective quality work is delivered; augmenting people and (automated) work; educating employees; capturing, transforming, and archiving knowledge; motivating, facilitating, and permitting employees; creating cultural conditions; providing IT-based infrastructure; providing knowledge sharing; coordinating KM efforts; conceptualizing, monitoring, guiding, and governing KM practices and results; and managing intellectual capital components.

3. Service paradigms describe what the enterprise, and individual units and people within it, ideally should be able to do for external and internal customers and how units and people should appear to customers through their behavior.

4. Wiig and Wiig (1999) discuss some existing approaches and the reasoning behind them.

5. For an excellent discussion of ontologies and their role in KM, see Chandrasekaran *et al.* (1999).

Appendix A

EXAMPLES OF KNOWLEDGE MANAGEMENT ANALYSIS APPROACHES

Knowledge management (KM) efforts must be viewed from two perspectives. The first and initial perspective is that of analyzing and identifying the organization's general and more specific knowledge-related significant issues and capabilities. That is the perspective of Appendix A. KM analysis approaches and tools, of which there are hundreds, are used mostly by short and intensive discovery projects to plan for new KM efforts. The exception is for approaches and tools that are used to monitor effectiveness and the like of continued knowledge-related practices and efforts. Such monitoring functions may be permanent.

The second perspective is that of initiating and operating the KM initiatives and practices, conducting KM to derive the benefits desired. That is the perspective of Appendix B. KM initiatives and practices are often long term or permanent and focus on improving personal and structural knowledge creation, availability, and effective utilization — the value realization of knowledge. KM, as such, encompasses both perspectives since they are interrelated and successful analyses regularly lead to permanent KM practices.

In the following, we have selected examples of classes of KM analysis approaches, with emphasis on approaches conducted by people. IT-based approaches are deemphasized, with a short list of sources presented at the end of the appendix. A table relating IT-KM tools to KM practices is also provided.

KNOWLEDGE VIGILANCE SURVEY APPROACHES

An organization's attitude toward KM and its readiness to pursue KM can often be measured by its level of "knowledge vigilance" (see Table A-1). Knowledge Vigilance Surveys are quick, high-level

Table A-1

Examples of knowledge management vigilance states.

State of Enterprise	Comprehensive Knowledge Management-Related Characteristics
Vigilant Attitude Is: Realistic, Automatic, and Tacit Knowledge Is Fully Internalized	■ Everyone in the enterprise understands how to be most effective — and pursues intelligent-acting behavior — for both their own and the enterprise's advantages by creating, capturing, building, and applying the best knowledge ■ Systems and approaches for transforming and deploying knowledge are everywhere ■ Culture and incentives are fully supportive of KM and are "Knowledge-Focused"
Proactive Attitude Is: Proactive and Pragmatic Based on Deep Insights	■ Most employees — and all top managers — have accurate understanding of how to create, use, and manage knowledge assets in support of enterprise goals and for personal gains ■ KM capabilities and activities are being implemented to bring about a broad KM vision ■ Culture and incentives are gradually being changed
Literate Attitude Is: Systematic but Dependent	■ Many employees — on all levels — understand how knowledge is created and transferred — and KM's value for sustained profitability and viability ■ They know KM is needed but cannot act without outside assistance ■ Culture and incentives are not yet supportive of KM
Aware Attitude Is: Idealistic and Innocent	■ Some employees — some top executives — are generally aware of the importance of knowledge ■ They don't know how to implement KM corporate-wide and can't make it a practical priority ■ Culture and incentives are not considered
Unconcerned Attitude Is: Not Caring	■ The value of knowledge is not explicitly recognized — only in isolated cases ■ Management and employees manage knowledge sporadically, intuitively, and individually ■ Culture is not cognizant of knowledge values

information-gathering tools that seek to obtain an initial overview of knowledge-related aspects of the enterprise's culture and the mentality of key people, including rank-and-file representatives.

Frequently, it is found that both management and rank-and-file agree that "knowledge is the most important success factor" for an organization. At the same time, there may be a general lack of understanding of how to pursue KM in ways that are both practical and can be fitted into schedules and efforts that already are overcommitted and priorities that are of crucial short-term importance. Knowledge vigilance surveys tend to bring such issues to the surface.

Purpose: Identify KM awareness levels and attitudes toward KM within parts of an organization as well as the whole enterprise. The main purpose is to identify major issues and start the process of raising knowledge-related issues and thereby initiate a KM dialogue among the people within the organization.

KNOWLEDGE SURVEYS AND KNOWLEDGE AUDITS

A knowledge audit provides a facts-based evaluation of where the enterprise must focus its KM efforts to attain its goals. The audit is a qualitative evaluation to identify the knowledge-related competitive effectiveness of the enterprise by identifying areas of strengths, weaknesses, opportunities, threats (SWOT analysis), and risks.

Typical Knowledge-Related Areas: Knowledge needs for operations and strategic efforts; existing knowledge assets and resources; important knowledge gaps; important knowledge flows within the enterprise and knowledge exchanges with outside parties; knowledge-related hurdles and other obstacles.

Purpose: Provide tangible evidence of the enterprise's knowledge-related strengths, weaknesses, opportunities, threats, and risks.

KNOWLEDGE ASSETS MAPPING — INTELLECTUAL CAPITAL INVENTORYING

Knowledge Asset Mapping (KAM) and Intellectual Capital (IC) Inventorying typically are performed to identify, locate, and assess knowledge and IC assets or resources in parts or all of the enterprise. KAM and IC inventorying are more in-depth than Knowledge Surveys and Audits and involve enumerating and categorizing tacit and explicit (including structural) knowledge. As an example, in a manufacturing firm, KAM may be performed separately for the Engineering Department or the factory operations. IC inventorying may be performed for the company as a whole. KAM and IC inventorying generally fulfill the same purpose and are similar to knowledge audits but focus on which assets exist and their state and importance — at times also their value.

Typical Tacit Knowledge Asset Categories: Who are the knowledgeable people, what is their level of expertise, how many are there, and where are they located; what knowledge and expertise do the people possess in terms of core knowledge, experience, and other qualifications; which jobs and functions do people perform; what new knowledge are people creating, sharing, learning — on the job, etc.

Typical Explicit Knowledge Asset Categories: Which structural knowledge and IC assets exist within the enterprise — numbers, types and categories of documents, databases, libraries, intranet web sites; where are the knowledge assets located — within departments and within repositories (such as databases, documents, etc.); how are the knowledge assets organized and represented, and how can they be accessed and utilized; why do these resources exist, how relevant and appropriate are they for that purpose, are they of good "quality" (e.g. up-to-date, reliable, evidence-based, etc.); what are the values of the knowledge and IC assets — market value; where and how are the assets utilized, and how much economic value do they create in utilization.

Purpose: KAM and IC are used to identify and categorize IC assets to understand opportunities and shortcomings for operation and overall enterprise success. In detail, the purpose is to provide information required to set priorities, to identify which actions need to be taken and which possibilities exist for leveraging IC assets.

Knowledge Landscape Mapping

Knowledge landscape mapping (KLM) is quite detailed and requires considerable effort over periods of a few weeks or stretching to several months in some instances. It provides important details for focusing on particular knowledge-related areas that need management attention. There are several reasons for undertaking KLMs.

When an enterprise first becomes concerned with KM, the major reason is to understand what the KM focus should be and to identify areas that should receive priority management attention. Later, after KM is an established practice, understanding the knowledge landscape is a requirement to shape the continued knowledge management effort — practices, programs, projects, infrastructure elements, policies and procedures, etc.

After the initial KM thrust has matured, regular KLM is required to monitor enterprisewide KM effectiveness and to discover new opportunities such as cross-departmental knowledge sharing and opportunities for new strategic directions.

What Is the Knowledge Landscape? The knowledge landscape (KL) of an operation or of the whole organization — similar to a physical landscape — is inordinately complex. From a high-level perspective, the KL shows general features of the terrain in ways important for enterprise governance. On an intermediate level, there are additional specifics pertaining to tactical programs and practices. On still closer view, details identify the nature of, and relationships between, specific KL components relating to the operation of the enterprise. The KL features that are of importance for enterprise governance must include the means to monitor the knowledge condition and where it is headed, the actual state of knowledge and knowledge-related processes and activities, and areas that will require management attention in one form or another.

Purpose: Obtain sufficient information about the "knowledge landscape" to support strategy setting, governance monitoring, and determination of required management actions ranging from budgeting and priority setting to creation of policies and incentive programs, and to identify specific needs and opportunities — all to secure the viability and profitability of the enterprise.

Knowledge Landscape Components within an Operation
1. Current and planned knowledge management practices and policies
2. Knowledge monitoring capabilities
3. Knowledge safeguarding capabilities and practices
4. Current practices and methods for knowledge-related benefit analysis
5. Knowledge-related incentives and disincentives
6. Knowledge infrastructure (existing, planned, opportunities for additional)
7. Specific knowledge processes (for securing, using, improving the knowledge itself, the work process, and the products and services)
8. Characterization and assessment of specific knowledge assets
9. Knowledge-related cultural issues
10. Notable roles of knowledge in operations

11. Notable roles of knowledge in creation and delivery of products and services
12. Notable roles of knowledge in customer relations, including marketing and sales
13. Other relevant aspects

Knowledge Mapping (K-MAPs)

Knowledge mapping covers several approaches to obtain an overview of the state of knowledge assets and knowledge flow within an area, the full enterprise, or within a region or country. Knowledge mapping may be part of, or combined with, other approaches such as knowledge surveys. Typical knowledge maps, in addition to providing descriptions of the knowledge assets and flows, will also provide pictorial maps that may indicate locations of assets, flows of knowledge, relationships between work flows and knowledge assets, and other significant aspects such as the quality or vulnerability of knowledge situations in different operating areas or for different business functions.

Examples of Knowledge Map Characteristics: Application of Knowledge — how knowledge is used, sold/licensed, created, shared, embedded in technology, etc.; **Knowledge Representation** — how knowledge is encoded in rules, stories, natural language, embedded, mental models, etc.; **Nature of Knowledge** — how knowledge exists such as topic knowledge, principles, schemata/scripts/metaknowledge, operational models, routines, prescriptive versus descriptive, conceptual versus concrete, granularity — precise (rule-based, facts, etc.) versus general, etc.; **Source or Destination of Knowledge** — how knowledge flows to and from external or in-house experts, customers, suppliers, practitioners, educational programs, customers, etc.; **Medium for Knowledge** — how knowledge is conveyed such as communicated person-to-person, assimilated on-the-job, embedded in knowledge-based system, included in policies/procedures, written in books and manuals, and documented in drawings.

Purpose: Identify the needs and availability of expertise (knowledge) within an operating area. KM may be undertaken to establish existing and expected requirements for knowledge to deliver the desired operational effectiveness and service paradigm, assess the present knowledge available to the unit, identify knowledge gaps, and spot the availability of valuable knowledge that may be underutilized. Secondary objectives are to arrive at an agreed characterization of the work to be performed (the service paradigm to be delivered) and obtain shared understanding of the knowledge situation within the unit.

Competitive Knowledge Analysis

Competitive knowledge analysis involves information gathering about and identification of particular areas of expertise and important IC assets that are part of competitors' strengths and successes. Competitive knowledge analysis is important for all organizations that aim at having a strong market position.

Purpose: Identify levels of competitive expertise and IC assets for reasons such as identifying where a competitor may be strong, requiring the enterprise to build comparable knowledge, or if the competitor has weak areas, that may point to opportunities that might be pursued. Other approaches include obtaining knowledge from competitors by examining patents and patent applications, performing reverse engineering, benchmarking, or exchanging knowledge in scientific articles and professional meetings, and so on.

Knowledge Flowcharting and Analysis (KFA)

A major challenge in KFA is to identify and characterize all the relevant sources of new knowledge. "Innovation is everywhere, the problem is learning from it" (Brown 1991). It is both impractical and undesirable to identify every innovation in an organization, particularly since people at all levels are full of ideas and continually invent new ways to improve their work. Many of these innovations are personal and may not apply to others. Nevertheless, valuable insights and many opportunities for improving knowledge flows are provided by identifying innovation sources and new knowledge and then charting paths from innovation to practical use. The goal is to identify areas of important improvements, and that is possible in spite of the problems that prevent us from being exhaustive.

Purpose: Find and describe opportunities for improving knowledge flows around selected areas of the organization in order to do business better. As a result, KFA involves investigating, characterizing, and describing how knowledge is used, held, built, and exchanged by individuals and entities such as work groups, departments, and the organization as a whole. Typically, KFA deals more with identifying the *paths*, *means*, and *utility* of aggregate knowledge flows than the flows of individual knowledge items, ideas, and innovations, although some of those may be used as examples of more general activities. KFA also deals with analyzing the strengths and weaknesses of existing knowledge flows and with identifying and synthesizing potential improvements.

Knowledge Diagnostics

Root-cause diagnosis of knowledge-related issues may be the least understood aspect of KM. Only advanced enterprises routinely pursue in-depth analysis and conceptualization — knowledge diagnostics — of target situations and use this expertise to develop candidates for intervention. Most enterprises still pursue conventional symptom-oriented "industrial engineering" diagnosis and devise remedial solutions accordingly. When such enterprises pursue KM, they may utilize KM surveys and screenings methods such as knowledge mapping, or they pursue KM based on what has been successful elsewhere without deep understanding of the knowledge-related mechanisms in the target situation.

Generally, knowledge-related problems or opportunities can only be observed indirectly. By their nature, they are different from traditional operational, tactical, and strategic issues. Knowledge-related situations involve how people think instead of what physically happens. They deal with determining which action is chosen and the reasons for why it is chosen, rather than just what happens. Enterprises often lack the ability to diagnose situations from knowledge perspectives and instead limit investigation to physical or observable characteristics, such as process flows, information flows and issues, and resource availabilities. Considerable understanding of underlying knowledge-related mechanisms and processes is needed to analyze situations and to conceptualize KM interventions and actions. It frequently is helpful to consider target situations in the form of critical knowledge functions (CKFs) that, to be conducted competently, require application of quality knowledge.

Effective KM diagnostics on the personal level requires understanding of how personal knowledge and other intellectual capital

(IC) assets are applied to produce work deliverables competently and competitively. On the organizational level, KM diagnostics requires analysis of structural knowledge-related factors that affect operations of business functions, the delivery and performance of products and services, and so on. In general, KM diagnostics requires awareness of representative knowledge-related issues by having familiarity with symptoms and underlying processes such as:

- Quality problems caused by assembly-line workers who make minute mistakes when they misunderstand how tolerances affect the field performance of products — when they do not understand how to identify when parts have problems — or when they do not know how to repair parts with minor problems and use them anyway.
- Low personal productivity and unnecessary delays caused by insurance underwriters who are uncertain about how to proceed in nonroutine cases when they only possess routine and operational knowledge while lacking broader script and schema knowledge that would allow them to operationalize such knowledge to apply to different cases and situations.
- Wrong customer advice provided by service representatives who misunderstand customer situations or lack sufficient knowledge of the enterprise's products, services, and systems and procedures and therefore address customer situations improperly.
- Inappropriate design solutions by engineers who misunderstand product application requirements because of insufficient knowledge of how to apply technology in the target context.
- Misdiagnosis and faulty repairs by office machine and instrument technicians who make hasty conclusions based on assumptions derived from limited experience.

Purpose: Identify and assess knowledge-related issues in target situations to determine whether better KM can improve the situation.

Typical Approaches: Identify pressing and priority operational and business symptoms and issues that then are pursued with in-depth analysis and aided by the use of Critical Function Analysis.

Critical Knowledge Function Analysis (CKFA)

Critical knowledge functions (CKF) analysis is a tool that many practitioners use to find knowledge-related areas that need attention.

A central issue in knowledge-related diagnostics and other knowledge analysis work is the capability to identify and characterize operational, professional, or managerial functions that in some way are critical — by being functional bottlenecks or vulnerable, or by being unrealized opportunities, etc. Examples of simplified CKF characteristics are presented in Table A-2 for four types of situations. CKFs are characterized by five descriptions:

1. The **type of knowledge** (or **expertise** or **skill**) involved in performing a function or task.
2. **Business use** of that knowledge.
3. **Constraint** that prevents the knowledge to be utilized fully, the **vulnerability** of the situation, or the **unrealized opportunity** that is not taken advantage of.
4. **Opportunities** and **alternatives** for managing (i.e., improving or correcting) the CKF.
5. **Expected** (incremental) **value** of improving the situation — release knowledge constraint, take advantage of (exploit) the opportunity to use knowledge differently.

Purpose: Find, characterize, and assess the potential value of knowledge-related improvements of critical knowledge functions.

Typical Approaches: Interviews of managers, supervisors, and line personnel to isolate potential CKF candidates. Particular in-depth interviews (sometimes with audio or video recording) of the people who operate the target function. Business analysis of operation around target functions at times using knowledge benefit analysis methods.

KNOWLEDGE (MANAGEMENT) BENEFIT ASSESSMENT (KBA)

Knowledge-related benefits are often difficult to analyze and substantiate. The benefits may be intangible, they may be masked by other improvement efforts that occur at the same time, and they may take a longer time than expected to be realized — before they "hit the bottom line." To illustrate, Figure 8-3 shows a generalized process for how the initial KM action may lead to intermediate effects and benefits before the results of the action produce the expected final benefits. Initially, KM efforts require the investment of time, attention, manpower, expenses, interruptions, and so on. The major

Table A-2
CKF characteristics for four example situations.

Examples CKF Characteristics	Example 1 Chemical Industry	Example 2 Truck Repair Services	Example 3 Engineering Department	Example 4 Financial Industry
Which *Type of* Knowledge Is Involved?	Chemical reactor operating expertise	Diagnostics expertise for truck diesel engines	Specialized mechanical engineering compressor design expertise	Securities trading expertise
What Is the *Business Use* of Knowledge?	Understand how to produce specialty chemicals for the commercial market	Provide effective repair of diesel powered trucks used by the organization	Develop, build, and sell high performance compressors to industrial customers	Increase the value of a retirement fund portfolio for mutual fund customers
Does the Situation Represent a *Constraint or Opportunity?*	There are too few proficient operators and as a result many reactors are not run well *— Constraint —*	The master diagnostician only has time to diagnose 25% of the trucks with problems and this leads to improper and expensive repairs that take too long *— Constraint —*	"Our design knowledge is superbly better than competition and we should offer a broad line of highly specialized custom designs to create a larger and more profitable market." *— Opportunity —*	The securities trader is operating in an environment that is too disruptive to allow him to search out and analyze the opportunities for each trade *— Constraint —*

Table A-2
(Continued)

Examples CKF Characteristics	Example 1 Chemical Industry	Example 2 Truck Repair Services	Example 3 Engineering Department	Example 4 Financial Industry
What Are Relevant *KM Alternatives?*	Create a KBS with expert reactor operator knowledge and make it available to all operators	Train more diagnosticians by apprenticing to the master diagnostician for six months	Introduce a new product line of compressors that are custom designed for specific situations	Support securities trader with a second trader and a KBS that performs initial market analyses of changes and screens trade opportunities
Which *Benefits* **Might We Expect?**	Increased profit, decreased costs, and increased market share	Reduce repair costs and time — to increase net profit and reduce capital investment (due to higher utilization factor of vehicles in fleet)	Increase revenues and profit margins to obtain higher net profits	Better selection of trading opportunities and faster executions increase revenues and profit margins to yield greater net profits

benefits from knowledge result later from the application of knowledge to create added value by improving quality, timeliness, or direction of work of some kind.

The assessment of benefits from KM actions requires first an estimate of the monetary or other costs of investments and second, the *assessment of incremental value* (again in monetary or other terms) from either (1) utilizing the expected improvement of knowledge in some work process, or (2) trading the knowledge in question (e.g., an IC asset such as a patent) in the marketplace.

Assessing the value of utilizing knowledge in work processes is inherently complex. It normally involves many stages for knowledge to be organized, communicated, mobilized (internalized and be readied for utilized) — and, when utilized, have the effects of translating the improved knowledge into intermediate improvements and benefits until the final benefits are realized. This is illustrated in Figure 8-3.

A major issue associated with knowledge benefit assessment, as a result of its complexity and intangibility, is to substantiate and establish the credibility of the analysis. It has been found helpful to represent the expected propagation of KM actions from beginning to end in a diagram such as Figure 8-3. The diagram is then used as a framework to discuss potential effects — activities involved, possible timetables, advantages, disadvantages, costs, benefits, etc. — with affected parties. Such discussions normally lead to better insights as to the best approaches to achieve the desired results as well as clear understandings of agreements and concerns. The outcome is a foundation for the credibility of the overall assessment.

Purpose: Prepare benefit analysis for potential knowledge-related initiatives to provide support for planning, action, and monitoring.

Information Technology-Based KM Tools

IT-based KM tools fall outside the scope of this book. However, extensive information on many different existing tools can be found by searching the Internet — for example, for the following companies which represent a fair cross section of what is available:

AI-CBR (www.ai-cbr.org)
Autonomy, Inc.(www.autonomy.com)
BackWeb Technologies (www.backweb.com)
CBR-Web (www.cbr-web.org)

Table A-3

Examples of IT application support of selected KM practices
Copyright © 2002 Knowledge Research Institute, Inc.

IT Applications/ Knowledge Management Practices	Common & Advanced E-Mail	Adv. Group-ware	Intranet Internet WWW	Knowl. Inventory Systems	Corp. Knowl. Maps	Knowl. Bases	Distance Learn. Systems	Global Knowl. Sharing Systems	CBR & KBS Expert Systems	Subject Matter Ontologies
Knowledge-Leveraging Mentality	✔		✔							
Integrative Management Culture	✔	✔	✔	✔	✔	✔	✔	✔		✔✔
Knowledge Capabilities, Needs Maps			✔	✔	✔	✔				✔
Measure Intellectual Capital Assets			✔	✔	✔	✔				✔
Create Intangible Asset Monitor			✔	✔	✔	✔				✔
Change Cultural Drivers	✔	✔	✔	✔			✔	✔		✔
Strengthen Intensive Knowledge-Work	✔	✔	✔	✔	✔	✔	✔	✔	✔	✔
Collaborative Work Practices	✔	✔✔	✔	✔	✔			✔		
Foster Communities of Practice	✔	✔	✔				✔	✔		✔
Foster Networks of Practice	✔	✔	✔				✔	✔		✔
Conduct Knowledge Cafés	✔					✔				

Communispace (www.communispace.com)
Convera / Excalibur Technologies Corporation (www.excalib.com)
Docushare Xerox Corporation (www.xerox.com)
Engenia Unity Desktop (www.engenia.com)
Fulcrum (www.888fulcrum.com)
Hummingbird (www.pcdocs.com)
IBM Lotus (www.lotus.com)
Intelligent Inference Systems (www.iiscorp.com)
Intraspect Software, Inc. (www.intraspect.com)

KDD	Speech Recognition	NLU	Concept-Based Knowl. Navigation	AI Operations-Related Software	Neural Net-works	Intelligent Agents	Complex Intelligent Systems	Genetic Algorithms	Evolutionary Computation
				✔					
		✔							
	✔	✔	✔	✔		✔	✔	✔	✔
	✔	✔	✔						

(*Continued*)

MAGI (www.projectmagi.com)
Open Text Corporation (www.opentext.com)
Plumtree Software (www.plumtree.com)
SageMaker (www.sagemaker.com)
Tacit Knowledge (www.tacit.com)
The Haley Enterprise (www.haley.com)

Table A-3 provides an overview of a selection of 20 common and emerging IT applications areas for 23 different KM practices. In this

Table A-3
(Continued)

IT Applications/ Knowledge Management Practices	Common & Advanced E-Mail	Adv. Group-ware	Intranet Internet WWW	Knowl. Inventory Systems	Corp. Knowl. Maps	Knowl. Bases	Distance Learn. Systems	Global Knowl. Sharing Systems	CBR & KBS Expert Systems	Subject Matter Ontolog
Capture & Share Expert Know-How			✔		✔	✔✔		✔	✔	✔
Capture Departing Personnel Expertise						✔✔		✔	✔	✔
Share Knowledge Widely	✔	✔✔	✔	✔	✔	✔	✔	✔	✔	✔
Transfer Expert Know-How	✔		✔				✔✔	✔✔	✔✔	✔
Capture Decision Reasoning										
Lessons Learned Systems										
After Action Reviews (AAR)	✔		✔							
Provide Outcome Feedback	✔	✔	✔			✔		✔		
Implement Expert Networks	✔	✔	✔	✔	✔		✔	✔	✔	✔
Discover Knowledge from Data						✔				✔✔
Deploy Knowledge-Based System			✔			✔			✔✔	✔
Deploy Knowledge Bases			✔			✔✔				✔

table single checkmarks (✔) denote IT applications that are of general value to a KM practice. Double checkmarks (✔✔) denote IT applications that are of pivotal value — where the success of the KM practice relies on the IT application.

KDD	Speech Recognition	NLU	Concept-Based Knowl. Navigation	AI Operations-Related Software	Neural Networks	Intelligent Agents	Complex Intelligent Systems	Genetic Algorithms	Evolutionary Computation
✔	✔		✔						
	✔								
		✔	✔						
✔		✔	✔						
✔		✔	✔						
✔		✔	✔						
✔		✔	✔						
✔	✔	✔	✔						
	✔	✔	✔	✔					
✔✔	✔	✔✔	✔		✔				
	✔	✔	✔	✔	✔	✔	✔		
✔		✔	✔						

Appendix B

EXAMPLES OF KNOWLEDGE MANAGEMENT PRACTICES AND INITIATIVES

When considering models for the different knowledge management (KM) approaches that enterprises pursue, we also need to be aware of the various interpretations of what KM entails. Some consider "knowledge" to be only a slightly different form of "information," whereas others consider knowledge and information to be fundamentally different and serve quite different purposes. Some pursue KM from a broad, general business focus, whereas others focus on intellectual asset or capital management, and so on. Here, we focus on five KM focus areas presented in the following pages.

There are virtually "1001" different approaches — practices and initiatives — for managing knowledge. Some focus on making people more knowledgeable, others on capturing expertise from competent people for immediate or later transfer to others, and still others on utilizing technology to communicate, capture, make available, or just store information about knowledge. KM practices and initiatives that focus on creating, building, deploying, and safekeeping knowledge are investments. KM practices and initiatives that focus on the application and exploitation of knowledge assets provide the benefits that the investments have targeted. In this appendix, we identify 20 different KM practices and initiatives of both kinds. Many authors provide excellent insights into powerful and effective KM approaches (See Dawson 2000, Denning 2000, Despres & Chauvel 2000, Dixon 2000, Hansen *et alia* 1999, Hoolsapple 2003a and 2003b, Klein 2002, Krogh *et alia* 2000, London 2003, Mittelstaedt 2003, Nonaka & Takeuchi 1995, Pfeffer 1994, Pinchot & Pellman 2000, Roos *et alia* 1998, Sveiby 1997, Ubogu 2001, Weick 2001, and Wiig 1995).

General Business Focus

Many advanced enterprises are able to pursue a combination of all the KM thrusts presented below. They explicitly and deliberately create, capture, organize, renew, share, use, and otherwise exploit knowledge — enterprisewide with all reasonable means possible. Their premise is that knowledge is the fundamental factor behind all of the enterprise's activities. The condition of its knowledge assets define the enterprise's future potential and its sustained viability. The enterprise's competitiveness and profitability depends directly on the competitive quality of its knowledge assets and the successful application of these assets in all its business activities; that is, the realization of the value of knowledge assets in conducting work and in other ways of leveraging these assets (Buckman 2004).

Purpose: Manage knowledge effectively to make people — and the whole enterprise — act intelligently to sustain long-term viability by developing and deploying highly competitive knowledge assets in people and in other manifestations. Make available and use best knowledge at each point of action for all plans, operations, and activities. The KM goal is to build and exploit intellectual capital effectively and gainfully.

Examples of Tools and Approaches: Knowledge landscape mapping to determine general needs, opportunities, and overall knowledge characteristics; knowledge strategy and priorities; dynamic Economic Value Added (EVA^{TM}) knowledge and knowledge-related activity evaluations; incentive programs; infrastructure supports; and KM monitoring capabilities. Knowledge management professionals provide a wide range of supportive and proactive services based on extensive understanding of how knowledge is developed, possessed, and used, and becomes valuable on both the personal and organizational levels.

Intellectual Asset Management Focus

Knowledge (personal and enterprisewide structural knowledge), from the perspective of being part of intellectual capital, can and must be managed as other enterprise assets with regard to investments, utilization, risks, renewal and maintenance, new exploitation opportunities, and so on, for the purpose of making appropriate allocations of resources and securing sustained enterprise viability.

Purpose: Manage intellectual assets (intellectual capital) — people-based knowledge, products, services, patents, technologies, practices, customer relations, organizational arrangements, and other structural assets. Increase and leverage (exploit) knowledge-related assets to enhance the economic value and potential viability of the enterprise.

Examples of Tools and Approaches: Identification of intellectual asset needs; intellectual capital accounting philosophy and system; evaluation of intellectual capital categories (patents, for example) with identification of exploitation opportunities. Knowledge management professionals assist by mapping knowledge landscape, evaluating intellectual assets, and identifying needs or opportunities for new ones.

INNOVATION AND KNOWLEDGE BUILDING FOCUS ("LEARNING ORGANIZATION")

An enterprise can remain in a leadership position (sustain its viability) only when it innovates and learns faster than its competitors. Effective innovation and learning require a supportive environment and extensive emphasis on internal opportunities and knowledge exchange and learning from all sources — particularly from external sources.

Purpose: Build better knowledge assets to be available within the enterprise for improved competitiveness through personal and organizational innovation, organizational learning and R&D, and acquisition of outside knowledge, supported by motivators to innovate and capture valuable knowledge.

Examples of Tools and Approaches: Programs for importing valuable external knowledge (benchmarking, collaborating with suppliers and customers, university relationships, etc.); environment and incentives to motivate employees to be practically creative and innovative. Knowledge management professionals support operating entities in creating and conducting knowledge acquisition and creation activities and capabilities.

Knowledge Sharing and
Information Transfer Focus

By having access to better knowledge throughout the enterprise, knowledge workers can innovate and adopt the most suitable practices and approaches and thereby deliver higher quality work. In addition, situation-handling is performed better when knowledge workers are provided with excellent, up-to-date information (*by being "informed that"*) on the most effective approaches, practices, and solutions. By using qualified knowledge management professionals, the knowledge transfer becomes more effective and valuable and demands less time and effort from the knowledge workers. Technology solutions provide these services with great effectiveness (Dixon 2000).

Purpose: Make available best available knowledge and facilitate its use at each point of action (PoA) to allow knowledge workers to deliver quality work for all activities, operations, and plans throughout the enterprise; facilitate communication between individuals; facilitate locating relevant information; screen information for appropriateness; reformat and organize information to facilitate end-use.

Examples of Tools and Approaches: Multiple approaches to transferring knowledge to points of action ranging from ad hoc to systematic and well-designed methods; comprehensive and targeted educational and knowledge distribution capabilities; identification of specific knowledge requirements in key functions for transfer of appropriate knowledge to PoAs. Knowledge management professionals act as knowledge-sharing facilitators by organizing knowledge sharing events, by conducting knowledge elicitation and organization for communicating knowledge to users (ranging from conducting and documenting knowledge acquisitions to creation of educational materials, including training program designers as well as instructors and the like). Knowledge management professionals assist in identifying and characterizing knowledge requirements for key functions. In addition, E-Mail/Intranet; Internet/WWW; Groupware to support widespread collaboration; Global Information Sharing System; "Yellow Pages" — Intranet homepages for each employee with competencies and interests. Information specialists provide information-facilitation services by obtaining requests for information.

INFORMATION TECHNOLOGY-BASED KNOWLEDGE CAPTURE AND DELIVERY FOCUS

Information technology (IT) provides capabilities to organize, reorganize, handle, store, locate, distribute, and present information faster, with greater precision, in greater volume, with better timeliness than otherwise possible. Technology-based approaches are used to mine and capture historical knowledge from well-known and routine tasks more effectively and comprehensively than people are able to do. Knowledge workers perform better when they have access to excellent, up-to-date knowledge (by *"understanding how"*) on the most effective approaches, practices, and solutions.

Purpose: Organize, structure, store, and deliver information with IT and automated to the largest practical extent; effectively capture knowledge with IT support; obtain knowledge from unorganized databases (such as implied rules for effective treatment of diseases, for handling of particular problems); organize knowledge to facilitate its application; distribute knowledge to point-of-action (PoA).

Examples of Tools and Approaches that Primarily Are Intelligent and Active: Knowledge and Information Navigation Tools; Office Management Systems; knowledge creation and transformation tools for knowledge discovery in databases (KDD, in contrast to "Data Mining") using methods such as machine induction and natural language understanding (NLU); automated lessons-learned-systems (LLS); Evaluation and Summarization Tools for Communications such as e-mail; intelligent agents; KBS/AI/Expert Systems); knowledge navigation tools based on NLU concept understanding; advanced computer-based educational systems with interactive multimedia delivery mechanisms; and specialized applications.

Examples of Tools and Approaches that Primarily Are Passive: Knowledge Inventory System; Information Inventory System; Corporate Knowledge Maps; Global Knowledge Sharing System; Corporate Memory Data Bases; Corporate Memory Knowledge Bases;[1] Distance Learning Systems.

20 KNOWLEDGE MANAGEMENT INITIATIVES AND PRACTICES

Knowledge management professionals, often with AI expertise, apply technical tools with understanding and judgment, create and facilitate operation of the technology-based capabilities, and provide technical support for maintaining them. We can outline different models for how enterprises approach and pursue what they consider KM as in the following selection of 20 initiatives and practices:

- **Promote Knowledge-Supportive Mentality and Culture.** When an enterprise builds and orchestrates an internal practice to deal systematically and deliberately with knowledge by having people share insights and seek assistance from one another, a new and open culture emerges. People open up and discuss difficult issues, emerging ideas, and tentative opportunities with one another. They take mental risks that would be unthinkable in conventional environments. They seek collaboration to achieve better results more quickly and build upon the ideas of others and let others build on their own ideas. By opening up to new approaches and perspectives, and by building on the capabilities of others instead of only relying on their own, they expand their action space. As people expand action spaces and become more effective through capable collaboration, the enterprise becomes more effective. Complex tasks are addressed better and faster, and innovations abound, making the enterprise more capable and able to engage in activities that previously were infeasible (Buckman 2004).
- **Measure Intellectual Capital and Create an Intangible Asset Monitor.** Provide overview by auditing the intangible assets of the enterprise with focus on the intellectual capital that can range from patents and product designs to human capital and explicit operating practices. Create a permanent IC management capability by implementing an intangible asset monitoring system for regular updates (Sveiby 1997).
- **Change and Facilitate Cultural Drivers.** Introduce more effective communication practices, peer reviews, and specifics such as incentives, guidelines, and policies, and corresponding employee evaluations to influence the behavior of people within an organization.
- **Create and Foster Collaborative Work Practices.** Many factors affect the capability to collaborate, some of which are associated with attitudes, others with understanding and knowledge, and

yet others with compatibility and sharing views, thinking styles, and backgrounds. A set of important factors for being able to collaborate includes sufficient, complementary, and diverse expertise for creativity, versatility, and flexibility; shared and well understood goals and objectives; shared knowledge to mutually understand the needs and nature of the situation; personal security and knowledge that collaborating is "safe"; understanding of others' expertise to accept the value and relevance of their potential contributions; mutual respect, tolerance, and trust; and compatible work styles and ability to work together.

- **Provide Formal Education and Training.** Utilize methods ranging from in-house courses and seminars with employees as instructors to external corporate university arrangements. The objectives are to provide employees with greater expertise in areas that are considered important for corporate success according to the reigning management philosophy. They can range from hands-on training classes to gain proficiency in performing concrete tasks to learning critical thinking and acquiring metaknowledge to general education in areas such as environmental and social systems.

- **Foster Communities and Networks of Practice.** Facilitate collaboration and socializing by people with similar or identical responsibilities within an organization (community of practice). The purpose is to enable these individuals to share experiences and insights and collaborate to find innovative solutions applicable to their daily work. Networks of practice are formed by people with similar functions from different organizations (Dawson 2003).

- **Conduct Town Meetings and Conduct Knowledge Cafés.** Town meetings refer to assemblies of many employees in one facility to be briefed on a topic (such as new corporate strategy) and to then discuss the topic and provide feedback on how it is perceived by the attendees. Knowledge cafés refer to group sessions in which a number of people (from a small number to several hundred) are assembled to discuss the implications of some topic that affects them and their organization. Typically, the knowledge café is conducted by presenting the topic and its background to the group. This presentation is followed by brief (5 to 15 minutes) discussions by small groups (five or fewer persons) of the implications and what they may mean for the participants. The groups are then scrambled, and discussions are repeated, often for four or five cycles before summaries are collected. Often, continued informal discussions are encouraged for days or weeks.

- **Build and Operate Expert Networks.** Provide formalized capabilities for workers in the field to consult or collaborate with topic experts on complex or unfamiliar tasks. Several mechanisms and infrastructure elements may be used to create and support an expert network. They include: (1) guides to "who knows what" in the form of "yellow page" systems on intranets, knowledge inventories, or knowledge roadmaps; (2) policies that permit knowledge worker access to experts; (3) budgets for experts to help knowledge workers; (4) communication channels that range from on-site expert visits, face-to-face meetings, telephone consultations, e-mail, groupware-based communication, video conferencing, and so on; (5) learnings capture systems to build frequently asked questions (FAQ) help systems; and (6) outcome feedback analysis and capture systems.

- **Capture and Transfer Expert *Know-How*.** Communicates concepts, judgments, and thinking by exceptional performers and experts to other knowledge workers to help them develop improved "*this is how we do it*" knowledge to perform better.[2] One approach uses experts to demonstrate, identify, and characterize their work methods. By observing experts at work and in simulated situations, the experts communicate directly with workers. They explain their approaches, thinking, and perspectives for handling routine and particularly, nonroutine, situations and engage less experienced workers in discussions and explorations. This approach allows these workers to learn by building and internalizing new knowledge. They particularly build mental models in the form of beginning routines, operational models, and scripts for how to perform the new tasks.

- **Capture and Transfer Expert *Concepts* to Other Practitioners.** Similar to the capture and transfer of know-how but instead of focusing on how to perform work, it focuses on the concepts, thinking, and reasoning foundations for why work may be performed in different ways under different conditions. A typical approach is for experts to describe, identify, and characterize their associations, concept hierarchies, mental models, content knowledge, and metaknowledge as best they can — first by telling the other practitioners and, as sessions evolve, by being drawn into discussions. This approach allows practitioners to build and internalize new knowledge by building mental models in the form of operational models, scripts, schemata, general abstractions, and metaknowledge.

- **Capture and Transfer Expertise from Departing Personnel.** This is a valuable practice when competent people retire or are promoted. Many approaches are used. For example, some use trained observers who document routine and semi-routine work in job descriptions, reports, or video recordings. Others utilize "self-elicitation" by writing or audio or video recording the departing individual as they perform their work or when they provide explanations of their expertise. Others use KM professionals to elicit and document pertinent knowledge. Still others use apprenticing or shadowing to learn on-the-job. Shadowing is particularly useful when the expertise covers a highly variable domain such as for managers, internal consultants, "troubleshooters," and similar broad fields.
- **Capture and Apply Decision Reasoning.** This is very important but rarely performed well. It involves identifying and making explicit the reasons why a particular decision was created and chosen and other pertinent aspects regarding the situation. Capture of what is behind the decision involves identifying the context and circumstance of the situation, as well as the perspectives that dominated the options that were considered and rejected, with reasons noted. The context also needs to be described. Decision reasoning is equally important for decisions that led to problems or dead ends.
- **Capture and Transfer Competitive Knowledge.** It is always important to allow the enterprise to understand new challenges and new opportunities. Capture of competitive knowledge may largely be achieved by following patent applications, participating in professional knowledge exchanges, learning from customers and suppliers, and, in some instances, acquiring and analyzing competitive products.
- **Create Lessons Learned Systems.** These systems are provided to support existing work and capture new knowledge, and they include procedures for sequestering the persons directly involved when a notable situation has occurred. They consist of several elements, including: (1) individuals involved in the target lesson learned (LL) situation; (2) procedures for the capture process; (3) repository for initial, unedited capture information; (4) editing process; (5) approval process for including LL into the final knowledge base (KB); (6) resulting KB consisting of all LLs; (7) KB access methods (such as Case-Based Reasoning, or CBR); (8) user community that will access and use the LLs in their

work; and (9) information technology environment in which LLS is implemented. The target LL situation may be a solved problem, a preventable mishap, a recognizable opportunity, and so on. LLS procedures call for quick assembly of participants to capture all relevant information, often in a predefined, structured format to make such knowledge available when required. The LLS may use CBR technology to store and locate applicable knowledge in the form of representative cases to provide guidance when a new situation arises (Wiig 1995, pp. 295–304).

- **Conduct After Action Reviews (AAR).**[3] AAR was first developed by the armed forces to learn from experience by identifying what the mission was, how it was approached, what went right, what went wrong, what the situation was relative to what was expected, and which learnings should be recognized. Three questions drive the AAR method: What happened? Why did it happen? and What should we do about it? The purposes of AAR are to improve the accuracy and detail of feedback available to sector leaders and employees; identify collective and individual strengths and how to leverage them; identify collective and individual deficiencies and how to correct them; reinforce and increase the learning that took place during a business activity; increase interest and motivation; guide the individuals and groups toward achieving performance objectives; identify lessons learned so that they can be applied to subsequent activities or tasks; increase confidence in performance capability; and increase the proficiency of all participants. These learnings are compiled, edited, and stored in a structured knowledge base for further studies and are to be available in future situations.

- **Provide Outcome Feedback.** Getting feedback on how work products perform in the external or internal customer environment is necessary information on which to base work performance assessments. Unfortunately, it frequently is not regularly available. Consequently, organizations and individuals have limited insights into how they may improve their performance, improve products and services, or otherwise innovate. Outcome feedback is provided in several ways. One approach is a formalized system for internal and external customers to evaluate received products or services. Use of questionnaires in merchandizing and many service industries is typical but is not considered very effective. Other, more effective approaches include on-site studies of how work products are utilized by recipients and how well they satisfy real requirements. For complex work products, highly effective outcome feedback includes studies of potentials for (1) innovation to improve product performance in customer environment; (2) including additional features in the products and services such as embedded or companion knowledge and expertise; (3) different products and services; and (4) education of users as to how better to use and leverage products and services.

- **Pursue Knowledge Discovery from Data (KDD).** KDD uses sophisticated statistical or automatic reasoning methods to identify patterns of interesting cause-effect relationships. An example is the discovery of intervention methods that had proven effective for treatment of mental disorders in large populations (United States and the Netherlands).
- **Implement and Utilize Performance Support Systems (PSS) and Knowledge-Based System (KBS) Applications.** Such computer-based systems contain explicit or implicit domain knowledge used specifically for reasoning about specific situations. Examples of KBSs are case-based reasoning (CBR) systems, expert systems, and neural nets. Recently, as a result of the systematic perspectives encouraged by explicit KM, the reliance of automated knowledge and reasoning has changed within many organizations. Instead of being considered as stand-alone or relatively isolated solutions to relieve particular critical knowledge-related functions, knowledge-based systems (KBSs) are now often considered as integral building blocks within a larger knowledge management (KM) perspective.
- **Build and Deploy Knowledge Bases.** A knowledge base (KB) is a component of a knowledge-based system that contains the system's domain knowledge in some representation suitable for the system to reason with. Knowledge in knowledge bases is typically represented in a standard format. KBs are important repositories for explicit knowledge. They can contain "knowledge" in the form of unstructured natural language documents, or many other representations. For unstructured KBs, editing ("rational reconstruction") of the acquired knowledge is needed. KBs are also equipped with retrieval mechanisms that can range from simple query languages to sophisticated intelligent agents.
- **Deploy Information Technology Tools for Knowledge Management.** A large number of IT tools are available for KM support. These tools are under constant development, and new capabilities are introduced repeatedly. A class of IT-based functions will operate on and support categorization and linking of natural language documents. Most of these tools will also create intranet

Table B-1

The relationship between typical KM initiatives and practices for five KM foci.

Knowledge Management Focus KM Initiatives and Practices	General Business Focus	Intellectual Asset Management Focus	Innovation & Knowledge Building Focus	Knowledge Sharing & Information Transfer Focus	Information & Technology-Based Knowledge Capture & Delivery Focus
Promote Knowledge-Supportive Mentality & Culture	X	X	X		
Measure Intellectual Capital & Create an Intangible Asset Monitor	X	X			
Change & Facilitate Cultural Drivers	X		X	X	X
Create & Foster Collaborative Work Practices	X		X	X	
Provide Formal Education & Training	X			X	
Foster Communities of Practice & Networks of Practice	X		X	X	
Conduct Town Meetings & Knowledge Cafés	X			X	

Table B-1
(Continued)

Knowledge Management Focus KM Initiatives and Practices	General Business Focus	Intellectual Asset Management Focus	Innovation & Knowledge Building Focus	Knowledge Sharing & Information Transfer Focus	Information & Technology-Based Knowledge Capture & Delivery Focus
Build & Operate Expert Networks	X			X	
Capture & Transfer Expert *Know-How*	X		X	X	X
Transfer Expert *Concepts* to Other Practitioners	X		X	X	
Capture & Transfer Expertise from Departing Personnel	X		X	X	X
Capture & Apply Decision Reasoning	X		X	X	
Capture & Transfer Competitive Knowledge	X	X	X	X	
Create Lessons Learned Systems	X		X	X	X
Conduct After Action Reviews (AARs)	X		X	X	
Provide Outcome Feedback	X		X		
Pursue Knowledge Discovery from Data (KDD)	X	X			X
Implement and Utilize PSS & KBS Applications	X			X	X
Build & Deploy Knowledge Bases	X	X			X
Deploy Information Technology Tools for Knowledge Management	X	X	X	X	X

portals. Many have limited natural language (concept) understanding and indexing capabilities.

For the limited number of examples provided above, we can identify which KM initiatives and practices may be pursued by the different KM focus areas. Such a representation of the relationships is presented in Table B-1. Clearly, most organizations do not show such a clear-cut selection of initiatives and practices. Many are in the process of expanding their KM efforts and are regularly adding new capabilities. Others have locally supported efforts that may fall outside the pattern and so on.

Notes

1. Corporate Memory Knowledge Bases differ from Corporate Memory Databases in content and form. Knowledge Bases contain "knowledge" such as "How-to Knowledge" and use knowledge representations such as rules or "case structures" to support automated reasoning. Databases contain descriptive data (ranging from transactional data to specific characterizations [as in personnel files] to natural language narratives) and are organized according to conventional data models.
2. Transfer of cognitive skills has proven difficult. Under the best of circumstances, at most 10 percent of expert knowledge can be elicited and transferred during a project period (Anderson 1981; Singley & Anderson 1989).
3. For a description of AAR, see, for example, <http://www.luminella.com/aar.htm> (May 22, 2000) and <http://www-dcst.monroe.army.mil/wfxxi/op-anx-f.htm> (May 22, 2000).

Appendix C

MEMORY AND KNOWLEDGE CATEGORIZATIONS

HUMAN MEMORY ORGANIZATION

When we communicate with the world outside ourselves, we use a system of highly complicated mental processes. Our senses provide inputs from our eyes, ears, nose, mouth, and from sensors in our skin and other parts of our body. This information is continually fed to working (or short-term) memories and similar faculties where we consciously or nonconsciously sort and classify it and transfer much of it to the longer-term memories to be remembered outright or processed further. Before being transferred to long-term memory, the mental objects created from received information may be retained temporarily in "buffer memory."

Mental objects are remembered as a result of long-term potentiation (LTP), where the synapses of certain neurons are strengthened by mental activity. It was believed that single, isolated synapses were strengthened and that this led to a "bit-like" memory as in digital computers. Instead, Bonhoeffer and his colleagues (1989) and others indicate that memory is produced by spreading potentiations of many neighboring synapses from numerous neurons. This leads to a much more complex — and more robust — memory system.

One of the difficult operational aspects of the memory system is the lack of a direct, conscious access to mental objects stored in long-term memory. Long-term memory apparently must be accessed through working memory, which then becomes a limiting factor. This is important when exploring what people know, since people do not normally know what they know. They often do not have access to particular knowledge until it is needed for use in a specific situation and are reminded — until they are "primed to use it." Priming has been established to be an important mechanism for recalling what we know.

312

A conceptual model of the human memory system is shown in Figure 4-2 (repeated below). In this highly idealized model, the communication paths between different memory areas are indicated with arrows. Communications with the sensory and motor systems are also indicated. The different memories are depicted as separate areas of the brain. This is not generally the case in reality, but it helps explain the functions. Our brain is organized to contain a large number of specialized areas such as vision, hearing, smell, language,

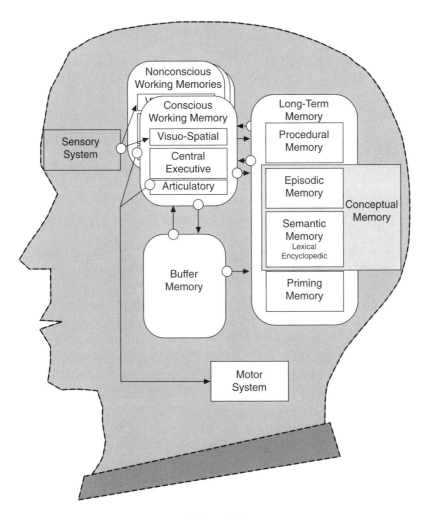

Figure 4-2
(Repeated). Conceptual model of the human memory system. (Copyright © 1993 by Karl M. Wiig. Reproduced with permission.)

number manipulations, and so on.[1] In addition, our right and left hemispheres serve distinctly different functions. Whereas the left hemisphere is dominant for processing language and conceptual and classificatory functions, the right hemisphere is dominant for processing spatial functions and detailed analysis and discrimination. Musical ability also is located in the right hemisphere. Hemispheric dominance is not always clear-cut, however. For example, although the numerical abilities, including understanding numerical relations and concepts, are located in the right hemisphere, the ability to read and produce signs of mathematics reside in the left hemisphere (Gardner 1983).

Working Memory

Working memory, or short-term memory, is considered to be the center of consciousness. Conscious and explicit reasoning takes place in working memory at the top level of attention. Hence, when I think about how I will drive across town to a particular address, I reason about it in my working memory. To help me, I retrieve from long-term memory images knowledge of the road conditions, different routes that I am familiar with, and similar material and use that to "think" consciously about what to do.

A noteworthy aspect of the present model is that people have the equivalent of many working memories which can operate on different levels of consciousness or attention. Of major interest is the working memory, which mostly operates on the conscious level. However, people have the ability to perform reasoning and other mental functions nonconsciously as when "suddenly getting a good idea" without having thought explicitly about, it or when they suddenly remember the name of a person that they met five minutes earlier but could not name at the time. Similarly, people perform a large number of activities in automatic or semi-automatic ways. For example, we can carry on a deep and highly conscious conversation with someone while driving a car, we can discuss difficult topics with someone while walking, or we can open and close doors automatically and analyze obstacles and make semiautomatic decisions on where to step.

In reality, the brain does not have a physically separate set of neurons that constitutes working or short-term memory. Instead, selective parts of the brain are activated when focusing on topics or functions handled by that area. When the brain is activated in this way, the target area becomes the focus of consciousness and will remain active for about five seconds after the conscious mind has shifted its focus elsewhere. That is conscious short-term memory.

To illustrate the way conscious or working memory functions, think of the following model: You are in a dark room with a flashlight. Wherever you shine the flashlight on the wall is where activity takes place, where consciousness is focused, and where you can perform short-term memory tasks. After you move the light beam elsewhere, the wall continues to glow with an afterglow that lasts some five seconds.

Another model — the "pinball machine model" — has been proposed to illustrate how people shift attention from one subject to the next. The pins are different subjects or concepts. The ball is the conscious focus. The focus bounces from one concept to another driven by associations, and reasoning results from the mental activities at the last stop.

We do not know what changes occur in the brain to transfer mental objects from working memory to long-term memory. It appears that the retention of mental objects in working memory is caused by temporary chemical changes in neurotransmitters and receptors. The initial chemical changes are later replaced by new, semipermanent, or permanent neural connections, which then result in long-term memory. What happens in between — that is, when the medium-term buffer memory is in effect — is not known. However, what is known is that much processing and integration of new knowledge takes place during sleep.

Working memory has been demonstrated to be a "serial processor," in general capable of handling only one issue or stream of conscience at the time. However, people often perform simultaneous multitasking by pursuing several lines of thought nonconsciously at any one time (as when we activate several of our nonconscious working memories to perform different tasks). Working memory is quite rapid, with access time and "object manipulation cycle" in the hundred millisecond range. We now consider this to be slow compared to modern computers; it allows us to make only a small handful of reasoning steps every second. However, although the capacity of working memory may only be of the order of five to nine "chunks"[2] or mental objects at a time, a chunk may be quite complex, ranging from a symbol, two to four digits in a group, an abstract concept, an image, or a phrase. Hence, since a vast amount of understanding and meaning may be encapsulated in a chunk, people can process tremendously complex reasonings in the blink of an eye. In situations where the mental objects that are reasoned with are complex abstract concepts, people adopt reasoning that is qualitative ("fuzzy," "approximate," or "inexact") rather than using crisp and precise logic and arithmetic, as when we add 2 + 2 and find that the result is 4.

When we speak deliberately about what we think or remember, we use working memory to select what we want to say. The material that we wish to communicate — facts, concepts, relations between them, etc. — is recalled from long-term memories into working memory, often facilitated by priming memory and primed by the concepts present in working memory. We consciously weigh and select what we want to say; we may even "think in words" as most, but far from all, people do. Next, we encode what we have selected to say into words and sentences and utter those as speech. Since working memory is a serial processor, and since speaking is a "linear process" that only allows presentation of one word and line of thought at a time, this is a relatively slow process.

When we consciously pursue one line of thought and recall related memory objects for processing the "next items," we may recall many objects, some of which have direct, while others have indirect, associations with the "thought" we want. As a result, our working memory may be presented with many simultaneous memory objects and become burdened by the need to process this wealth of facts, perspectives, and concepts that often are at different levels of abstractions and, therefore, require considerable processing to be compatible. The working memory, in effect, becomes a significant bottleneck in our attempts to communicate what we know when we are fortunate enough to recall the relevant memory objects. The first time we have to communicate something that we know well, we may find it difficult to select which concepts to present first — what we want to say. If we talk repeatedly about the same issue, it becomes easier for us to explain. We may even have remembered a sequence of statements (a "party line") that expresses what we wish to communicate. In the end, that tendency may lead to inflexible, rigid explanations and positions that can be a liability when the world around us changes.

When we know a subject extremely well, we normally have *automated* or *compiled* our knowledge. Therefore, it is no longer necessary to access what we know in detail. In fact, the details may no longer be available to working memory, making it impossible for us to explain what we know. How this happens has not been established.

Conscious working memory is considered to be divided into three specialized functions: (1) The *central-executive* function controls what we think about. (2) The *visuo-spatial scratch pad* holds the memory units (chunks and associations) while we work with them. And (3) the *articulatory loop* (or "phonological" loop) is the mechanism we use to speak, write, and express other physical behavior, including nonverbal gestures and facial expressions, to the external world (Baddeley 1992a). The articulatory loop is coupled very closely to the motor system. We may have the capacity to operate what appear to be several parallel working memories, which we use at different levels of consciousness to perform more or less automatic mental functions and tasks, some of which can be very complex.

Medium-Term Buffer Memory

"Buffer memory" plays the role of a medium-term memory where we store a large number of mental objects that we work with right now, or have worked with during the last several hours. Mental objects stored in the buffer memory are easily accessed by working memory. At the same time, they are also easily forgotten. We all can relate to the store manager's statement about two customers who just left that "I know they were in here before and that they looked at the jacket they just bought. But I cannot remember if it was last night or this morning."

On the way to becoming transferred to long-term memory, the mental objects we create from received information may be retained temporarily in buffer memory where they reside for some time after working memory has forgotten (or released) them. The notion of "buffer" or "medium-term" memory is not uniformly accepted but is required to explain human professional work functions. It has no known physiological basis but explains the intermediate state of memorization. Retrieving memory objects from buffer memory is easier and quicker than obtaining them from long-term memory. After some hours, the mental objects in this intermediate memory are typically no longer available but must be retrieved from long-term memory if we want access to them again.

People retain mental objects stored in their buffer memory differently. Some may remember facts accurately but cannot remember what was said or how statements were phrased; others remember verbal statements precisely but cannot remember facts per se; and still others remember neither facts nor verbal statements but know what the underlying concepts were on a much broader basis than the other two groups. This variability is worth remembering when we work with what our coworkers know and how they obtain and use new knowledge.

Long-Term Memory

Long-term memory stores information and knowledge as mental objects for long periods. It may be created by permanent links that somehow represent what we know. Long-term memory is thought to have "limitless" capacity for things to be remembered. It is located throughout the brain, presumably in the areas where the various functions for vision, speech, and so on, are located. The memory objects that we store in long-term memory are not directly accessible but must be accessed by activating working memory. As indicated above, this often creates a significant bottleneck.

Long-term memory is organized functionally into at least four separate kinds of memory which serve quite different purposes: *procedural, episodic, priming,* and *semantic* tasks. Semantic memory is further divided into *lexical* and *encyclopedic* memories. Some researchers also suggest that the episodic and semantic memories together form *conceptual* memory. Other researchers suggest that the distinction between semantic and episodic memory is wrong, that there is semantic content in episodic memory, that conceptual memory is episodic in nature, and that lexical memory contains knowledge of syntax.

The domain of procedural memory is thought to be behavior, whereas the domain of episodic, semantic, and priming memories is cognition. All these memory functions have properties that are both interesting and important when we work with what our coworkers know, how they reason, how they differ, and how they gain access to their knowledge, as well as when we consider how we can manage knowledge in daily situations.

Procedural Memory

Procedural memory is where we remember how we do things: the procedures we follow when we perform tasks we are familiar with and skilled in. Our procedural memories keep such mental objects as schemata, scripts, and routines as well as specific ways of acting. It is believed that our procedural memory holds knowledge of methods and scripts in the form of mental models that include sequential steps or as chains of events where the outcome of one event feeds into and controls the behavior of the next. The sequential steps can be distinctly discrete steps, or they can be similar to "waves" of activities whereby one activity wave gradually changes into the next with seamless transitions.

Typically, we cannot explain what we know from our procedural memory. When we recall mental objects from procedural memory, the recollections are expressed as actions rather than explicit thought. We can only "act out," or perform, the tasks we have memorized in this part of our memory. And we may only be able to perform the task under special circumstances. For example, we may have to be *primed* to perform a certain task as when we are led to perform it as a natural extension of our present situation. We may also be led to perform the task by a *cue* such as seeing a particular situation, hearing a certain word, or thinking about something very specific. In some instances, an expert can be led to document, or tell, how a procedural task is performed by recalling a realistic scenario and then explaining it step-by-step from the beginning. The expert essentially simulates the performance of the task.

Conceptual Memory

Conceptual memory is considered to consist of both episodic and semantic memories as shown schematically in Figure 4-2. Everything we remember of what has happened and of things that mean something takes the form of *concepts*. Concepts are considered to be language-free, highly abstracted, and partly codified to fit into our mental organization and be used as our mental and associative building blocks.

Episodic Memory

Episodic memory stores recollections of personally experienced episodes and events as they occurred without further analysis or integration into what we know. Tulving (1972) proposed that the mental objects we store in episodic memory are not yet knowledge. Tulving suggested that objects in episodic memory are contrasted with knowledge since they are not "tied down" and connected and integrated with the main knowledge in our brains. Later, Tulving and Schacter (1990) provided additional insights into other memory systems, including priming memory, which typically includes mental models and may represent complex episodes that depict images and verbal communications of a chain of events, including what we thought and felt at the time.

Tulving's position that episodic memory contains *information* about an event, rather than *knowledge* about the event, is founded on the premise that this version of the event has not been analyzed and internalized, although it has been represented in a concise and efficient form. Since it has not been abstracted and nothing has been learned about it or from it, it is information, not knowledge. To become knowledge, whatever is abstracted and learned from the event will be re-represented and stored in semantic memory. Episodes that we observe and remember, our experiences, are highly subjective. We are not good observers. In all situations, we narrow our focus according to a particular perspective and only seem to remember that aspect to the exclusion of everything else.

Semantic Memory

Semantic memory is where we keep factual knowledge in the broadest sense and where we attach meanings to this knowledge. It contains abstract, mental (cognitive) representations and mental models of everything we know: facts, concepts, words, expectations, schemata, and many other forms of knowledge. In semantic memory, we also keep our notions about relations between the different mental objects. We have associations and categorizations. Mental objects recalled from semantic memory are expressed as abstract thoughts (cognitions) rather than behavior. Semantic memory is thought to be divided into lexical memory and encyclopedic memory.

Lexical Memory

Lexical memory is where we hold all our knowledge about language: words, idioms, syntax, common expressions, and other structural and detailed information that we use to parse and decode incoming messages. It contains the "semantic labels," that is, the words we associate with and use to describe specific concepts.

Lexical memory may also contain selected aspects of metaknowledge — *knowledge of what we know.* It is, in effect, an abstracted overview of our knowledge, a lexicon of the knowledge that we have. It is *about* knowledge.

From a Western perspective, where we operate with written, often phonetic versions of the words we pronounce, we tend to forget the symbolic-conceptual relations of the ideographs of written Chinese or Japanese, and similarly, the signs used by the deaf, or icons used in modern computer graphic interfaces. These symbolic-conceptual relations are also stored in our lexical memory and may bear no relationship to the conventional semantic labels that we use as words in our spoken language.

The organization of lexical memory may differ significantly from person to person. Some have highly developed language representations of their concepts — they also "think in language" — whereas others (perhaps some 20 percent of all people) do not have strong semantic labels for their concepts and do not think in words and language. They may think with "concepts," "pictures" (i.e., visual representations), or even models such as interrelated and dynamic systems objects.

Since people are quite different, they have considerably different strengths. However, the absence of capabilities that the majority of the population possesses often are considered "weaknesses." This distinction is important when considering a person's competence. Lexical memory — as all other memories — displays specific characteristics. When one characteristic becomes dominant (such as the ability to keep track of semantic labels), it normally means having fewer capabilities in other areas, and vice versa. These differences in degrees of dominances indicate that individuals will present a broad diversity of capabilities and mental emphases (Gardner 1983).

Encyclopedic Memory

Encyclopedic memory contains the details of knowledge — encoded in abstract representations whose form we can only guess but which we picture as consisting of hierarchies of chunks and concepts, schemata, scripts, relational and associative nets, and so on. Many researchers subscribe to the opinion that encyclopedic memory is where language-free concepts are stored. As for other memories, location of encyclopedic memory is likely spread throughout the cortex, with separate areas specializing in particular functions.

Priming Memory

Priming memory is a nonconscious memory, which identifies and recognizes, conceptually or perceptually, words and mental objects as cues. When a valid cue is recognized, it triggers a larger, associated "chunk" that can be quite extensive and complex and can serve as a pointer for long-term memory retrieval. "Priming is a type of implicit memory; it does not involve explicit or conscious recollection of any previous experience. It has affinities to both procedural and semantic memory" (Tulving & Schacter 1990, p. 301).

Conceptual priming occurs when planning a complex project and discovering resource contentions between critical tasks. We then automatically recall how we handled similar situations in the past. We associate the new situation with the previous ones and remember the concepts for how to deal with it. *Perceptual priming* occurs when, for example, we drive and see brake lights go on in the car ahead, and automatically start applying the brakes in our own car.

Our priming memory is full of associative links, which point to knowledge stored in semantic and other memories. For performance of expertise and for use of knowledge in decision situations and the like, priming memory is of utmost importance. From this point of view, priming memory is the major repository of context-dependent cues and hence contributes heavily to our capability to perform and exercise our expertise as part of our daily work, particularly if we are "practical knowledge workers" — which most of us are. We compile and automate the knowledge that we are experts in, and the automated scripts and schemata may subsequently be stored as strings of cues in our priming memory.

Abstract Knowledge Objects

Routines, Operational Models, Scripts, Schemata, General Principles, and Metaknowledge

In our minds, and when we work with explicit knowledge, we represent situational and procedural concepts with varying degrees of abstraction. An example of how we go about hiring a new employee illustrates how we can characterize knowledge in each of these categories. For hiring, routines may apply only to hiring many people to fill similar positions (See Figure 3-10). Hiring one or a few people may not become routine, and the hiring process may instead be governed by scripts, and in more unusual situations, by schemata or even metaknowledge. For hiring, proceeding from specific routines to general principles and metaknowledge, the characterizations will be something as follows.

Routines

Routines are generally automatized, nonconscious, concrete, and deterministic. Routines may allow room for variance to accommodate branching when different, but understood and expected, conditions materialize. In the case of hiring a competent professional, routines consist of rigid steps that might cover many of the tasks of the hiring process. Some tasks may still require explicit reasoning.

As we become very familiar with a work process such as hiring a particular type of professional, much of the process becomes automatic, resulting in a routine. However, we may never routinize all steps in a procedure for how to handle a situation. Instead, we may routinize the way we handle selected episodes that often are repeated.

The actual routine may start earlier in the process than illustrated. It also may extend beyond the steps shown in the example and will generally consist of hundreds of subevents. A simplified routine for hiring tasks may be described by the sequence of the main events within the procedure:

- Identify job requirement with function manager and write job standard description.
- Research salary range from peer groups within organization and specify salary level and job class.

- Obtain approval for hiring from personnel department, function manager, and general manager using standard procedures.
- Contact the designated employment agency and authorize them to start search.
- Receive resumes that have been pre-screened by agency.
- Screen resumes, first in personnel department, then with function manager.
- Invite selected candidates for interviews.
- Interview candidates, by personnel department, function manager, and associates.
- Evaluate candidates and rank them, and decide what initial offers should be.
- Check references for the two best candidates.
- Send formal offer letter to best candidates, and hold off communications to the remainders until one candidate accepts position.
- Receive response from candidate.
- Negotiate salary and relocation terms, start date, and so on, with candidate, obtain approval of renegotiated terms, write and send revised offer letter.
- Candidate accepts — first verbally and then in writing.

Operational Models

Operational Models are applicable for situations and tasks that are less known than routine work. They provide particulars on how to perform tasks for specific purposes or situations. Operational models are often generated by operationalizing scripts to handle new tasks for which routines do not exist. Operational models are not automatized like routines and may also be explicit instead of the non-conscious nature of routines.

An operational model for hiring may include particulars for individual tasks such as:

- Particulars for soliciting applications for applicants.
- Particulars for obtaining and evaluating applications from applicants.
- Particulars for how to undertake negotiations that involve non-standard considerations and issues.
- Particulars for appropriate interview follow-up and next steps.

Scripts

Scripts consist of the general event sequence that underlies a referenced type of situation. Scripts are flexible and somewhat abstract, and include general expectations and directions. Typically, scripts consist of several steps made up of episodes and events. They are similar to routines and operational models but are more general, broad, and flexible compared to specific and unvarying steps of operational models and routines.

A hiring script may cover the responsibilities of different positions, and not just competent professionals. Examples of a hiring script may be:

- Determine the need for additional staff (perhaps ascertain approval).
- Specify characteristics of person(s) to be hired (perhaps ascertain approval if not obtained earlier).
- Identify where and how candidates can be identified.
- Search out candidates and communicate with them by mail to obtain resumes, phone conversations, interviews, references, and so on.
- Identify individual(s) to be approached for hiring (maybe ascertain approval if not obtained earlier).
- Contact selected candidate(s), negotiate, and secure acceptance.

In the hiring script, the sequence of events may also vary considerably as indicated for when to obtain approval. Scripts are more concrete and specific than schemata and can be generated from schemata to form more definite expectations for evolutions of specific situations.

Schemata

Schemata are broader sets of general approaches and tactics (Mandler 1979, p. 263) and are abstract models for how to deal with generalized situations or challenges. They consist of broad and conceptual plans or schemes for a class of situations and consist of concepts and mental models by which either static or dynamic situations can be characterized, understood, and approached from one or more general perspectives. Examples of hiring schemata may include components such as:

- General approaches to determine needs for additional resources to perform different kinds of operations — staff, access to other departments, outside contractors, better office automation, and so on.
- Nature of strategies to evaluate and select which of several approaches should be pursued to cover resource requirements.

Event details such as "obtain approval" are not likely to be explicit in a schema. Instead, a schema may include features that deal with "making results acceptable." Since many details are assumed to be part of "general operating practices," they may be part of the context or a more detailed script instead of serving as an explicit part of the schema itself.

General Principles

General Principles are mental models of underlying principles within a target domain. Whereas schemata provide models for general approaches for how to deal with situations or challenges, general principles provide the conceptual and factual bases, characteristics, behaviors, processes, mechanisms, and expectations within target domains. Examples of general principles for hiring may include components such as:

- Legal principles associated with retaining employees.
- Principles governing competitive compensation and enterprise guidelines.
- Considerations for hiring expertise to cover knowledge gaps and provide people-capabilities to support enterprise strategy.

Metaknowledge and Metacognition

Metacognition in people is developed gradually starting at about three years of age (Kuhn 2000). The resulting metaknowledge and the ability to reason with it (metacognition) is a cornerstone for intelligent functioning — for all knowledge work. Metaknowledge covers many areas (most likely all facets of human reasoning) and has many functions, all of them highly abstract. For the reasoning example, we provide indications of associated metaknowledge below.

On the lowest abstraction level, metaknowledge can be divided into the following (Kuhn 2000):

- *Procedural metaknowledge* is about know-how and strategies for how to proceed toward the task goal.
  - Example: High-level and tacit generic strategies for how to explore, investigate, and judge people, particularly as applicants and potential employees or coworkers. Many factors are involved and must be blended, typically "on the fly," and they range from considering competence to ethics, personalities, and practical considerations.
- *Declarative metaknowledge* is about having tacit declarative understanding of what is known — know-what.
  - Example: Tacit awareness of aspects such as personal or enterprise capabilities to perform the hiring process competently. This would include which hiring expertise "I" have and which hiring expertise my coworkers have.

Metacognition

On the highest abstraction level, metaknowledge consists of metacognition; that is, the capability to reason with mostly tacit high-level mental models to "regulate" — or provide evaluation, planning, strategy and methodological and monitoring guidance for — regular ("first order") cognition, be it tacit or explicit.

Metacognition can be divided into the following (Kuhn 2000):

- *Metastrategic knowing* provides strategies such as methodologies and perspectives to address the task goals provided by metatask knowing.
  - Example: General approaches and points of view for how to achieve the criteria and expectations for the hiring task.
- *Metatask knowing* provides particulars — objectives, expectations, perspectives — for goals for target situations and tasks.
  - Example: Knowing what constitutes a "good" employee, a desirable candidate, an equitable match between a candidate's expertise and the needs of the enterprise, and a well-executed hiring process.
- *Metacognitive knowing* is metaknowledge about declarative knowing.
  - Example: Having a tacit understanding of how good, complete, and appropriate the declarative metaknowledge for hiring is.

NOTES

1. A thorough discussion of the brain's organization can be found in Posner (1989), Chapter 8.
2. George A. Miller (1956) reported the capacity of working memory in his famous study, "The magical number seven, plus or minus two."

GLOSSARY

Abductive Reasoning: A special case of inductive reasoning resulting in specific assertions that imply the available information in the context of the background knowledge without logical certainty. Example: Premise: "Those dogs are mastiffs." Background knowledge: "All Erik's dogs are mastiffs." Hypothesis: "Perhaps those dogs are Erik's."

Acquisition: Knowledge may be acquired and represented for inclusion in a knowledge model. Acquisition can be performed by eliciting knowledge from a domain expert, inducing knowledge from examples, porting knowledge from databases, and by other methods. Also see Knowledge Acquisition.

Actor: An agent that perform actions — predominantly a person but can be an organizational entity or a computer programmed to handle situations.

Action Space: The realm, the "space," within which a person — or enterprise — is competent, willing, comfortable, or otherwise prepared to make decisions and act. The action space is not a passive domain with fixed boundaries. It is formed by the creative capabilities, methodologies and attitudes, mentalities, and motivations that allow actors to perform regular tasks and consider novel actions and innovate within the boundaries of what they find to be permissible and acceptable and is closely related to what is considered to be allowable.

Adjacent Function: A business function that exchanges (provides or receives) consultation or collaboration resources, information, or secondary work products with the target function.

Artificial Intelligence (AI): A subfield of computer science concerned with pursuing the possibility that a computer can be made to behave in ways that humans recognize as "intelligent" behavior in each other. Applied AI becomes a broader field than AI, including cognitive, social, and management sciences.

Asset Management Mentality: Management attitude and practice that is required to manage intangible assets with the same objectives as for tangible assets. The mentality to focus on operational and strategic objectives to create, renew and maintain, safeguard, and utilize and leverage tangible and intangible capital throughout the enterprise.

Automated Knowledge: Explicit knowledge that has been embedded in an automatic device (such as a computer).

Automatic or Automatized Knowledge: The lowest abstraction level of tacit knowledge. People know this knowledge so well that it has been automated and is used to perform tasks automatically — without conscious reasoning.

Basic Knowledge Analysis (BKA): A relatively extensive analysis and characterization of the knowledge in the task environment. It focuses on how knowledge is held, used, etc., and it encompasses Task Environment Analysis (TEA), Critical Knowledge Function Analysis (CKFA), business function analysis, and knowledge acquisition — or knowledge elicitation and modeling.

Blackboard Systems: Knowledge-based systems that consist of several separate reasoning processes that use a "blackboard" to post intermediate results or information that needs to be communicated between the various systems. Blackboard systems may be used for multiple-hypothesis reasoning.

Case-Based Learning: Approach to learning using "cases" (stories, scenarios, descriptions of real events, etc.) to illustrate the material to be internalized. Case-based learning is supportive of building mental reference models.

Case-Based Reasoning (CBR): A reasoning approach often used by people but also implemented as knowledge-based system (KBS) reasoning strategy. In case-based reasoning we compare the present situation or condition to previously experienced situations (reference cases) and interpolate between the most likely ones to arrive at conclusions for how to handle the present case.

CBT: See Computer-Based Training.

Certainty Factor: Either a number supplied by an expert system to indicate the system's level of confidence in the conclusion or a number supplied by the user of an expert system to indicate the user's level of confidence in the validity of the information supplied to the system.

Chunking: A mental activity that allows aggregating several (typically five to nine) entities such as concepts into a single, new concept.

CKF: See Critical Knowledge Function.

CKFA: Critical Knowledge Function Analysis.

Closed System: A system-theoretic concept — a system that is isolated from its environment such that its final state is determined by its initial state. Many physical systems are examples of closed systems that in addition have manipulated and observable input variables that will change their states. The states of such closed systems are "observable." Hence they are "identifiable" and "controllable" in contrast to open systems.

Codification: Dealing with obtaining, characterizing, and validating knowledge. It includes elicitation or acquisition, analysis, and synthesis (rational reconstruction) of knowledge to generate internally consistent knowledge models that are congruent with domain knowledge as held by experts or existing as previously codified bodies of knowledge.

Cognition: The act or process of knowing (Webster 1986).

Cognitive Engineering: A recently coined term to denote the professional field concerned with analysis and synthesis of systems which interact with human cognitive functions. Cognitive engineering encompasses human behavior in the real target world; ecological aspects of that world; semantic contents of the target domain; behavior and performance; and implications of changing cognitive-related aspects of the target domain.

Cognitive Science: The field that investigates the details of the mechanisms and processes of human intelligence (such as learning, memory, recall, decision making) to determine the procedures and functions that produce and utilize that intelligence.

Cognitive Style: An individual's mental approach and reasoning style. Cognitive styles include preferences for graphic or verbal representations of concepts, hemispheric dominance, etc.

Competence: The capacity and capability of a person or other actor to function with a desired effectiveness — the ability to deliver quality work within a particular domain.

Completed Staff Work: The study of a problem and presentation of a solution, with alternatives, to a manager, so that all that remains for the manager to do is to indicate approval or disapproval of the completed action.

Computer-Based Training (CBT): Training program delivered by interactive computers. Modern CBTs include multimedia (sounds, video clips), hyperlinks, and may also have embedded intelligence to guide or challenge students. Some CBTs allow students to react to simulated, real-life situations (such as being confronted by an angry customer) and will record student behavior as the computer changes the path of interaction.

Concept: An abstract or general idea often generalized from specific instances. A concept can be a mental model and be tied to other concepts through associations.

Concept Hierarchy: A hierarchy of related concepts, particularly as they relate to a particular position, role, task, or activity. Concept hierarchies build on concepts that are consolidated through chunking and are related to semantic nets and knowledge maps.

Concept Net: A net(work) of related concepts, often pertaining to particular situation. The connections between concept nodes may be specified as to relation type.

Conceptual Blending: The human capability to integrate and find new meaning in large amounts of knowledge coming from different sources and that may be semantically distant from one another.

Conceptual Knowledge: Abstract mental models of the world. *Concepts, perspectives*, and *Gestalts* are metamodels for complex situations built from observations and available facts and data. Conceptual knowledge includes abstract images such as how to view the economic situation and how to think about behavior and the operating status of difficult chemical plants (when the operator says: "It is unstable today"). The frame of reference applies to a particular competitive situation, and so forth.

Critical Knowledge Function (CKF): Knowledge-related situation or condition that warrants KM attention. CKFs can be characterized by five factors: (1) type of knowledge (understanding, expertise, or skill) involved in performing a task; (2) business use of that knowledge; (3) constraint that prevents knowledge to be utilized fully, the vulnerability of the situation, or the unrealized opportunity that is not exploited; (4) opportunities and alternatives for managing (i.e., improving) the CKF; and (5) expected incremental value of improving the situation — release knowledge constraint, exploit (take advantage of) the opportunity to use knowledge differently.

Critical Thinking: Effective mental methodologies, strategies, and representations people use for handling situations, decision making and acting, learning and innovating.

Customer Capital: Part of intellectual capital that includes customer goodwill and relations and nonfinancial aspects of customer contracts and obligations.

Decision-Making Knowledge: See Pragmatic Knowledge.

Declarative Knowledge: Facts about, and relations between, objects (such as abstract concepts or physical objects), events, and situations stated in some representation such as rules or clauses.

Deductive Reasoning: Reasoning to deduce information about the situation under analysis, such as deducing facts or premises from hypotheses and rules, given the background or domain knowledge.

Deutero-Learning (DL). Learning that occurs when organizations learn how to carry out single-loop and double-loop learning (Argyris and Schön 1978).

Domain: A bounded part of a larger system. It may be a specific area of knowledge such as "the domain of financial knowledge." At times, it may be the knowledge or expertise area of a knowledge-based system.

Domain Expert: A person with expertise in the domain of the target knowledge area, such as a knowledge-based system being developed. The domain expert often works closely with the knowledge engineer (particularly the knowledge professionals) to allow capturing the expert's knowledge for codification into a knowledge model, which can then be encoded into a knowledge base.

Double-Loop Learning (DLL). Learning that occurs when, in addition to detection and correction of errors, the organization is involved in the questioning and modification of existing norms, procedures, policies, and objectives. DLL involves changing the organization's knowledge base or firm-specific competencies or routines (Dodgson 1993). DLL is also called higher-level learning (Fiol and Lyles 1985), generative learning, or learning to expand an organization's capabilities (Senge 1990), and strategic learning (Mason 1993). (Argyris and Schön 1978.)

Downstream Function: A function that receives the target function's work products.

Economic Value Added™ (EVA™): A measure of financial performance calculated by determining net operating income and subtracting charges for capital expended to produce that income. (Economic value added = net operating income – capital charge.)

Effective Behavior: Behavior that achieves implementation of objectives and goals.

Elicitation: The process of obtaining domain knowledge from experts through one of several elicitation methods such as interviews, observation, and simulation.

Encoding: Encoding of knowledge involves translating codified knowledge models to a representation such as that required for an expert system tool or shell. Encoding is similar to "programming" and may often include computer programming to augment tools or shells. Encoding may fully be a programming task as when an expert system is directly implemented in LISP, Prolog, or another computer language.

Episode: A relatively independent incident or scene that occurs in the context of a larger situation — a script or story line. As such, episodes have intrinsic meaning that may not have been analyzed and internalized. An episode is the collection of distinct steps we observe as the situation unfolds. We may choose to divide a situation into many episodes, depending on which detail we wish to work with. Or episodes may be relatively aggregate entities consisting of several events.

Episodic Memory: Human memory that stores recollections of personally experienced episodes and events as they occurred without further analysis or integration.

Event: An isolated occurrence within a particular situation. Events are concrete and detailed — the numerous distinct steps that occur as a situation unfolds. Events are normally observable and are typically, by themselves, without context and meaning.

Expectational Knowledge: Human expectations, judgments, working hypotheses, associations, and beliefs are derived mental models and connections that lead to opinions on how situations — both simple and complex — might evolve and how to handle them. Expectations are based partly on working hypotheses for how the situations work and what influences them. They include our associations that often become premises and reasoning stepping stones for potential conclusions and interpretations of contexts. Beliefs are formed by expectations and working hypotheses and are based on concepts, perspectives, and facts and confirmed data.

Expert Networks: A formal or informal arrangement that allows people with operational problems access to experts for assistance.

Expert System: A knowledge-based computer program containing expert domain knowledge about objects, events, situations, and courses of action, which emulates the reasoning process of human experts in the particular domain. The components of an expert system include the knowledge base, inference engine, and user interface. Types of expert systems include rule-based systems and model-based systems.

Explicit Knowledge: Knowledge that has been explicated and made available for examination such as personal knowledge about which a person can talk or write or as knowledge captured in documents, video clips, computer programs through oral or written language, expert system rules, computer programs, diagrams, or in any other manner. Structural knowledge is often explicit.

Factual Knowledge: Our knowledge of what we "know to be true" consists of facts, confirmed data, known causal chains, and remembered sensory inputs and episodes. Much of it is retrieved from memory in the form of declarations. It is semantic knowledge pertaining to particular domains and is organized to be relevant to particular contexts. When we elicit and codify knowledge in external knowledge bases, most of the initial knowledge is of this type. It is knowledge of isolated facts — data and information — and of relations between facts and concrete and reality-connected details. (Example: knowing the constants of the metric system and how they relate.) Also see Pragmatic Knowledge.

Forward Chaining: A search technique used in production (i.e., "if-then" rule) systems, which begins with the condition clause of a rule and works "forward" through a chain of rules in an attempt to activate implied action rules (also termed data-driven reasoning or bottom-up search). During forward chaining, the inference engine searches for if-condition matches in other rules in the knowledge base when new values are generated by then-action in rules that have been "fired."

Fuzzy Logic: A formal logic that is defined to work with fuzzy operations.

Fuzzy Reasoning: A fuzzy logic reasoning model similar to qualitative reasoning.

Fuzzy Systems: Knowledge-based systems that employ fuzzy reasoning.

General Principles: Mental models of underlying principles within a domain.

Goal-Setting Knowledge: See Idealistic Knowledge.

Hermeneutics: The branch of epistemological philosophy that deals with methodological interpretation of the intended meanings, often of written or verbal communication.

Human Capital: Human capital is part of intellectual capital. The enterprise's human capital consists of the knowledge, understanding, skills, experience, and relationships of its employees. Human capital is the property of employees and is only leased or rented by the enterprise.

Idealistic Knowledge: The highest abstraction level of conceptual knowledge at which we hold vision and paradigm knowledge. Part of this knowledge is well known to us and explicit — we work consciously with it. Much of it — our visions and mental models — is not well known; it is tacit and only accessible nonconsciously.

Implicit Knowledge: Knowledge that is contained implicitly in oral or written language, actions (also when videotaped or provided as part of a hypermedia system), trained neural networks, embedded in technology, culture, practices, and so on.

Implicit Learning: The process of learning without intending to learn (by being engaged in an activity or by passive observation), without being aware of learning, and resulting in tacit — and mostly inaccessible — knowledge.

Inductive Reasoning: Reasoning to generate hypotheses based on background or domain knowledge and information such as premises, statements, or facts. Example: Premise: "The engine is powerful." Background knowledge: "The engine is part of a car." Hypothesis: "The car is powerful." Inductive reasoning can also be used to generate hypotheses from background knowledge and other hypotheses. Rules are often used to perform inductive inference.

Information: Description of a particular situation, circumstance, or case. Information consists of facts or data that are descriptive of particulars that may be concrete, abstract, certain, uncertain, etc. Information may be used by knowledge to interpret or reason about a particular situation, circumstance, or case.

Integrative Management Culture: A new and open culture that emerges when an enterprise builds and orchestrates an internal practice to deal systematically and deliberately with knowledge by having people share insights and seek assistance from one another. People open up and discuss difficult issues, emerging ideas, and tentative opportunities with one another. They take mental risks that would be unthinkable in conventional environments. They seek collaboration to achieve better results more quickly, and they build upon the ideas of others and let others build on their own ideas. By opening up to new approaches and perspectives, and by building on the capabilities of others instead of only relying on their own, they expand their action space. As people expand action spaces and become more effective through capable collaboration, the enterprise becomes smarter and more effective. Complex tasks are addressed better and faster, and innovations abound, making the enterprise more capable and able to engage in activities that previously were infeasible.

Intellectual Capital: The sum of the enterprise's human capital, customer capital, and structural capital. Intellectual capital is part of the enterprise's intangible capital.

KMap: See Knowledge Mapping.

Knowledge: Operational definitions for this book: (1) The content of understanding and action patterns that govern sensemaking, decision making, execution, and monitoring. (2) Knowledge consists of facts, perspectives and concepts, mental reference models, truths and beliefs, judgments and expectations, methodologies, and know-how. (3) Knowledge is used to interpret information about a particular circumstance or case to handle the situation. Knowledge is about what the facts and information mean in the context of the situation. (4) Knowledge is possessed and represented on many conceptual levels, in many forms, many types, and many domains.

Knowledge about Knowledge: Understanding which knowledge is available; what knowledge is about; and how it is created, used, and structured, as studied by the field of epistemology. Also see Metaknowledge.

Knowledge Analysis: A general term for investigating, characterizing, and structuring (modeling) knowledge as possessed by experts or other knowledge workers, required to deliver quality work, used in practice, and so on. Knowledge analysis may involve the use of specific methods, including basic knowledge analysis (BKA), critical knowledge function analysis (CKFA), knowledge mapping (KMap), knowledge use and requirements analysis (KURA), knowledge scripting and profiling (KS&P), knowledge flow analysis (KFA), and so on.

Knowledge Audit: Survey and characterization of the status of knowledge in an organization. Knowledge audit may refer to identifying specific knowledge assets such as patents and the degree to which these assets are used, enforced, and safeguarded.

Knowledge Base (KB): The component of a knowledge-based system which contains the system's domain knowledge in some representation suitable for the system to reason with. Knowledge in knowledge bases is typically represented in a standard format.

Knowledge Engineers: Specialists responsible for analyzing knowledge-intensive functions to design appropriate knowledge management activities such as technical development of a knowledge-based system. Knowledge engineers may be *knowledge technologists*, focusing on the content and functionality of knowledge use in a knowledge-based function, or *AI technologists*, focusing on implementation of a knowledge-based system. Only rarely is a knowledge engineer both an AI technologist and a knowledge technologist.

Knowledge Engineering: The professional activities associated with acquiring or eliciting, codifying, and encoding knowledge, conceptualizing and implementing knowledge-based systems, and engaging in activities to formalize knowledge and its use, particularly through the application of artificial intelligence.

Knowledge Flow Analysis (KFA): Explicit analysis of existing or potential flows of knowledge within an organization. KFA may focus on threats, opportunities, weaknesses, and strengths of knowledge flows, and on flows in four dimensions: (1) application of knowledge to work objects; (2) learning to perform work better; (3) application of knowledge to improve the system of production and service; and (4) application of knowledge to improve the products and services themselves.

Knowledge Holder: The person (domain expert) who holds the knowledge of interest. Knowledge holders can behave in different ways and can be classified as professional practitioners, practical knowledge-workers, performers, or communicating negotiators.

Knowledge Management Activity: Distinct knowledge-related changes to manage knowledge such as analyzing a situation using KM analysis tools, creating and implementing KM capabilities, practices, and initiatives, or engaged in KM practices, utilizing or operating KM capabilities.

Knowledge Management: The systematic, explicit, and deliberate building, renewal, and application of knowledge to maximize an enterprise's knowledge-related effectiveness and returns from its knowledge and intellectual capital assets. The field covers deliberate and systematical analysis, synthesis, assessment, and implementation of knowledge-related changes to attain a set of objectives and to check that KM activities are carried out appropriately and meet their objectives. It comprises activities needed to facilitate direct knowledge-related work. KM includes fostering the "knowledge asset management mentality" required to create, maintain, and utilize appropriate intangible capital.

Knowledge Mapping (KMap): Methodologies followed to generate knowledge maps.

Knowledge Model: A model that take many forms. It may be documentation of domain knowledge on paper, in a computer-based knowledge base, or a videotaped "show-and-tell" for performing a particular task. Knowledge models may be represented using a formal "knowledge representation"; it may be in natural language as a narrative, a set of diagrammatic representations, and so forth.

Knowledge Professional: A professional who focuses on optimal creation, organization, availability, and use of knowledge in a domain or within a business function. Knowledge professionals have an applied understanding of task environment analysis, various KM approaches, business use of knowledge, and support of knowledge workers with automated reasoning and other means. Knowledge professionals may be trained in cognitive sciences, artificial intelligence, philosophy, and management sciences.

Knowledge Profiling: A method to characterize particular knowledge domains in terms of specific knowledge areas (often less than 20) and the levels of existing or desired proficiency for individual roles or persons in each of these areas. A polar coordinate graphical display (Kiviat diagram) is often used to portray the resulting "profiles."

Knowledge Representation: The formal structures used to store information in a knowledge base in a form that supports the reasoning approach to be employed. Knowledge representation techniques include "production rules" ("if-then rules"), logic (often "first-order logic"), semantic networks, frames, and scripts.

Knowledge Script: A step-by-step representation of knowledge-related work processes. Knowledge scripts may specifically focus on knowledge-intensive activities to ensure that they are properly represented.

Knowledge Scripting and Profiling (KS&P): A method for explicating K-I work performing a function and describing the particular knowledge, skills, and personal characteristics required to deliver routine and exceptional work. KS&P is used to identify the requirements for different work-roles. KS&P produces knowledge scripts and profiles.

Knowledge Technologist: A professional who focuses on codification and automation of knowledge content in a domain. The knowledge technologist must have applied understanding of knowledge elicitation, analysis, and modeling, and support of knowledge workers with automated reasoning. Knowledge technologists may be trained in cognitive sciences.

Knowledge Use and Requirements Analysis (KURA): A method to identify and characterize the knowledge required to deliver quality work and the actual use of knowledge in the target work functions. KURA relies on several other knowledge analysis and characterization methods such as BKA, KFA, and knowledge profiling.

Knowledge Vigilance: The degree to which an enterprise exhibits knowledge awareness and pursues explicit and systematic knowledge management, with the understanding that such pursuits are vital for success and viability.

Knowledge Work: Work that requires the application of knowledge to a work object. Knowledge work may involve highly abstract knowledge, such as when a judge or lawyer assesses the applicability of a precedence, or it may involve concrete knowledge, such as when a machinist selects feed speed to match a tool to the material to be turned. Knowledge work may be routine, as when an underwriter reviews a standard life insurance application, or it may require anomalies as when a marketing specialist faces a totally new situation.

Knowledge Worker: An individual who makes her/his contributions through exercising intellectual expertise and understanding.

Knowledge-Based System (KBS): A computer-based system that contains explicit or implicit domain knowledge used specifically for reasoning about specific situations. Examples of KBSs are case-based reasoning (CBR) systems, expert systems, and neural nets.

Knowledge-Intensive Activity (K-I Activity): An activity that requires extensive knowledge to perform appropriately. As a result of the depth of knowledge required, the knowledge may be internalized (and automated) by the performer. Consequently, many K-I activities will be executed within the performer's mind — hidden from outside observation — and are therefore difficult to identify and characterize.

Knowledge-Intensive Work: A characteristic of all work. All work is invariably knowledge-intensive (K-I), often some part of it has become tacit and automatic. K-I situation-handling may require focused thinking and explicit reasoning and may involve nonroutine conditions that require expertise. Highly automatic clerical work, such as "uncomplicated" correspondence filing, requires extensive judgment and concept knowledge, although much is so familiar that proficient office workers have automated it and perform complicated activities within seconds.

Learning Models: In the learning sciences, a large number of different types of individual learning have been distinguished; for example, incidental learning, implicit learning, learning by reflection, simulation-based learning, case-based learning, learning by exploring, and goal-directed learning.

Machine Learning: An area of AI research that investigates techniques for creating computer programs that can learn from their own experience.

Machine Translation: An area of AI research that attempts to use computers to translate text from one language to another. Machine translation programs often use combinations of natural language understanding and natural language generation techniques.

Menu-Based Natural Language: An approach to natural language understanding in which the computer helps build a natural language sentence by presenting "menus" (options lists) of choices that are available in each context and allowing the user to select the options that meet the user's requirements.

Mental Model: The conceptual and operational representation in the mind of situations, events, etc. that has been experienced or learned from other sources. This is a "real mental model." "Imaginary mental models" result from thought experiments and self-imagined situations. (See Chapter 3.)

Mental Reference Model: Mental model that can act as a principle, guide, template, or example.

Metacognition: Cognition that reflects on, monitors, or regulates first-order cognition (Kuhn 2000).

Metacognitive Reasoning: Reasoning that allows a person (or an inanimate system) to know what it knows — and what it does not know.

Metaknowledge: Normally considered to be "knowledge about knowledge" possessed by people or descriptions of knowledge in a physical knowledge base. Much of a person's metaknowledge is tacit, which on the lowest conceptual level consists of procedural metaknowledge and declarative metaknowledge. On a higher conceptual level, metaknowledge is metastrategic knowing consisting of metastrategic knowledge, metatask knowledge, and metacognitive knowing.

Methodological Knowledge: Knowledge that provides our methodological approaches and reasoning strategies with the metaknowledge for how to think and reason within particular contexts and situations, given information about the situations and the background knowledge in terms of facts, data, perspectives, and judgments.

Model-Based Expert System: A type of expert system, usually intended for diagnostic purposes, which is based on a model of the structure and behavior of the device or system it is designed to "understand."

Model-Based Reasoning: Complex reasoning strategies that allow the use of mathematical or logical models as representations of the domain knowledge.

Natural Language (NL): A language in common use by people to communicate among themselves (Example: Chinese or English).

Natural Language Generation: The part of natural language-processing research that attempts to have computers present information to their users in a natural language.

Natural Language Interface (NLI): A computer program that allows the user to communicate with a computer in a natural language. An NLI may incorporate both natural language-understanding and natural language-generation capabilities. An NLI is sometimes called a natural language front end.

Natural Language Processing (NLP): An area of AI research that allows computers to use a natural language. Natural language processing is divided into natural language understanding and natural language generation.

Natural Language Understanding: The part of natural language-processing research that investigates methods of allowing computers to understand a natural language.

Neural Nets: A family of reasoning strategies and knowledge representations that are patterned on the neural architecture of the brain. Neural nets often consist of a large number of nodes connected by links that attenuate, amplify, and transmit signals. Neural nets must be "trained" using examples to modify the strength of the couplings between nodes to change the net's reasoning behavior. Neural nets are used in a number of applications where the knowledge is amorphous and ill understood, like handwriting interpretation, seismic data interpretation, and so on.

Nonmonotonic Reasoning: A reasoning method that allows the retraction of hypotheses, conclusions, or facts given new (and better) information or understanding. Also, this method often supports multiple lines of reasoning (multiple-hypothesis reasoning). Nonmonotonic reasoning is useful where knowledge is not well understood, information is unreliable, or the situation is dynamic.

Open System: A system-theoretic concept — a system that is integrated with, and continually influenced by, its environment. Many open systems, such as human and social systems, have scores of unobservable inputs. Moreover, dimensions of their internal states are large and not fully observable. Their internal states cannot be observed or measured. Open systems are "unidentifiable" and "uncontrollable."

Operational Model: A mental model of procedures for how to perform certain tasks. An operational model is more abstract than a routine and less general than a script. In specific situations beyond prior experience, operational models may be generated by operationalizing scripts.

Organizational Learning Models: Three types of organizational learning is described by Argyris and Schön (1978). Learning that occurs when errors are detected and corrected and firms carry on with their present policies and goals. According to Dodgson in 1993, single-loop learning (SLL) can be equated to activities that add to the knowledge-base or firm-specific competencies or routines without altering the fundamental nature of the organization's activities (Argyris and Schön 1978). A second type of organizational learning, double-loop learning (DLL), occurs when, in addition to detection and correction of errors, the organization is involved in the questioning and modification of existing norms, procedures, policies, and objectives. DLL involves changing the organization's knowledge-base or firm-specific competencies or routines (Dodgson 1993). DLL is also called higher-level learning (Fiol and Lyles 1985), generative learning or learning to expand an organization's capabilities (Senge, 1990), and strategic learning (Mason, 1993) (Argyris and Schön 1978). The third type of organizational learning, deutero-learning (DL), occurs when organizations learn how to carry out single-loop and double-loop learning (Argyris and Schön 1978).

Pattern-Matching: A reasoning method that recognizes similarities between patterns and objects or events.

Pragmatic Knowledge: The next lowest abstraction level of conceptual knowledge at which we hold **Decision-Making and Factual Knowledge.** Decision-making knowledge is practical and mostly explicit. It supports everyday work and decisions, is well known, and is used consciously.

Procedural Knowledge: Knowledge and information about courses of action that may be sequential in nature. It may in particular refer to the sequential steps of a procedure or methodology.

Production Rule: A rule in the form of an "if-then" or "condition-action" statement often used in the knowledge base of an expert system. A production rule typically represents a single heuristic. The **If** (Condition) is called the "antecedent," and the **Then** (Action) is called the "consequent."

Production System: A knowledge-based system that relies on a reasoning approach that uses knowledge representation in the form of production rules. Production systems consist of a rule base, an inference engine, and a user interface.

Proficiency: Capability to perform.

Qualitative Reasoning: A reasoning method that is based on qualitative relations. Example: Background Knowledge: "All **attractive**

products, while **priced slightly high**, will **sell well.**" Premise: "The present product is **very attractive** and **priced slightly high.**" Conclusion: "The present product will **sell very well.**"

Reference Methodology Knowledge: Knowledge of how to proceed with particular activities — what to do next. Reference methodology knowledge is often possessed in the form of procedural knowledge and is used to govern planning as well as real-life actions at the time of execution.

Routine: A regular, often unvarying procedure for what to expect and how to handle a specific kind of situation. A routine is detailed, concrete, and inflexible. It consists of numerous and relatively deterministic, rigid steps that might cover many of the tasks in the process. Other tasks may still require explicit reasoning (they are still part of the script that underlies the routine).

Routine Working Knowledge: See Automatic Knowledge.

Schema: A broad and conceptual plan or scheme for a class of situations. Schemata are concepts or mental models by which a static or dynamic situation can be characterized and understood. They are abstract models of a generalized situation. Scripts are more concrete and specific than schemata and can be generated from schemata to form more definite expectations for evolutions of specific situations. A schema is a generalized concept that defines our understanding of the underlying structure, nature, or principles of a general type of story, situation, or "system."

Schema Knowledge: Abstract and generalized knowledge that provides an understanding of underlying principles and generic attributes of complex domains.

Script: A general event sequence that underlies a referenced type of situation. Scripts are flexible and somewhat abstract, and include general expectations and directions. Typically, scripts consist of several steps made up of episodes and events. Scripts are similar to, but more general than, operational models and routines. Scripts and their steps are general, broad, and flexible compared to the routines' specific and unvarying steps. Accordingly, hiring scripts, for example, may cover a range of positions — not just competent professionals as covered by a routine.

Semantic Network: A graphic knowledge representation method for representing associations between mental objects using a network of nodes with arcs between the nodes. The nodes represent mental objects (such as concepts or events), and the arcs represent the relations between the objects. Semantic networks are related to concept hierarchies and knowledge maps.

Single-Loop Learning (SLL). An organizational learning that occurs when errors are detected and corrected and firms carry on with their present policies and goals. According to Dodgson in 1993, SLL can be equated to activities that add to the knowledge-base or firm-specific competencies or routines without altering the fundamental nature of the organization's activities (Argyris and Schön 1978).

Situational Awareness: The functional proficiency by which a person is aware and makes sense of a situation. Any time a person encounters a situation, she observes it by obtaining, decoding, analyzing, interpreting, and accepting information about it.

Structural Capital: Structural capital is part of intellectual capital and includes all of the enterprise's intellectual property and intellectual property rights. It includes factors such as technology, practices, organizational structure, patents, and copyrights.

System: A group of entities that interact partially or completely with each other.

Systematic Knowledge: The next highest abstraction level of conceptual knowledge at which we hold **System, Schema, and Reference Methodology Knowledge.** Our knowledge of underlying systems, general principles, and problem-solving strategies is, to a large extent, explicit and mostly well known to us.

Systems Theory: The transdisciplinary study of the abstract organization of phenomena, independent of their substance, type, or spatial or temporal scale of existence. It investigates both the principles common to all complex entities, and the (usually mathematical) models that can be used to describe them (Heylighen and Joslyn 1992).

Systems Thinking: A broad and comprehensive perspective of how components of larger entities (systems) work together and how their activities need to be coordinated to facilitate effective and smooth operation without conflicts and inefficiencies. Systems thinking embraces concepts for projecting implications of changes and behaviors of dynamic situations where many parallel activities are coupled and affect each other over time in complex, often nonlinear, ways. (Does not refer to "information systems.")

Tacit Knowledge: Knowledge that a person possesses unconsciously. Tacit knowledge may be inaccessible to conscious recall and reasoning because it (1) is not well understood; or (2) is highly routinized and automatic and has transgressed the recall barrier.

Talk-Aloud: Narrative produced by a person while performing an activity to reflect aspects under consideration at the time. It is related to "Think-Aloud," which is narrative that reflects the thoughts and reasoning of a person while undertaking a K-I activity. "Verbal Protocol" is the talk-aloud narrative produced by knowledge workers while undertaking K-I tasks.

Task Environment Analysis (TEA): In-depth investigations of how knowledge workers perform business tasks and the conditions under which they work. The focus is on knowledge, its manifestations, presence, use, etc., and how important knowledge is, given the environment's driving forces. Its focus is on how the task is performed, what its inputs and deliverables are, and, to some extent, how it is used by "customers." Most TEAs also take the next step of considering how deliverables may be used as business and operating practices change, and how the task may be modified and strengthened by changing its organization or operation or by introducing different perspectives or different support systems.

Thinking about Thinking: Being consciously able to engage in meta-reasoning and to understand mental processes such as strategies and models.

Upstream Function: A function that supplies the target function with work products.

User Interface: The facility of a knowledge-based system that supports bidirectional communication between the system and its user. Most user interfaces use natural language-processing techniques and bit-mapped graphics.

Work Role: The often complex role that a knowledge worker is given or assumes. The role reflects the passive-active and learner-teacher behavior. Examples are: expert and team leader; apprentice and project assistance; and quality controller.

Work-Domain Knowledge: Knowledge that pertains directly to performing primary work such as a design engineer's engineering knowledge and knowledge of systems and procedures for performing design work. Also see Domain Knowledge.

REFERENCES

Ackoff, Russell L. (1978). *The Art of Problem Solving Accompanied by Ackoff's Fables*. New York: Wiley-Interscience Publication.

Ackoff, Russell L. (1994). *The Democratic Corporation*. New York: Oxford University Press.

Ackoff, Russell L., and Emery, Fred E. (1972). *On Purposeful Systems*. Chicago: Aldine-Atherton.

Amidon, Debra M. (2001). *The Intellectual Capital of Nations*. http://www.entovation.com/whatsnew/ic-nations.htm.

Amidon, Debra M. (2003). *The Innovation Superhighway: Harnessing Intellectual Capital for Sustainable Collaborative Advantage*. Newton, MA: Butterworth-Heinemann.

Anderson, John R. (1981). *Cognitive Skills & Their Acquisition*. Hillsdale, NJ: Lawrence Erlbaum Associates.

Anderson, John R. (1983). *The Architecture of Cognition*. Cambridge, MA: Harvard University Press.

Anonymous. (1998). "It Is the Manager, Stupid." *The Economist*, August 8, p. 54.

Anonymous. (2000). "Pioneer of the Big Picture — Profile: Roger Martin." *Financial Times*, September 11, p. 10.

Anonymous. (2001a). *CIO* 14, no. 16, June 1, p. 66.

Anonymous. (2001b). "Flaws Appear as Companies Turn to Computer-Based Training." *The Wall Street Journal*, July 3, p. A1.

Argyris, Chris, and Schön, Donald A. (1974). *Theory in Practice: Increasing Professional Effectiveness*. San Francisco, CA: Jossey-Bass.

Argyris, Chris, and Schön, Donald A. (1978 and 1996). *Organizational Learning II: Theory, Method, and Practice*. Reading, MA: Addison-Wesley.

Badaracco, Joseph L. (2002). *Leading Quietly: An Unorthodox Guide to Doing the Right Thing*. Boston: Harvard Business School Press.

Baddeley, A. (1992a). "Working Memory." *Science* 255, January 31, pp. 556–559.

Baddeley, A. (1992b). "Is Working Memory Working?" The Fifteenth Bartlett Lecture. *The Quarterly Journal of Experimental Psychology*, 44A, no. 1, pp. 1–31.

347

Bartulovitch-Richards, Regina. (2000). Effective Collaboration — Roles That Make It Work. hsfo.ucdavis.edu/download/Effective_Collaboration.pdf.

Bechara, Antoine; Damasio, Hanna; Tranel, Daniel; and Damasio, Antonio R. (1997). "Deciding Advantageously Before Knowing the Advantageous Strategy." *Science* 275, pp. 1293–1295.

Bennis, Warren. (1994). *On Becoming a Leader.* Cambridge, MA: Perseus.

Bennis, Warren, and Biederman, Patricia Ward. (1997). *Organizing Genius: The Secrets of Creative Collaboration.* Cambridge, MA: Perseus.

Bennis, Warren, and Thomas, Robert J. (2002). *Geeks & Geezers: How Era, Values, and Defining Moments Shape Leaders.* Boston: Harvard Business School Press.

Bereiter, Carl. (2002). *Education and the Mind in the Knowledge Age.* Mahwah, NJ: Lawrence Erlbaum.

Boden, Margaret A. (1990). *The Creative Mind: Myths & Mechanisms.* New York: Basic Books.

Boden, Margaret A. (1996). *Dimensions of Creativity.* Cambridge, MA: The MIT Press.

Bonhoeffer, Tobias, Staiger, Volker, and Aertsen, Ad. (1989). "Synaptic plasticity in rat hippocampal slice cultures: Local 'Hebbian' conjunction for pre- and postsynaptic stimulation leads to distributed synaptic enhancement." *Proc. Natl. Acad. Sci.* 86, pp. 8113–8117.

Bossidy, Larry, and Charan, Ram. (2002). *Execution: The discipline of getting things done.* New York: Crown Business.

Brase, Wendell C. (2001). *Sustainable Performance Improvement.* www.abs.uci.edu/spi/index.html.

Brown, John Seely. (1991). "Research That Reinvents the Corporation." *Harvard Business Review* 69, January–February, pp. 102–117.

Brown, John Seely, and Duguid, Paul. (2000). *The Social Life of Information.* Boston: Harvard Business School Press.

Buckman, Robert H. (2004). *Building a Knowledge-Driven Organization: Overcome the Resistance to the Free Flow of Ideas: Turn Knowledge into New Products and Sevices; Move to a Knowledge-Based Strategy.* New York: McGraw-Hill.

Cannon-Bowers, Janis A., and Salas, Eduardo. (1998). "Team Performance and Training in Complex Environments: Recent Findings from Applied Research." *Current Directions in Psychological Research*, March, pp. 83–87.

Chandrasekaran, B., Josephson, John R., and Benjamins, V. Richard. (1999). "What Are Ontologies, and Why Do We Need Them?" *IEEE Intelligent Systems* 14, no. 1, pp. 20–26.

Chatzkel, Jay. (2002). *Intellectual Capital.* Oxford, England: Capstone.

Checkland, Peter B. (1999). *Systems Thinking, Systems Practice*. New York: John Wiley.

Christensen, Clayton M., and Raynor, Michael E. (2003). *The Innovator's Solution: Creating and Sustaining Successful Growth*. Boston: Harvard Business School Press.

Collins, Harry M., and Kusch, Martin. (1998). *The Shape of Actions: What Humans and Machines Can Do*. Cambridge, MA: MIT Press.

Collins, James C. (Jim). (2001). *Good to Great: Why Some Companies Make the Leap and Others Don't*. New York: Harper Business.

Craik, K. (1943). *The Nature of Explanation*. London, New York: Cambridge University Press.

Csikszentmihalyi, Mihaly. (1990). *FLOW: The Psychology of Optimal Experience*. New York: Harper.

Damasio, Antonio R. (1994). *Descartes' Error: Emotion, Reason, and the Human Brain*. New York: Grosset/Putnam.

Damasio, Antonio R. (1999). *The Feeling of What Happens: Body and Emotion in the Making of Consciousness*. New York: Harcourt-Brace.

Damasio, Antonio R. (2003). *Looking for Spinoza: Joy, Sorrow, and the Feeling Brain*. New York: Harcourt-Brace.

Davenport, Thomas H., and Beck, John C. (2001). *The Attention Economy: Understanding the New Currency of Business*. Boston: Harvard Business School Press.

Davenport, Thomas H., and Glaser, John. (2002). "Just-in-time delivery comes to knowledge management." *Harvard Business Review* 80, July, 107–111.

Dawson, Ross. (2000). *Developing Knowledge-Based Client Relationships: The Future of Professional Services*. Boston: Butterworth-Heinemann.

Dawson, Ross. (2002). *Living Networks: Leading Your Company, Customers, and Partners in the Hyper-Connected Economy*. New York: Financial Times Prentice Hall.

de Bono, Edward. (1978). *Teaching Thinking*. Harmondsworth, England: Penguin.

de Bono, Edward. (1992). *Serious Creativity: Using the Power of Lateral Thinking to Create New Ideas*. New York: Harper Business.

de Bono, Edward. (2000). *New Thinking for the New Millennium*. New York: New Millennium Press.

De Geus, Arie. (1997). *The Living Company: Habits for Survival in a Turbulent Business Environment*. Boston: Harvard Business School Press.

Denning, Stephen. (2000). *The Springboard: How Storytelling Ignites Action in Knowledge-Era Organizations*. Boston: Butterworth-Heinemann.

Dixon, Nancy M. (2000). *Common Knowledge: How Companies Thrive by Sharing What They Know*. Boston: Harvard Business School Press.

Dodgson, Mark. (1993). "Organizational learning: A review of some literatures." *Organization Studies* 14, no. 3, pp. 375–394.

Drucker, Peter F. (1993). *Post-Capitalist Society.* New York: Harper Business.

Drucker, Peter F. (1999). *Management Challenges for the 21ˢᵗ Century.* New York: Harper Business.

Edvinsson, Leif. (2002). *Corporate Longitude: What You Need to Know to Navigate the Knowledge Economy.* New York: Financial Times — Prentice Hall.

Edvinsson, Leif, and Malone, Michael S. (1997). *Intellectual Capital: Realizing Your Company's True Value by Finding Its Hidden Brainpower.* New York: Harper Business.

Fahey, Liam, and Prusak, Lawrence. (1998). "The Eleven Deadliest Sins of Knowledge Management." *California Management Review* 40, no. 3, Spring, pp. 265–277.

Fauconnier, Gilles, and Turner, Mark. (2002). *The Way We Think: Conceptual Blending and the Mind's Hidden Complexities.* New York: Basic Books.

Feldbaum, A. A. (1960, 1961). "Dual Control Theory, Parts I and II." *Automation and Remote Control* 21, no. 9, April, pp. 874–880 and 21, no. 11, May, pp. 1033–1039. (Russian originals in *Automatika i Telemekhanika*, September 1960, pp. 1240–1249 and November 1960, pp. 1453–1464.)

Fiol, C. M., and Lyles, M. (1985). "Organizational Learning." *Academy of Management Review* 10, no. 4, pp. 803–813.

Gardner, Howard. (1983). *Frames of Mind: The Theory of Multiple Intelligences.* New York: Basic Books.

Garvin, David A., and Roberto, Michael A. (2001). "What You Don't Know About Making Decisions." *Harvard Business Review* 79, no. 8 September: pp. 108–116.

Gazzaniga, Michael S. (ed.) (2000). *Cognitive Neurosciences: A Reader.* Oxford, England: Blackwell.

Gilhooly, K. J. (1988). *Thinking: Directed, Undirected and Creative* (2nd Edition). New York: Academic Press.

Glimcher, Paul W. (2003). *Decisions, Uncertainty, and the Brain: The Science of Neuroeconomics.* Cambridge, MA: MIT Press.

Gorman, Christine. (2003). "The New Science of Dyslexia." *Time,* July 28, pp. 52–59.

Halpern, Diane F. (1989). *Thought and Knowledge: An Introduction to Critical Thinking* (2nd ed.). Hillsdale, NJ: Lawrence Erlbaum.

Hammon, John S., Keeney, Ralph L., and Raiffa, Howard. (1999). *Smart Choices: A Practical Guide to Making Better Decisions.* Boston: Harvard Business School Press.

Handy, Charles. (1997). *The Hungry Spirit: Beyond Capitalism — A Quest for Purpose in the Modern World*. London: Hutchinson.

Handy, Charles. (1999). *Waiting for the Mountain to Move: Reflections on Work and Life*. San Francisco, CA: Jossey-Bass.

Hansen, Morten T., Nohria, Nitin, and Tierney, Thomas. (1999). "What's Your Strategy for Managing Knowledge?" *Harvard Business Review* 77, no. 2, March–April, pp. 106–118.

Helander, Martin. (1990) (Editor). *Handbook of Human-Computer Interaction*. Second Edition. Amsterdam: Elsevier Science Publishers.

Herzberg, Frederick. (2003). Quoted in "Profit Machines Where People Come First." *Financial Times*, Interview by Simon London, September 26, p. 14.

Heylighen, F., and Joslyn, C. (1992). What is systems theory? [WWW document] F. Heylighen, C. Joslyn and V. Turchin (editors): Principia Cybernetica Web (Principia Cybernetica, Brussels), Retrieved February 13, 2004 from http://pespmc1.vub.ac.be/SYSTHEOR.html.

Hymowitz, Carol. (2002). "In the Lead," *The Wall Street Journal*, April 24.

Ivry, Richard B., and Robertson, Lynn C. (1998). *The Two Sides of Perception*. Cambridge, MA: MIT Press.

Janis, Irving L. (1989). *Crucial Decisions: Leadership in Policymaking and Crisis Management*. New York: The Free Press.

Janis, Irving L., and Mann, Leon. (1977). *Decision-making: A Psychological Analysis of Conflict, Choice, and Commitment*. New York: The Free Press.

Johnson-Laird, Philip N. (1983). *Mental Models: Towards a Cognitive Science of Language, Inference, and Consciousness*. Cambridge, MA: Harvard University Press.

Johnson-Laird, Philip N. (1988). *The Computer and the Mind: An Introduction to Cognitive Science*. Cambridge, MA: Harvard University Press.

Johnson-Laird, Philip N., and Byrne, Ruth. (2000). http://www.tcd.ie/Psychology/Ruth_Byrne/mental_models/.

Kahneman, Daniel, Slovic, Paul, and Tversky, Amos. (1982). *Judgment under Uncertainty: Heuristics and Biases*. New York: Cambridge University Press.

Kahneman, Daniel, and Tversky, Amos. (2000). *Choices, Values, and Frames*. New York: Cambridge University Press.

Kalman, Rudolph E. (1960a). "A New Approach to Linear Filtering and Prediction Problems." *Trans. ASME*, Series D, *Journal Basic English*, 82, March, pp. 35–45.

Kalman, Rudolph E. (1960b). "On the General Theory of Control Systems." *Proceedings of the First IFAC Congress in Moscow* 1. London: Butterworth, pp. 481–492.

Keeney, Ralph L., and Raiffa, Howard. (1976). *Decisions with Multiple Objectives: Preferences and Value Tradeoffs.* New York: John Wiley.

Kelly, Kevin. (1996). "The Economics of Ideas." *Wired* 4, no. 6, p. 149.

Klein, David A. (1998). *The Strategic Management of Intellectual Capital.* Boston: Butterworth-Heinemann.

Klein, Gary. (1998). *Sources of Power: How People Make Decisions.* Cambridge, MA: MIT Press.

Klein, Gary. (2002). *Intuition at Work: Why Developing Your Gut Instincts Will Make You Better at What You Do.* New York: Doubleday.

Kleiner, Gary. (2003). *Who Really Matters: The Core Group Theory of Power, Privilege, and Success.* New York: Dobleday.

Kotter, John P., and Cohen, Dan S. (2002). *The Heart of Change: Real-Life Stories of How People Change Their Organizations.* Boston: Harvard Business School Press.

Krogh, Georg von; Ichijo, Kazuo; and Nonaka, Ikujiro. (2000). *Enabling Knowledge Creation: How to Unlock the Mystery of Tacit Knowledge and Release the Power of Innovation.* New York: Oxford University Press.

Kuhn, Deanna. (2000). "Metacognitive Development." *Current Directions in Psychological Science* 9, no. 5, pp. 178–181.

Lakoff, George. (1987). *Women, Fire, and Dangerous Things: What Categories Reveal About the Mind.* Chicago: University of Chicago Press.

Landes, David S. (1999). *The Wealth and Poverty of Nations: Why some are so rich and some so poor.* New York: W.W. Norton & Co.

Lawler, Edward E., III. (2003). *Treat People Right! How Organizations and Individuals Can Propel Each Other Into a Virtuous Spiral of Success.* San Francisco, CA: Jossey-Bass.

Lev, Baruch. (2001). *Business Week,* June 18, p. 30D.

Littler, Craig. (1978). "Understanding Taylorism." *British Journal of Sociology* 29, pp. 185–207.

Loehr, Jim, and Schwartz, Tony. (2003). *The Power of Full Engagement: Managing Energy, Not Time, Is the Key to High Performance and Personal Renewal.* New York: The Free Press.

Lowen, Walter. (1982). *Dichotomies of the Mind: A Systems Science Model of the Mind and Personality.* New York: John Wiley.

Malone, Thomas F., and Yohe, Gary W. (2000). "Knowledge Partnerships for a Sustainable, Equitable, and Stable Society." *Journal of Knowledge Management* 6, no. 4.

Mandler, J. M. (1979). "Categorical and Schematic Organization in Memory." C. R. Puff (ed.), *Memory Organization and Structure.* New York: Academic Press, pp. 259–299.

Matta, Nadim F., and Ashkenas, Ronald N. (2003). "Why Good Projects Fail Anyway." *Harvard Business Review*, September, pp. 109–114.

Miller, George A. (1956). "The magical number seven, plus or minus two: some limits on our capacity for processing information." *Psychological Review* 63, pp. 81–97.

Mintzberg, Henry. (2002). "Heretic in the Ranks." *Scotland on Sunday*, June 9.

Mintzberg, Henry. (2003). Quoted in "In Search of a Balanced Society." *Financial Times*, Interview by Michael Skapinker, September 16, p. 14.

Mittelstaedt, Robert E. (2003). "Why Don't They Understand Our Strategy?." *Financial Times*, August 20, p. 9.

Moore, Brian E., and Ross, Timothy L. (1978). *The Scanlon Way to Improved Productivity.* New York: John Wiley.

Nadel, Lynn. (ed.) (2003). *Encyclopedia of Cognitive Science.* London: Nature Press.

Neves, D. M., and Anderson, John R. (1981). "Knowledge Compilation: Mechanisms for the automatization of cognitive skills." *Cognitive Skills and Their Acquisition.* J. R. Anderson (ed.). Hillsdale, NJ: Lawrence Erlbaum.

Nonaka, Ikujiro, and Takeuchi, Hirotaka. (1995). *The Knowledge-Creating Company: How Japanese Companies Create the Dynamics of Innovation.* New York: Oxford University Press.

Oliva, Loredana. (2003). "A Lesson in Staying Ahead of the Game." *Financial Times*, November 3, p. 9.

Pfeffer, Jeffrey. (1994). *Competitive Advantage through People: Unleashing the Power of the Work Force.* Boston: Harvard Business School Press.

Pfeffer, Jeffrey. (2003). Quoted in "Profit Machines Where People Come First." *Financial Times*, Interview by Simon London, September 26, p. 14.

Pinchot, Gifford, and Pellman, Ron. (2000). *Intrapreneuring in Action: A Handbook for Business Innovation.* San Francisco, CA: Berrett-Koehler Publishers.

Pinker, Steven. (1997). *How the Mind Works.* New York: W. W. Norton.

Polanyi, Michael. (1966). *The Tacit Dimension.* Garden City, NY: Anchor Books, Doubleday.

Posner, Michael J. (1989). *Foundations of Cognitive Science.* Cambridge, MA: MIT Press.

Quinn, James Brian; Anderson, Philip; and Finkelstein, Sydney. (1996). "Managing Professional Intellect: Making the Most of the Best." *Harvard Business Review*, March–April, pp. 71–80.

Ready, Douglas A. (2002). "How Storytelling Builds Next-Generation Leaders." *Sloan Management Review* 43, no. 4, Summer, pp. 63–69.

Romer, Paul. (1993). "Idea Gaps and Object Gaps in Economic Development." *Journal of Monetary Economics* 32, no. 3, pp. 543–573.

Roos, Johan; Roos, Göran; Edvinsson, Leif; and Dragonetti, Nicola C. (1998). *Intellectual Capital: Navigating in the New Business Landscape.* New York: New York University Press.

Sardina, G. D., and Vrat, Prem. (1987). "A Model for Productivity Measurement in a Multi-Product Organization Using Programming and Multi-Attribute Utility Theory." D. J. Summanth (ed.), *Productivity Management Frontiers I*, p. 3548. New York: Elsevier Science.

Schön, Donald A. (1983). *The Reflective Practitioner: How Professionals Think in Action.* New York: Basic Books.

Schön, Donald A. (1987). *Educating the Reflective Practitioner: Toward a New Design for Teaching and Learning in the Professions.* San Francisco, CA: Jossey-Bass.

Schrage, Michael. (1995). *No More Teams! Mastering the Dynamics of Creative Collaboration.* New York: Currency Doubleday.

Schwartz, Jeffrey M., and Begley, Sharon. (2002). *The Mind and the Brain: Neoplasticity and the Power of Mental Force.* New York: Regan Books.

Shellenbarger, Sue. (2001). "New Training Methods Allow Jobs to Intrude Further into Off Hours." *The Wall Street Journal,* July 11, p. B1.

Sherman, David K., and Cohen, Geoffrey, L. (2000). "Accepting Threatening Information: Self-Affirmation and the Reduction of Defensive Biases." *Current Directions in Psychological Science* 9, no. 4, pp. 119–123.

Simon, Herbert A. (1945, 1957). *Models of Man, Social and Rational: Mathematical Essays on Rational Human Behavior in a Social Setting.* New York: John Wiley.

Simon, Herbert A. (1976). *Administrative Behavior: A Study of Decision-Making Processes in Administrative Organizations* (3rd ed.). New York: The Free Press.

Simon, Herbert A. (1977a). *The New Science of Management Decision* (rev. ed.). Englewood Cliffs, NJ: Prentice-Hall.

Simon, Herbert A. (1977b). *Models of Discovery and Other Topics in the Methods of Science.* Vol. 54, Boston Studies in the Philosophy of Science, R. S. Cohen and M. W. Wartofsky (eds.). Boston: D. Reidel.

Singley, Mark K., and Anderson, John R. (1989). *The Transfer of Cognitive Skill.* Cambridge, MA: Harvard University Press.

Snowden. (2000). "The Social Ecology of Knowledge Management." *Knowledge Horizons: The Present and the Promise of Knowledge Management.* Charles Despres and Daniele Chauvel (eds.). Boston: Butterworth-Heinemann.

Sohlberg, Ragnhild. (2000). Personal Communication.

Solomon, Joan. (2000). "The Importance of Stories." *BSHS conference Science Communication*, Education and the History of Science, the Royal Society, Paper 8.1, 12–13 July 2000. Retrieved February 13, 2004 from http://216.239.37.104/search?q=cache:0J9XnCazHPwJ:www.bshs.org. uk/conf/2000sciencecomm/papers/solomon.rtf+Solomon,+Joan+(2000) +"The+Importance+of+Stories"&hl=en&ie=UTF-8.

Sowell, Thomas. (1980). *Knowledge and Decisions*. New York: Basic Books.

Stafford, Sue. (2002). Personal Communication.

Stein, Joel. (2003). "Just Say Om." *Time*, August 4, pp. 48–53. (On meditation).

Stewart, Thomas A. (1991). "Brainpower." *Fortune* 123, no. 11, June 3, pp. 44–60.

Stewart, Thomas A. (1997). *Intellectual Capital: The New Wealth of Organizations*. New York: Currency Doubleday.

Stewart, Thomas A. (2002a). "How to Think with Your Gut." *Business* 2.0, November, pp. 98–104.

Stewart, Thomas A. (2002b). *The Wealth of Knowledge: Intellectual Capital and the Twenty-First Century Organization*. London: Nicholas Brealey.

Suchman, Lucy. (1995). "Making Work Visible." *Communications of the ACM* 38, no. 9, pp. 56–65.

Sullivan, Gordon R., and Harper, Michael V. (1997). *Hope Is not a Method: What Business Leaders Can Learn from America's Army*. New York: Broadway Books.

Sveiby, Karl Erik. (1997). *The New Organizational Wealth: Managing & Measuring Knowledge-based Assets*. San Francisco, CA: Berrett-Koehler.

Sveiby, Karl-Erik, and Lloyd, Tom. (1987). *Managing Knowhow*. London, England: Bloomsbury.

Thor, Carl. (1988). *Productivity Brief 5*. Houston, TX: American Productivity and Quality Center.

Treacy, Michael, and Wiersema, Fred. (1993). "Customer Intimacy and Other Value Disciplines." *Harvard Business Review*, January/February, pp. 84–93.

Tulving, E. (1972). *Organization of Memory*. E. Tulving and W. Donaldson (eds.). New York: Academic Press.

Tulving, E., and Schacter, D. L. (1990). "Priming and Human Memory Systems." *Science* 247, pp. 301–306.

Ubogu, Felix U. (2001). *Knowledge Management for Decision Making: Tools, Institutions and Paradigms*. Proceedings of Second Meeting of the Committee on Development Information (CODI), Addis Ababa, September. New York: UN's Economic Commission for Africa.

von Bertalanffy, (Karl) Ludwig. (1969). *General Systems Theory: Foundations, Developments, Applications.* (rev. ed.). New York: George Braziller.

Weber, Rosina, Aha, David W., and Becerra-Fernandez, Irma. (2001). "Intelligent Lessons Learned Systems." *International Journal of Expert Systems Research & Applications* 20, no. 1, pp. 17–34.

Webster's Ninth New Collegiate Dictionary. (1986). Springfield, MA: Merriam-Webster Inc.

Weick, Karl E. (1995). *Sensemaking in Organizations.* Thousand Oaks, CA: Sage Publications.

Weick, Karl E. (2001). *Making Sense of the Organization.* Malden, MA: Blackwell.

Wellman, Barry. (1999). "Living Networked in a Wired World." *IEEE Intelligent Systems* 14, no. 1, pp. 15–17.

Wiig, Elisabeth H., and Wiig, Karl M. (1999). *On Conceptual Learning.* KRII-WP-1999-1. Arlington, TX: Knowledge Research Institute.

Wiig, Karl M. (1993). *Knowledge Management Foundations: Thinking about Thinking — How People and Organizations Create, Represent, and Use Knowledge.* Arlington, TX: Schema Press.

Wiig, Karl M. (1995). *Knowledge Management Methods: Practical Approaches to Managing Knowledge.* Arlington, TX: Schema Press.

Wiig, Karl M. (1999): "Successful Knowledge Management: Does It Exist?" *The European American Business Journal,* Autumn, pp. 106–109.

Wiig, Karl M., and Jooste, Adriaan. (2003). "Exploiting Knowledge for Productivity Gains." *Handbook on Knowledge Management: 1. Knowledge Matters.* Clyde W. Holsapple (ed.). Berlin: Springer.

Wilson, R. A., and Keil, F. C. (eds.) (1999). *The MIT Encyclopedia of the Cognitive Sciences.* Cambridge, MA: MIT Press.

Winograd, Terry. (1988). *Byte* 13, no. 11, December, p. 256.

Wright, Andrew. (2000). "Stories and their importance in Language Teaching." *Humanising Language Teaching.* 2; Issue 5; September 2000.

Wright, Robert. (1994). *The Moral Animal — Why We Are the Way We Are: The New Science of Evolutionary Psychology.* New York: Pantheon.

INDEX

357